Girls and Their Comics

Finding a Female Voice in Comic Book Narrative

Jacqueline Danziger-Russell

THE SCARECROW PRESS, INC.
Lanham • Toronto • Plymouth, UK
2013

Published by Scarecrow Press, Inc.
A wholly owned subsidiary of The Rowman & Littlefield Publishing Group, Inc.
4501 Forbes Boulevard, Suite 200, Lanham, Maryland 20706
www.rowman.com

10 Thornbury Road, Plymouth PL6 7PP, United Kingdom

British Library Cataloguing in Publication Information Available

Library of Congress Cataloging-in-Publication Data

Danziger-Russell, Jacqueline.
 Girls and their comics : finding a female voice in comic book narrative / Jacqueline Danziger-Russell.
    p. cm.
 Includes bibliographical references and index.
 ISBN 978-0-8108-8375-8 (cloth : alk. paper) — ISBN 978-0-8108-8376-5 (ebook)
 1. Comic books, strips, etc.—United States—History and criticism. 2. Women—Comic books, strips, etc. 3. Comic books, strips, etc.—Japan—History and criticism. 4. Women in art. I. Title.
 PN6725.D196 2013
 741.5'0973—dc23   2012014543

∞™ The paper used in this publication meets the minimum requirements of American National Standard for Information Sciences—Permanence of Paper for Printed Library Materials, ANSI/NISO Z39.48-1992.

Printed in the United States of America

To Mom, Dad, and Nana for
instilling in me
a lifelong love of reading,
and to James for being my
love and my rock, always.

CONTENTS

Acknowledgments vii

CHAPTER ONE   Girls and Their Comics: A Brief History 1
In the Beginning 2
Comic Books' Evolution from Working-Class Literature
    and the Marginalization of Comics 6
The History of Comic Books for Girls 10
Comics—Now! 31

CHAPTER TWO   Comics as a Hybrid Art Form, or
    The Mysterious Case of the Picture Book. 37
Defining the Picture Book 37
The Graphic Text and Reader-Response Theory. 38
The Dynamic Interaction of Image and Text 40
Comics' Influence on the Picture Book. 63

CHAPTER THREE   The Power of Visual Narrative. 73
Why Visual Literacy Is Important 77
The Value of the Visual Text. 77
The Mechanics of Comics 83
Comics Giving a Voice to the Underrepresented Female 92

CHAPTER FOUR   The Appeal of Manga 129
Manga's History 131
Shōjo Manga: A Tradition of Girls' Comics 137
Manga in America. 147
Manga's Future Influence in America. 159

CONTENTS

CHAPTER FIVE   Girls' Comics Today: Different Formats,
  Expanding Readership 171
The Validation of Comics through the Graphic Novel Format 171
What Is a Graphic Novel? Taking a Step Back through History 176
Marketing Comics as Literature 179
New Heroes: The Maturation of the Female Role in Comics 181
Beyond Graphic Novels: The Digital Age of Comics Has Arrived 196
Conclusion 218

Bibliography 227
Index 235
About the Author 247

ACKNOWLEDGMENTS

I would like to thank all of the people who helped make this book possible: Dr. Lisa Sainsbury at Roehampton University for her encouragement when I first began to research this topic, as well as Dr. Gillian Lathey, Dr. Pat Pinsent, and everyone from the NCRCL. I am thankful to Dr. Rita Ray for lighting a spark so many years ago, and I am also grateful to Professor Pamela King and Professor Emeritus Michael Warren for their helpfulness when I was still an undergrad. Thank you to Brian Schulte for the advice and reassurance, and to Sharon Segal, owner of Sweet Briar Books. To Laurence Herman, thank you for generously giving me your Elfquest collection. My gratitude also belongs to Katie Brute for her assistance.

Many thanks to my interviewees, Justin Azevedo, Chelsea Couillard, Leigh Dragoon, Davi Gabriel, Qiuning Huang, Hope Larson, and Jared Rudy for their kindness and candor. Thank you to Davera Gabriel and Naoko McHale, who were both instrumental in facilitating some of these interviews. I am also grateful to the creators and publishers that have allowed me to use the images that appear in this book.

Special thanks to my editor, Patty Campbell, for her patience and good advice.

Most importantly, I want to thank my family and friends who have empowered me to write this book. Thank you Sharon Danziger, Frederick Danziger, Juliette Bennett, Josephine Simmonds, and Liisa Russell for always believing in me and helping me along the way. Thank you

ACKNOWLEDGMENTS

Ian Russell, Gerry Russell, and Alexis Kreiberg for encouraging me. Thank you Teresa Bizarro, J. Karl Metts, Ryan House, and Lorna Jones for your steadfast friendship. Thank you to Katie Brute for the advice and friendship when I needed it the most. I am extremely thankful to my husband, James Russell, for all of the love and encouragement he has given me throughout this process.

GIRLS AND THEIR COMICS
A Brief History

The term *comic book* has long been associated with the adolescent male in America. It is a label considered synonymous with low art and juvenile machismo; comics have even been criticized as detrimental to literacy and literary appreciation. Yet comics can transcend these stereotypes. They are not just about men in tights and bulging underpants (or the occasional codpiece) rescuing damsels in distress. Rather, comics constitute a mode of art and literature that has the potential to reach female readers and allow them to connect with strong and complex female characters. The amalgamation of art and narrative that is referred to simply as "comics" encompasses many genres that can be artistic, political, and challenging and are not necessarily biased toward a male readership.

While there have been many positive examples of female characters throughout the history of comics, for many years the majority of publications have been produced *primarily* for male consumption and have often shown women and girls in weaker roles than their male counterparts. However, all of this is changing. Comic books such as Barry Deutsch's *Hereville: How Mirka Got Her Sword* (2010), Ted Naifeh's *Courtney Crumrin* series, and Castellucci and Rugg's *The Plain Janes* (2007) are representing girls in a positive light and investing them with power. These comics feature female protagonists in active roles, sometimes adopting the cape of the superhero and reinventing a genre that has been known to be typically male-oriented. Others represent the feminine in the realist "slice of life" genre, as in Mariko and Jillian Tamaki's *Skim* (2008) or Daniel Clowes's *Ghost World* (1993–1997). Still others explore what it is to be female in works of fantasy.

The medium of sequential art, to borrow Will Eisner's term, is a special creative space that can be used to explore feminist themes and issues and represent marginalized people, including girls and adolescent females. Furthermore, the expression and exploration of what it means to be female is often discussed more directly in independent comics that depart from the mainstream. Independent comics are the art books of the comics world; published by a small press or an individual, they frequently take a more experimental approach to the art form. This means that, through new usage of comics structure and narrative, they have the potential to break down the barriers imposed by a male-oriented society. The goal of this book is to examine how the unique combination of visual and textual narrative found in the underground art form of comics works as the perfect medium to give voice to and empower subaltern females.

In the Beginning

This book intends to explore and explode the myths surrounding the field of comic books, their implied readership, and the gendering of the field. When investigating comic books and their relationship with the girls who read them, it is necessary to consider the history of this connection, the myths surrounding the art form, and its reception by the critics. This book will argue that the prejudice against comics is rooted in history and that it stems from a general distaste on the part of the literary establishment for working-class art and popular culture. This is a bias that remains today and is perpetuated by those who have not read widely in the field.

In order to examine the importance of the comic book in the literary diet of girls, as well as its establishment as an art form, we must first recognize why the form has been so maligned. Comics are no new mode of expression. In fact, the history of comic books goes back quite a long way. However, there is some debate over just how the art form began. Some comic book historians like Scott McCloud claim that comics find their ancestry in ancient Egyptian paintings. In his book *Understanding Comics: The Invisible Art* (1993), McCloud suggests that Egyptian paintings have much in common with comic books and visual narrative. He also gives examples of what he claims are a form of early comics dating back to "a pre-Columbian picture manuscript 'discovered' by Cortez around 1519"; and, using his own panel illustrations, he explains how it can be read today.[1] He also examines the Bayeux Tapestry, which tells the story of the Norman Conquest of England. The tapestry dates back to 1066, which McCloud notes would establish sequential art as a historical fact.

Mario Saraceni, author of *The Language of Comics* (2003), appears to delve further into the origin of pictorial storytelling, suggesting that hieroglyphs are one of the earliest forms of telling a story in pictures. He comments:

> We think of comics as very modern texts, but it is possible to see connections between them and the communication systems of early civilizations. For example, the Egyptians used combinations of images and hieroglyphics, while narratives composed of sequences of pictures were common in other ancient cultures.[2]

With this statement, Saraceni appears to challenge McCloud's earlier assertion that hieroglyphs tell us only about the history of the written word, and not of pictorial storytelling: "These glyphs represent only *sounds*, not unlike our alphabet."[3] However, in his book *Comics and Sequential Art: Principles and Practices from the Legendary Cartoonist* (1985, 2008), Will Eisner validates the pictograph (see fig. 1.1) as a form of storytelling through image, confirming that it is not merely a phonetic unit:

> Words are made up of letters. Letters are symbols that are devised out of images, which originate out of familiar forms, objects, postures and other recognizable phenomena. So, as their employment becomes more sophisticated, they become simplified and abstract.[4]

Therefore, the origins of sequential art and the pairing of image and narrative (written or expressed by the image alone) remain unclear.

What Saraceni, McCloud, and Eisner all seem to agree on is that the world has a history of communicating through a combination of words and pictures, and the comic book form is another effective mode of communication and expression that transmits human experience. However, what we think of as modern-day comics has a more recent history. Saraceni states that

> comics in the form we know now were first created in the last half of the nineteenth century in England. The first regular comic strip appeared in 1884 and featured the first comics hero, Ally Sloper. A few years later, in 1890, *Comic Cuts* appeared, which many consider to be the world's first regularly appearing comic.[5]

While Saraceni establishes that "Ally Sloper" and *Comic Cuts* were the forerunners of the field, he also acknowledges that "American comics historians generally cite The Yellow Kid as the first comics character, which first appeared in 1896 in the Sunday edition of *The New York World*."[6] Depending upon the angle from which one approaches the history of the field broadly referred to as "comics," the beginnings of the modern comic are subject to debate. Perhaps this is because the recording of history is imperfect, and each nation has their own version of "the truth"; or perhaps it is because the genre of comics, though an old form of art, is only recently enjoying a rise in status, and therefore its history is still being established.

McCloud, through all of this confusion, has a very practical approach to the history of the comic book, citing the invention of the printing press in Europe by Johann Gutenberg, c.1450, as the biggest step in its development. In 1474 William Caxton printed the first book in English: his translation of *The Recuyell of the Historyes of Troye*. This would open the floodgates for distribution of the written word throughout Britain. The printing press was the real catalyst for developing what we now know as comics, as it allowed literature and art to be replicated and distributed,

Figure 1.1. *Comics and Sequential Art: Principles and Practices from the Legendary Cartoonist*, **1985, 2008, page 8. Eisner illustrates how the pictograph transmits narrative.**
From *Comics and Sequential Art* by Will Eisner. Copyright © 1985 by Will Eisner. Copyright © 2008 by Will Eisner Studios, Inc. Used by permission of W. W. Norton & Company, Inc.

making it accessible to more classes of people, rather than just "the rich and powerful,"[7] as McCloud puts it. He also singles out Rodolphe Töpffer and William Hogarth as instrumental in contributing to comics today, specifically Töpffer's cartoons and Hogarth's paintings "A Harlot's Progress" (1731) and "A Rake's Progress" (1735). This suggests that comics found its beginnings in the social and political satire of cartoon and caricature. These first works of satire would later spawn the tradition of the comic strip,[8] forever associating comics with humor. Comics, however, have developed far beyond what are considered "funnies."

In America, the history of the modern comic book started with newspaper comic strips such as *The Yellow Kid* (1896) and *Krazy Kat* (1913). Saraceni says of the strip comics: "Encouraged by their increasing popularity, in the early 1930s some publishers began to collect newspaper comic strips into books, hence the term 'comic book.'"[9] This collation of comic strips took off, and in 1935 *New Fun Comics*—the first comic book that contained all new material—was printed.[10] Shortly after came the beginning of the superhero genre, the genre that comics are best known for in America today. According to Saraceni,

> The first costumed hero was The Phantom, which appeared in *Ace Comics* in 1938. In June of the same year, Superman, the most famous superhero, made his debut in the first issue of *Action Comics*. Another famous superhero, Batman, first appeared the following year in *Detective Comics*.[11]

During these early years that are often referred to as the Golden Age, comics often cost only a dime and were printed on low-quality paper. As Trina Robbins, author of *From Girls to Grrrlz: A History of Female Comics from Teens to Zines* (1999), aptly puts it:

> In those days, before television, comics provided a less expensive alternative to movies—they only cost a dime!—and they were disposable. You could roll up a comic book and stash it in your back pocket; better yet, you could conceal it in your loose-leaf notebook and read it beneath your desk during math class.[12]

After the superhero craze starting with *Superman* began to quiet down, comics of the late 1940s turned toward darker subject matters; the crime and horror genres became new hits. This gave rise to the idea that an increase in violence in comics—reading materials that many children enjoyed as well as adults—would lead to an increase in violent behavior in young people. Saraceni comments, "The most important figures in the expression of these worries were Dr. Frederic Wertham in America and George Pumphrey in Britain. The concerns over the presumed harmful influence of comics on children spurred campaigns against comics both in America and in Britain, which led to censure in the mid-1950s."[13] These fears and comics' reputation for "ensnaring youth" in the manner mentioned by Robbins became a matter of concern for some critics, and this is a prejudice that comics still struggle with today.

Comic Books' Evolution from Working-Class Literature and the Marginalization of Comics

Perhaps there is a deeper reason behind the bias against comics, a reason that goes back further into history than has been previously assumed. The moral concern fueled by the popularity of horror and crime comics in America mirrors the demonization of one of modern comic books' predecessors: the penny dreadfuls of Victorian England (sometimes referred to as "bloods" or "shilling shockers"). Alongside the caricature and the comic strip, chapbooks and Victorian penny dreadfuls could be viewed as predecessors to the modern comic book form in the West. Chapbooks were books made cheaply (the term itself may have been a corruption of the words "cheap book") and were sold for a small sum from the sixteenth to early nineteenth century. According to *The Concise Oxford Dictionary of Literary Terms* (1990), chapbooks consisted of "ballads, fairy-tales, old . . . romances, accounts of famous criminals, and other popular entertainments."[14] The chapbook and another type of working-class fiction, the penny dreadful, emerged in the early 1820s with titles such as *The Tell-Tale* and *Legends of Horror*.[15] The penny dreadful is closely related to the modern-day comic book. They were inexpensive publications typically sold for a penny apiece (hence the name) and were serialized into episodes, featuring stories of adventure and horror, often representing anti-heroes. These penny dreadfuls might have appealed to the working class because they frequently championed an unprivileged character, which would have been attractive in a time of class stratification in Britain.

The penny dreadfuls were not examples of what Eisner would term "sequential art," but featured illustrated stories with a short text, usually penned by hack writers but sometimes written by better known "respectable" authors, often under pennames. According to anthologist Peter Haining, "one of the most important 'selling' features of these publications were the lurid engravings—'fierce' plates as they have become known—which decorated the front page of each issue."[16] Haining notes that while the illustrations were well executed, the text was sometimes lacking in continuity and that "by modern standards, most of these works were atrociously written, appallingly printed and ephemeral to the last degree. Yet their influence and format have been enduring."[17] By the 1860s there was a significant change in the marketing of penny dreadfuls toward young people.[18] Haining quotes Margaret Dalziel, who states, "'It is true that from the sixties onwards "Penny Dreadfuls" were directed toward a juvenile public—but, of course, this included many adults, just as the readers of comics do today!'"[19] Another way in which comics show similarities to their ancestors is that the physical dimensions of the average penny dreadful are similar to those of the modern-day comic book, and many late examples featured a full-color illustration on the front, as do comics.

In his book titled *Youth, Popular Culture, and Moral Panics: Penny Gaffs to Gangsta-Rap, 1830–1996* (1998), John Springhall describes the penny dreadful in a way not unlike the reaction to comic books today: "They represent what most late Victorian and Edwardian juveniles actually *chose* to read, as opposed to the improving 'reward book' literature which adults in power over them felt that they *should* read."[20] Of course, the unseemly subject matter of this new form of entertainment became fodder for criticism by the upper classes of society. Youth crime and other social disorders were blamed on this form of popular fiction. The bigotry of class hierarchy flared to the point where the penny dreadfuls were being implicated in actual court cases. Stephen Humphries explains this social elitism and hysteria in his book *Hooligans or Rebels? An Oral History of Working-Class Childhood and Youth, 1889–1939* (1995):

> Conformity, with its associations of low intelligence and poor taste . . . has been another concept popular with critics, who have detected in the

mass culture of working-class youth a particular gullibility and a tendency to imitate the antisocial behavior retailed, for example, by comics, cinema and television. Thus in the late nineteenth century the dramatic growth of juvenile literature, especially the penny dreadfuls, aroused moral panic among sections of the middle class, which linked these pernicious influences directly with resistance to authority and crimes committed by working-class youth.[21]

The assumption that these products of popular culture have a negative impact on social behavior displays a bias against the working class. Popular art and entertainment is often derided and erroneously blamed for social ills, while it is common to ignore the true origin of often deeply buried societal problems. Also, when the working class begins to have a literature that unites it, and the act of reading is no longer reserved for the upper classes, it might feel like a rising threat to order. Springhall notes, "The most vociferous critics of new forms of entertainment for the young were recruited from the ranks of the expanding professional middle class and the intellectual clerisy rather than from the manufacturing or business middle class."[22] This "moral panic" and vilification of popular art and literature was nothing more than a thin veil over social bigotry. Springhall continues:

> Misrepresentation of the dangerous effects of such highly stylized and melodramatic fiction on the young suggests that Victorian reporters, magistrates, policemen and watch committees preferred to target a convenient cultural scapegoat for outbreaks of delinquency, rather than lend credence to more fundamental social and economic explanations . . . Official and press reaction to cheap fiction . . . tells us more about adult middle-class impressions of working-class youth culture than about the actual dimensions and causes of juvenile crime.[23]

Just as it happened then, so does it happen now that popular forms of entertainment are wrongly blamed for inspiring juvenile delinquency. Despite this official scorn for working-class literature, the popularity of this kind of entertainment was not dampened, and the notoriety induced by these moral panics may have actually enlivened interest in the art form.

The need for these popular narratives was not a specifically British occurrence. In America in the nineteenth century, the "dime novel" arose as a form of working-class literature. Dating back to the 1840s,[24] the story paper and the cheap library were forerunners to the dime novel and are sometimes lumped in with the term. However, the first true examples arrive in 1860[25] and are attributed to publishers Beadle and Adams. These dime novels were heavily influenced by the penny dreadfuls. In fact, historian Merle Curti explains that

> contrary to the general impression, the dime novel did not spring full-grown from [the minds of publishers Erasmus and Irwin Beadle] when in 1860 they published *Malaeska: The Indian Wife of the White Hunter*. . . . Nor was the rise of this proletarian literature a uniquely American phenomenon: enterprising publishers in this country sometimes pirated whole series of English equivalents, the "shilling shockers."[26]

Unsurprisingly, dime novels suffered the same cultural stigma as their British cousins. Nyberg writes that "the decline in the literary quality of the stories, along with the addition of more lurid cover illustrations, led to an attack on dime novels by vice societies, formed in many major cities in the years following the Civil War."[27] Nyberg goes on to explain how these "vice societies" led to the demise of many of these works, and the status of the dime novel suffered as a consequence of the attacks.[28] In 1884, this moral panic was further inflamed by a book titled *Traps for the Young*, written by Anthony Comstock, in which he blasts the dime novel.[29] Nyberg comments that this book instigated "the first major controversy in the history of American children's culture."[30] Later, comic strips would be attacked, as well as another new form of popular culture—the motion picture.[31] As comic books developed and began to increase in popularity, they were likewise attacked. According to Nyberg,

> The first national attack on comic books came from Sterling North, literary critic for the *Chicago Daily News*. In an editorial on May 8, 1940, headlined "A National Disgrace," North noted that almost every child in America was reading comic books. . . . He examined 108 comics available on the newsstands, concluding that at least 70 percent of them contained material that no respectable newspaper would think of accepting. He argued that the old dime novel could be considered classic literature compared to the comic book.[32]

North's scathing editorial marked the beginning of the debates about comic books that would later lead to the widespread censorship of the field.

The tendency to blame popular entertainment for social ills can still be recognized today. Violent video games and Marilyn Manson music were implicated in the Columbine High School massacre committed by Eric Harris and Dylan Klebold. It seems unlikely that the music and video games were significant contributors to the boys' actions, but popular culture and media are an easy scapegoat when parents, authority figures, and social institutions have trouble addressing their own shortcomings. Like the current demonization of popular music, comics and their forerunners were publicly reviled. This contempt for certain forms of popular culture seems even more apparent when the art form is cheap, readily accessible to the working class, and generally distinguished as "lowbrow" entertainment, rather than looked at as expressing the voice of the proletariat. In essence, they are a product of a classist attitude, and a kind of "social imperialism"[33] is at work. Although this bigotry is becoming more obvious, comics are still looked at with disdain by many a critic. As Scott McCloud says, "For much of this century, the word 'comics' has had such negative connotations that many of comics' most devoted practitioners have preferred to be known as 'illustrators,' 'commercial artists,' or, at best, 'cartoonists'!"[34] The snobbery of critics regarding these inexpensive, serialized publications has kept the esteem for comics down, but all of that is in the midst of change right now, as comics are gaining respect and are becoming an undeniably important mode of expression in our postmodern era.

The History of Comic Books for Girls

If the value of comic books has been overlooked, then so has their appeal to the female reader. Even among the penny dreadfuls, there were titles such as *Jenny Diver, the Female Highwayman* and *Alice; or, The Adventures of an English Girl in Persia*, featuring female protagonists, even though many penny dreadfuls were adventure or horror stories written to attract male readers. Girls and women would have been interested in the printed fare that was intended for their male counterparts when journals for women such as *Girl's Own Paper* (1880–1956) instructed heavily on domestic duties and preached about how to become an "angel in the house." As Kimberley Reynolds asserts in *Girls Only? Gender and Popular Chil-*

dren's Fiction in Britain, 1880–1910 (1990), "There is a noteworthy contradiction between what girls actually read, the prohibitive rhetoric which laid down what they ought and ought not to be reading, and what in fact it was tacitly accepted that girls read."[35] The media prescribed for females at the time could not have appealed to every woman and girl since some human interests are universal, even if considered crass or unseemly. There is also a history of females as the creators of working-class narrative. This is unsurprising because females' tastes don't always coincide with society's values. In *The Penny Dreadful Or, Strange, Horrid & Sensational Tales!* there is an engraving depicting a gruesome scene of cannibalism illustrating the story of Sawney Beane, an influence on the creation of the famous Sweeney Todd character.[36] The caption exclaims, "*The Terrific Register* published in 1825 was one of the very first Penny Dreadfuls. The bloodthirsty engraving was the work of a woman, Mary Byfield!"[37] This proves that not only did females read such publications, but they also had a hand in creating them. There is no doubt that penny dreadfuls would have appealed to girls—they were thrilling, enticing in their serial form, and, above all, inexpensive. This tendency has of course persisted, as girls have been reading comics oriented toward males for many years. According to Martin Barker's book *Comics: Ideology, Power and the Critics* (1989), "The Penny Dreadfuls were widely read by both girls and boys (as the Victorian critics noted to their dismay)."[38] Evidence also suggests that, in America, dime novels would have been attractive reading fare for females as well. A fine example of a dime novel that certainly would have had appeal to female readers, cites Curti, is

> the story of Deborah Sampson, born of poor and inferior parents, who had as an indentured servant learned to read tolerably well. Donning soldierly attire, she fought unsuspected in the ranks until sickness led to the discovery of her secret. Her name, we read, became venerated as that of a self-made woman whose great gifts the War of Independence had released for a great cause.[39]

Similarly, girls have always been interested in that later form of popular fiction, the comic book, whether or not the target audience was male. While there is little doubt that some girls would have been interested in comics featuring male characters, it is even more likely that girls would have been drawn to and even influenced by comics starring a female protagonist.

One of the most fascinating females in early comic books, Sheena, Queen of the Jungle, made her debut in 1937.[40] Sheena fought villains with strength, skill, and her sharp wits. She also had a sharp knife and was not afraid to use it—she was an expert in all manner of combat. The golden-haired jungle queen also holds the distinction of being the first female character in comics to star in her own series.[41] However, Will Eisner and S. M. Iger's fierce jungle warrior was not created specifically for the enjoyment and empowerment of female readers. Although she was represented as a strong and powerful female, Sheena resembled a pin-up model, designed for the male gaze. Though she would fight and often kill her opponents brutally, yet efficiently, she would do all of this with her statuesque form clad in only the scantiest, often ragged or torn leopard-hide bathing suits. *Sheena, Queen of the Jungle* belongs more to the pulp tradition of adventure stories than girls' or women's cartoons, though, undoubtedly she was read by many females and her success spawned a whole genre of jungle-woman comics.

However, there is a long history of American comic books published specifically for the female consumer. Wonder Woman was the first female superhero created with the *intention* of providing a strong role model for girls. Some of the first female superheroes, such as *Fantomah* (1940) and *The Woman in Red* (1940), predated the well-known *Wonder Woman*, which was published in 1941.[42] However, according Petersen, "Wonder Woman was the first conceptual superhero specifically designed to send a feminist message."[43] Psychologist William Moulton Marston devised the character with the help of his wife, Elizabeth Holloway Marston, also a psychologist. The Marstons were an unconventional couple; they helped to develop the lie detector test (its powers echoed, remarkably, in the abilities of Wonder Woman's Lasso of Truth), and they were involved in a long-term polyamorous relationship.[44] Also, Elizabeth was a career woman, as well as a mother, in a time when many women were expected to give up their work once they were married. Therefore, it is not surprising that the Marstons, having revolutionary views of sexuality and the role of the woman, would invent such a boundary-breaking character.

This all began when the comic book publishers, who would later merge to become the modern incarnation of DC Comics, approached

William Moulton Marston. Interested in his expertise, the company recruited Marston to contribute to an "Editorial Advisory Board."[45] Marston's involvement in the comic book industry would put him in an ideal position to create his own character, and the idea for a new type of superhero was born. Petersen states: "Marston saw an opportunity to provide a new role model for girls by creating a vigorous and bold female archetype in comic books."[46] However, it was Elizabeth Holloway Marston's suggestions that shaped the creation of what would become one of comics' most enduring characters. Reportedly, it was her input that decided the gender of this new character. In her 1993 obituary (she lived to be one hundred years old), the *New York Times* acknowledged Elizabeth Holloway Marston's influence on the invention of the popular character, quoting the Marstons' son, Peter, saying, "When he [William Moulton Marston] was developing the idea for a cartoon character, he sought his wife's advice. She told him, 'Come on, let's have a Superwoman! There's too many men out there.'"[47] Her suggestion not only helped to construct a character that appealed to girls but to boys as well. Through Wonder Woman's broad attraction, the Marstons were able to disseminate their early feminist message to an entire generation and beyond. In her book, *Reading Comics: Language, Culture, and the Concept of the Superhero in Comic Books* (2000), Mila Bongco notes that *Wonder Woman* was one of the few superhero comics to continue "without a break in publication during the lean years of the early 1950s when interest had shifted to crime, western, and in particular 'horror and gore' comics."[48] To this day, Wonder Woman has remained a mainstay comic book character. Moreover, the influence that she has had on girls is undeniable. Feminist activist Gloria Steinem even used an image of Wonder Woman for the cover of the first issue of *Ms. Magazine*, proving that Wonder Woman has had a strong and lasting effect on the girls who grew up with her.

While *Wonder Woman* was one of the earliest comics to be written with girls in mind, it was never meant to be *exclusively* for girls. Boys enjoyed her adventures as well. Nevertheless, comic books made specifically for girls would soon appear in abundance. Strangely enough, this trend began with *Archie* (1941–present), a comic book that was not specifically written for girls. *Archie* featured the day-to-day adventures of a teenage boy; "Archie Andrews, his pal Jughead, and a wistful blond named Betty made their debut in issue no. 22 of *Pep*, dated December 1941 . . . For the next seventeen years, teen comics ruled the roost."[49] What was so different about Archie was that he was a normal teenage boy—no superpowers, no cape, no secret identity. He was just a boy whose main interests were girls, cars, and having fun with his friend Jughead. In *From Girls to Grrrlz*, Robbins theorizes why superhero comics were on the decline, giving rise to the teen comics boom:

> *Archie*'s success was a case of the right teenager at the right time. Superhero comics, which dominated the market during the war, had been steadily losing their audience. Perhaps the returning GIs, who had made up a large part of the comic-reading market, were now more interested in buying homes on the GI bill and raising families, or perhaps the general public was tired of violence after almost five years of war. Whatever the reason, soon after the war DC Comics' superhero line was reduced by more than half, and other companies followed suit. The departing superheroes left a gap on the newsstands that was quickly filled by horror comics, westerns, . . . and teen comics aimed at girls.[50]

This shift would see the rise of an era of girls' comics. It had quickly become apparent that girls made up a large percentage of Archie's readership. Robbins observes, "The majority of *Archie* readers were girls, ages six to thirteen."[51] Popularity increased for the girls' market, and by the mid-1940s the newsstands were filled with girls' comics. Some of these comic books featured strong female characters, such as Millie the Model (1945) and Katy Keene.[52] Katy Keene, who originated in the *Wilbur* comics, received her own comic book series in 1949.[53] Katy was a career woman (an actress), and, due in part to the interactive style of the comic books, which included games and puzzles, photos of fans, as well as paper dolls and pinups featuring fan-made designs, and more, *Katy Keene* had a popular fan club.[54] By 1950, Archie's girls got their own comic book, *Betty and Veronica*, which, according to Robbins, would become "the best-selling title in the *Archie* comics line."[55] However, Betty, Veronica, and many of their derivatives were not always the most positive role models for girls: they were often boy-crazy, shallow, and obsessed with their looks. Even Robbins admits that Katy Keene was often shown competing with another girl, Gloria Grandbilt, for men's affections.[56]

The stereotyping of females in early girls' comic books is exemplified by the way in which Betty and Veronica are drawn (see fig. 1.2). If Veronica's

Figure 1.2. *Archie Comics Digest Magazine*, no. 38, October 1979. Veronica and Betty. In the Archie universe, women are depicted similarly.
Courtesy of Archie Comics™.

sleek, dark coiffure was swapped for Betty's bouncy blonde locks, it would soon be apparent that the hairstyle and color are their only distinguishing characteristics, while Archie and Jughead are drawn as distinctly different characters with definitive facial features (see fig. 1.3). Female characters were given to jealousy and a desire to "catch a man," which led to comical situations in these stories.

However, the popularity of teen comics did not survive beyond the 1950s. Aside from a few comics such as *Millie the Model* and *Patsy Walker*, as well as the *Archie* line, which retained steady popularity, teen comics only lasted from the early 1940s through the late 1950s, when a great upheaval occurred within the comics industry.[57] In 1954, a psychiatrist by the name of Dr. Fredric Wertham published his now famous book, *Seduction of the Innocent*, which, according to journalist and historian David Hajdu, "indicted comics as a leading cause of juvenile delinquency."[58] This

Figure 1.3. *Archie Comics Digest Magazine*, no. 38, October 1979. Archie and Jughead are physically distinct from each other.
Courtesy of Archie Comics™.

eerily echoed the concerns of Comstock over the dime novel, published seventy years before Wertham's book. In the aftermath of the publication of *Seduction of the Innocent*, the Senate Subcommittee on Juvenile Delinquency began its attack on the comic book industry.[59] In 1954, a three-day congressional hearing was held, and twenty-two witnesses were brought in, including Dr. Fredric Wertham and publishers such as William Gaines, head of Entertaining Comics (EC), one of the leading purveyors of crime and horror comics.[60] Even though the Senate Subcommittee on Juvenile Delinquency did not ultimately find comics responsible for increases in juvenile delinquency, and only suggested that the violence of these publications be toned down, it was obvious that the comic book industry had lost this battle. Wertham was a highly esteemed witness, and Gaines was young and perhaps ill-prepared for such an attack on his products.[61] Nyberg relates how Gaines floundered when he was asked, "Is there any limit you can think of that you would not put in a magazine because you thought a child should not see or read about it?"[62] His reply would soil his reputation and condemn comics further. He insisted that he worked within the limits of what he considered "good taste."[63] However, the opposition was armed with some damningly graphic and violent comic book covers. Gaines was unable to wiggle out of his previous statement. When asked "'Do you think that is in good taste?' Having just said he would publish anything he felt was in good taste, Gaines had no choice. He answered, 'Yes, sir, I do, for the cover of a horror comic.'"[64] The comic book in question featured a woman's severed head, eyes rolled back, and blood dripping from her mouth. At this moment in the hearing Gaines discredited himself, coming across as amoral, and the media ran wild with the sensational reports. Other negative examples of EC publications were taken out of context to condemn Gaines and the industry that he represented.[65] As a result, comics were further lambasted as crude and violent.

Although the Senate's report did not end up with any conclusive evidence that comics were harmful to children, the report suggested that the publishers should take responsibility for their products and that the industry should publish material that "measures up to its standards of morality and decency."[66] The wounded comic book industry developed its own form of self-censorship in response to the dilemma stirred up by Wertham and the Senate Subcommittee on Juvenile Delinquency. The Comics Code Authority (CCA) was born. Nyberg claims that the establishment of such a watchdog committee was the agenda of the Senate all along. She says, "[T]he intention of the hearing from the beginning was to force (or frighten) the publishers into adopting a self-regulatory code like that of the film industry."[67] The fallout of the hearings not only curbed the Senate's intended target—horror and crime comics—it forever changed the entire industry. The scandal led many parents to disallow comics to their children. Furthermore, many comic book authors and illustrators lost work or never worked again in the field.

Today, historians disagree on whether or not the comics industry should have taken it upon themselves to censor their publications and whether the impact that the Comics Code Authority made upon the field was a positive or negative one. In her book, *The Great Women Cartoonists* (2001), Trina Robbins discusses the enforcement of the Comics Code and how it affected the industry, asserting that it led directly to the demise of "most of the comic book companies" and affected comics for young women.[68] Robbins states:

> As with any industry slump, many artists were let go, and as with any industry, the first fired were women. *Patsy Walker* comics died in 1967. *Millie the Model* . . . hung on until 1974. By this time, neither book had been drawn by a woman for over twenty years.[69]

In the appendix to *The Ten Cent Plague: The Great Comic-Book Scare and How It Changed America*, Hajdu makes it a point to catalogue the comic book creators who never worked again in the comics industry after the Comics Code was created, and the list includes a great number of women.[70] According to Robbins, it appears that there is a link between the departure of female artists and writers from the comic book field and the decline of comics for females. She notes sadly:

> The two major comic book publishers that survived the comics depression of the mid- to late 1950s were Marvel and DC, and both companies had, since the mid-1960s, been gearing themselves toward super heroes and the young male market. Female-oriented comic books were slowly being phased out.[71]

In contrast, however, Martin Barker suggests that girls' comics enjoyed a boom due to enforcement of the Comics Code. In the aftermath of Wertham's book and the Senate hearings, a wealth of new titles aimed at teen girls and women cropped up, reflecting the values of a censorship culture that dictated how good girls should think and behave. An era of romance comics was born. This genre did not initially meet with friction from critics because romance and love were acceptable topics for young women to be interested in. At this point, gender separation in comics became even more marked. Barker explains this phenomenon: "On each occasion when the definition of a 'comic' came under threat, one of the first responses was to reinforce the gender separation of readers. . . . One of the first acts of the new comics producers was to enforce a clear distinction."[72]

How could critics like Wertham complain about comics that featured the topic of love? Romance comics were viewed as safe because no one could possibly blame juvenile delinquency on comic books that focused on love and romance. The romance titles quickly replaced many horror and crime books in a flurry of love. Hajdu writes, "That the romance books were, at first, seen as harmless—just love stories, only girl stuff—allowed them to flourish in an era when other comics were held in suspicion."[73] Though there were many positive examples of women within the romance genre, there was also an abundance of comics with pages filled with stereotypes: women who could not live without a man and women who would give up their careers, their ambition, their *independence*, to be at his side.

There were exceptions to the boy-crazy stereotypes, however. Many earlier comics featured female characters who were strong, and even got the better of the boys in their story lines—with comics such as *Little Lulu* (1945). Marjorie Henderson Buell (known by her penname, "Marge") created her sassy character, Little Lulu Moppet, in 1935 as a single-panel cartoon for the *Saturday Evening Post*.[74] However, in 1945, Marge's feisty Lulu made the transition from newspaper to comic books where John Stanley became the writer and arranged the layouts.[75] Henderson Buell didn't draw Lulu for the comic books, though she did retain the rights to Lulu until 1971.[76] Working with artist Irving Tripp, Stanley augmented the Lulu character and created continuing story lines that spread out over separate issues.[77] The successful Lulu comic book series was known as *Marge's Little Lulu*.

In a time when girls were expected to be timid and grow up to be subservient, Lulu offered an alternative message to girls. For example, *Marge's Little Lulu*, no. 8, February 1949, contains a story called "Beautiful Lulu." In this episode, Lulu, looking for her playmates, walks over to the boys' clubhouse. As she approaches, she begins to hear the boys talking about how pretty some of the other neighborhood girls are. However, when the boys get around to talking about Lulu, they laugh and describe her as "homely."[78] Devastated, Lulu runs home crying and hides under her bed. When her mother finds out what had happened, she says, "I think I can show you how *silly* boys are."[79] Her mother proceeds to give Lulu a sophisticated new hairdo, and dresses her up in a fashionable frock. When she sees the neighborhood boys again, they change their attitude toward Lulu. They can't seem to stop complimenting Lulu and fawning over her.

Lulu's smile shows how pleased she is with her and her mother's experiment, until the boys start fighting each other over her.[80] Lulu extricates herself from this situation and runs home where her mother asks her if the boys liked her and if they found her to be pretty. Lulu replies, "I guess so . . ."[81] When her mother remarks, "Well, you don't seem to be very *happy* about it," Lulu states, "I don't think I *want* to be pretty after all, mother. / You were right about boys being *silly!* / I'm going up to my room to change."[82] When she reemerges from her house, the old, rough-and-tumble, curly-haired Lulu has returned. She happily starts to play a carefree game of leapfrog with the "fellers."[83] Transcending the pressures that our society exerts upon girls to dress in ways that are attractive to the opposite sex, this story sends the message that girls need not change a thing—they are fine the way that they are. Although the boys make fools of themselves over the artifice of her makeover, in the end Lulu is accepted by the boys without having to alter her appearance and please the eye. Lulu's fun-loving personality is magnetic enough without the addition of frippery.

In the story, "A Wrong Move," from *Little Lulu,* no. 9, March 1949, Lulu is outdoors playing with a ball when the neighborhood boys walk by and announce that they are having a meeting at their clubhouse. When Lulu asks if she can join in, she is told cruelly, "Of course not, stupid!" only because she is not a boy.[84] One of the boys demeans her saying, "Go change your dolly's diaper!" insinuating that all girls do is play with dolls in practice for a life of domestic responsibilities.[85] However, Lulu does not want to play with dolls and diapers. She just wants to play with the boys and be treated as an equal. The "fellers" walk off to their clubhouse leaving Lulu alone to play with her ball. The next panel contains no words, but it is obvious that Lulu is angry. She continues her game with the ball, but her mouth has become a large frown and her brows are knitted together. Three large, dark clouds rise from her head like smoke as she fumes at the way in which she has been treated.[86] In the subsequent panel, Lulu can no longer contain her anger, and she shouts out, "Phooey! Who cares!" in the boys' general direction.[87]

Meanwhile, one of the boys proclaims, "Anybody who tries to get a girl in our club gets kicked out right away!"[88] The boys all stare at Tubby, Lulu's friend, and it is obvious that this comment is directed at him. Instead of defending his friendship with Lulu, Tubby replies, "You bet!"[89] When the boys get to their clubhouse, they find that the empty lot where they had built it is slated for development. The clubhouse needs a new home, but no one can think of a place to move it to, until Tubby comes up with an idea: if they ask Lulu to join the club, then they can use *her* backyard. The boys, desperate to find a new home for the clubhouse, resign themselves to bringing a girl into their club, after all. Nevertheless, the plan does not go so smoothly when they approach Lulu. When Tubby is sent to ask her to join the club, Lulu refuses, having been stung by the earlier rejection. However, Tubby, being resourceful, whispers to Lulu, offering her presidency of the club. He says, "You'll be the boss an' you can do anything you want!"[90] Lulu agrees. They start to sing "For She's a Jolly Good Fellow" to Lulu, but soon depart to start work on moving the clubhouse, leaving Lulu singing her victory song all by herself.[91]

Lulu, not understanding what is going on, has to run to catch up with them. Miffed at not knowing what the group is up to, she demands to know what is happening, but Tubby snaps at her, "*Quiet*! Can't you see we're *busy*?" to which Lulu, frustrated, yells, "But *I'm* the *president*!"[92] In response, the boys then decide that, because she is their president, she should have the *honor* of helping them tow their clubhouse away using a rope and wagons. When they get to the street, they find that the clubhouse (which, ironically, still sports a sign that says, "No girls allowed" on its side) moves more easily, so the boys jump inside and demand that their president tow them the rest of the way.[93] When they finally arrive at their destination, Lulu, exhausted, falls flat on her face. Once she sits up, she is surprised to find herself in front of her own house. By now, Lulu knows that she's been duped. When Lulu gets angry, the boys try to convince her that they had decided to move the clubhouse for *her* convenience, since she is the new president.[94] Lulu is not convinced. She watches as the boys raid her kitchen and make a big mess before they run off to get to a ball game to which Lulu is not even invited.[95]

Later, Lulu's father comes home, complaining about the price of wood for a workbench that he was going to make for himself, and Lulu has a bright idea. She remembers the words that Tubby had said about her being president of the club: "you can do *anything you want!*"[96] She asks her dad if he would like all the wood that he needs for fifty cents and shows him the clubhouse. Happily, her father dismantles the structure. Later that day, when the boys return, they are puzzled by the disappearance of the clubhouse, until Lulu informs them that she sold it for fifty cents because Tubby had told her that she could do whatever she wanted as president. The boys, infuriated, run off, chasing after Tubby, who cries for his "ma."[97] Clever Lulu had turned an empty promise into a profit. The boys, thinking that they had been smart in manipulating Lulu to get what they wanted, pay for their behavior when the ingenious Little Lulu outwits them. This story pokes fun at sexist attitudes, as well as highlighting the capability of females—and all this in the 1940s, well before the second wave of feminism.

A year before Lulu made her transition from newspapers to comic books, Timely Comics (later to become Marvel Comics) created Miss America (1944), a female superhero. But the superhero format was soon transformed: "By its second issue Miss America had become a girls' magazine featuring fiction, fashion and beauty tips, chatty articles about pop stars, and comics."[98] American girls' magazines featuring comics first began in 1941 with the magazine *Calling All Girls*.[99] Both *Calling All Girls* and *Miss America* (which was aimed at older teen girls) contained at least some typical magazine fare such as letters pages and advice columns, contests, jokes, short stories and featurettes, advertising, and even paper dolls—a major preoccupation of these magazines being fashion and popular culture, as well as comics. Many of these magazines promoted positive role models for young women, even though these magazines often featured such gender-stereotypical articles and advertising as makeup and fashion tips.

The September 1942 issue of *Calling All Girls* includes comics that feature many strong, proactive female characters. "Daughter of Free France"[100] tells the story of Eve Curie, daughter of Marie Curie, who traveled the world and went to the front lines to report on World War II. "The Unsinkable Molly Brown"[101] tells the story of legendary philanthropist Margaret Brown, hero and survivor of the Titanic disaster. The serial "Judy Wing: Air Hostess No. 1"[102] relates the adventures of a (fictional) character working as an airline "hostess" who is also studying for her pilot's license. This issue also includes a section titled "Girls in the News."[103] While it is not a comics feature, it presents short paragraphs with accompanying photos about *real* girls and young women who are engaged in various activities. Many of the blurbs feature the patriotic role of young women in America at that time: the "students of Isaac E. Young High School, New Rochelle, N.Y., build wooden model planes to be used in teaching aircraft spotters recognition of military aircraft,"[104] and "two Girl Scout mariners of the "Whaler" unit of Greenwich, Conn., learn to operate a telephone switch board. The girls enjoy this landlubber's job because it will make them useful to welfare and war agencies."[105] Within the pages of these early comics magazines there are many colorful examples of active and brave females.

Perceptions of American girls and women can be charted across the issues of these comic book magazines. The pages of the 1942 issue of *Calling All Girls* promotes a "you can do it" attitude in girls. The females of these comic book stories are active and resourceful. They display examples of women who have *jobs*, women who don't just settle for getting married and keeping a house. During the era in which these pieces were written, young women were being galvanized to take up new roles for the first time in America. Women were needed in the workforce. They were needed by their country to work in factories and fill the void that would be left by the men who went away to fight a war on foreign shores. The patriotism and strength of the women and teenage girls portrayed in the magazines and comics of this era reflect the country's need, at that time in history, to prepare teenage girls for a world in which they would have to contribute to the workforce and be involved in the war effort. Later issues of the same publication and its contemporaries such as *Miss America* portray a very different attitude toward the role of the young woman.

If we examine the covers of some of these postwar examples of the comic book/magazine combination, we can see how gender was structured for readers of this literature. The September 1958 (vol. 1, no. 92) issue of *Miss America* (see fig. 1.4) features the hero, Patsy Walker, in a roller skating rink leaning back on a young man (her boyfriend, Buzz) while two other girls make comments about Patsy's "skating ability." Her rival, a raven-haired girl named Hedy, remarks, "Humph! You'd think Patsy would be *smart* enough to *know* how to skate by now!" while Patsy's best friend, Nancy, retorts, "She *does* know . . . but she's smart enough not to *admit* it!"[106] This exchange not only portrays a sense of petty rivalry between teenaged girls as they compete for male affection but also implies that girls should hide how intelligent they are in order to attract the opposite sex. This attitude suggests that females should "play dumb" and that they may even be less attractive to males the more capable they show themselves to be. Only two years after World War II was over, the

Figure 1.4. *Miss America*, September 1958, vol. 1, no. 92 (cover image).
Courtesy Miss America, copyright and trademark Marvel Entertainment, LLC; used with permission.

September 1947 (vol. 7, no. 2) edition of *Miss America* contains vacuously boy-obsessed stories featuring the magazine's most popular character, Patsy Walker, and others. In this issue, Patsy becomes infatuated with a man that she sees on a bus, even though she has a devoted boyfriend, Buzz Baxter. She winds up following this stranger as he goes home. Later in the story, she manages to get herself invited into the gentleman's mansion to deliver a package, and while she is there, she steals a framed photograph of the young man. Not only does this story promote unhealthy obsessions and dangerous behavior, but Patsy never apologizes for stealing the portrait, nor is she punished. Patsy actually uses the portrait to make Buzz jealous, but this plan backfires when she finds out that the man from the bus has a sweetheart—her nemesis, Hedy. In a jealous rage, Patsy smashes the framed picture over Hedy's skull.

In its own strange way Patsy's behavior can be viewed as liberating. When Buzz exclaims, "I thought you said you wouldn't go *out* with other boys," she replies, flippantly, "Ohh . . . I have my moments!"[107] This shows that Patsy does not feel that she has to be tied to one relationship, or one image of how a young woman should behave. Nevertheless, when Patsy finds out that she has no chance with the man from the bus, she decides that she still wants to be with Buzz. She lies and tells poor Buzz that the whole debacle was "just a little *joke*"[108] and suggests that they go out for a movie. Buzz may not be what Patsy really wants, but at least she has a man! Not only does this episode of "Patsy Walker" normalize disturbing behavior, but it also sends a dangerous message to girls that it is better to settle for an imperfect relationship than to be alone.

Even more interesting are the changes that took place in postwar issues of *Calling All Girls*. Where real girls were once featured on the cover of this comic book magazine, illustrations began to appear. While many of the illustrations for *Calling All Girls* were innocuous, some appear overly suggestive for a magazine aimed at pre-teens. The October 1960 edition (fig. 1.5) displays a girl dressed up for Halloween in a tiger costume. She is posed kneeling while the magazine's mascot, a dachshund, is shown holding the severed tail of her costume in his mouth while the young woman gazes at her own posterior. This image can be viewed as sexualized not only because of the submissive kneeling pose but also because of the image's content. Felinity has long been associated with a sexist notion of female temperament and sexuality. Her lips are full and red and her

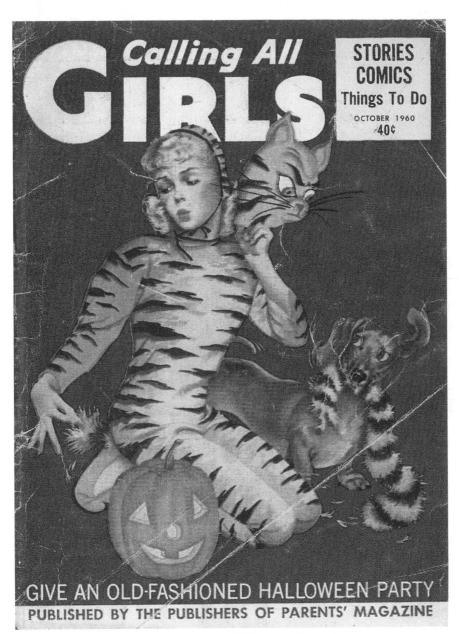

Figure 1.5. *Calling All Girls*, **October 1960 (cover image).**
Illustrated by Freeman Elliot and originally published in *Calling All Girls*® magazine.

costume clingy. If the artwork featured on the covers of these later issues looks familiar to you, then perhaps you have previously encountered the work of the pin-up artist Freeman Elliot. In his introduction to *Patriotic Pin-ups*, a collection of various pin-up artists, Max Allan Collins describes typical Elliot subject matter: "Elliot's girls were gorgeous, impossibly long-stemmed creatures, often involved in whimsically compromising situations. . . . Other Elliot subjects might be found answering the phone in a towel, painting the house in a bikini, cooking in the kitchen wearing nothing but a tiny apron."[109] It is not hard to imagine that Elliot's talent was more attuned to drawing racy pin-up art rather than the covers for a pre-teen girls' magazine. The May 1959 edition of *Calling All Girls* (fig. 1.6) shows a scene in which a young woman with rouged lips is posed emerging from a doghouse, vacuum-cleaning wand in hand, silently rebuking her dog, which has chewed her tennis shoe. It seems innocent enough, yet her face is illustrated in a sophisticated manner that does not belong to any pre-teen girl and the vacuum cleaner's wand looks strangely phallic. Again the subject is shown on her knees. It seems that though Elliot may have been a versatile artist who could be hired to create mainstream art as well as erotica, a little of the pin-up artist peeps through in these covers for *Calling All Girls*. There is no doubt as to their sexualization of the young female, as low-key as it might seem at first glance.

In addition to the covers, the postwar content of *Calling All Girls* was questionable as well. The recurring "Tizzie" comics focus on the hijinks of a pre-teen girl named Leticia, or Tizzie for short. On one hand, Tizzie is a tomboy and is frequently drawn wearing pants instead of skirts or dresses. Many of the stories involve Tizzie in active adventures, often playing with the boys (or showing them up). However, the authors seem torn between characterizing Tizzie as a strong girl and painting her as the 1950s standard of girlhood. In an episode called "Tizzie's Private Practice Session," Tizzie is incensed when a boy tells her that females are no good at sports.[110] Tizzie sets out to put the record straight. We cheer for Tizzie when she makes a home run and the boys ask her to join their team. But soon we find that Tizzie had her eyes closed and the hit was just a stroke of luck. Tizzie has enough pluck to request baseball lessons from her father, but her diligence doesn't pay off—Tizzie is still lousy at baseball. This seems to preserve the myth that girls have no place in competitive, male-oriented

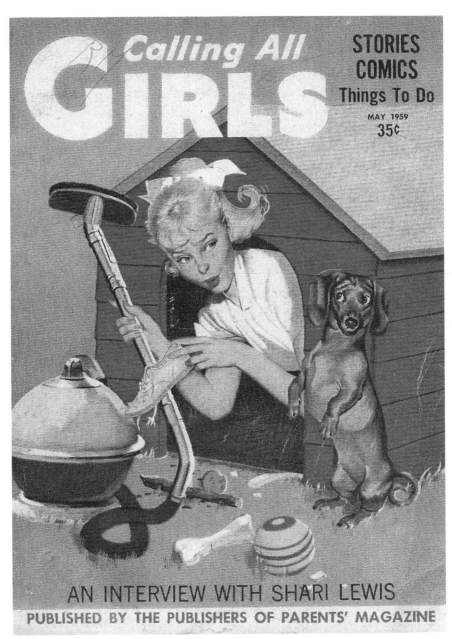

Figure 1.6. *Calling All Girls*, May 1959 (cover image).
Illustrated by Freeman Elliot and originally published in *Calling All Girls®* magazine.

sports and attempts to put young females in "their place." The most retrogressive scene in "Tizzie's Private Practice Session" comes when Tizzie's mother hurts her arm while playing catcher, and her father wrenches his back from pitching for Tizzie's practice lessons. Tizzie then jumps at the opportunity to use this as an excuse not to play in "the big game." Instead of giving it her best and trying to face the boys, she decides that playing the role of "nurse" to her parents takes precedence over competing with males.[111] This sends a message to girls that their duties lie in the home first and that they are far better suited to traditionally feminine jobs such as nursing. In the final two panels we see that Tizzie even changes her appearance from a trouser-clad tomboy to a uniformed nurse, complete with white apron and starched hat (see fig. 1.7).

Another regular feature in *Calling All Girls* was the nationally syndicated "Penny" comics by Harry Haenigsen. The "Penny" comics offered little vignettes from a week in Penny's world. "Penny" originated as a

Figure 1.7. *Calling All Girls*, April 1959, page 21. From "Tizzie's Private Practice Session."
Originally published in *Calling All Girls*® magazine.

syndicated strip comic. In *Calling All Girls*, the strip typically contains four to ten panels with the last panel containing the punch line. The eponymous comics offer light humor and feature the teenage Penny and characters such as her pipe-smoking father. Sometimes the Penny cartoons are so fluffy that it makes the protagonist seem shallow and vacuous. In the October 1957 issue of *Calling All Girls*, Penny appears in a four-panel gag in which her father is upset because he had left an important message for her on the bulletin board, which she did not notice. When confronted about this, Penny admits to her father, "Oh, I never look at that old thing."[112] Her perpetually frustrated father then has a brilliant idea: he turns Penny's mirror into her message center. In the last panel Penny is shown fixing her hair in the mirror. Only then does she notice her father's messages. "Weeps," she cries, "a message from Father!"[113] This suggests that teen girls are typically obsessed with vanity and not the practical side of life. Comics such as "Penny" and "Patsy Walker" send young women the message that it is normal behavior, and even expected of them, to be image-obsessed and boy-crazy. In *Comics and Magazines* (1984), Judith Hemming and Jane Legget attempt to bring criticism of comics and magazines into focus. They suggest that "times have changed, but girls' images of themselves haven't. And where do they get those from? You've guessed it. . . . Comics have an enormous influence on children."[114] Popular forms of media have incredible sway over how teens perceive themselves, from body image to their role in society. Hemming and Legget comment that in comics magazines like these, teens "learn that trendy girls don't do their homework. They're too busy dreaming about boys."[115]

While Hemming and Legget's analysis of comics' influence on girls is valid, the historical context of these early comics for girls should not be ignored. While Patsy Walker and her ilk may appear to be obsessed with boys and cleave to other sexist stereotypes and roles, they also often represented girls and women who were clever and tough. Comics have always reflected the times in which they have been written. Mass media has always had an influence on the public, and girls' comics and magazines of the past are no exception. Whether these comics were suggesting that young women seek to learn new skills and serve their country, or be preoccupied with fashion, boys, and household ties, comics have mirrored the sociopolitical climate of their times.

Today, comics still represent the identity of girls in America and their current concerns, and they increasingly reflect what teenaged girls think in a more realistic manner—especially since the advent of independently released comics that are less influenced by advertisers and the mass media. Through independent comics, we begin to see a revolution taking place: the clear voices of young women are shining through this medium with more personal and imaginative forms of storytelling. The women's movement of the 1960s took a little while to permeate the world of comics, but at long last, in the 1970s, the field took a more enlightened turn with the rise of underground comics, better known as "comix." The comix realm had been dominated up until 1970 by males, but the wave of feminism finally broke upon America's western shore. Trina Robbins remarks,

> Despite the general male antipathy, 1970 saw an explosion of feminist underground newspapers all over America. . . . The San Francisco Bay Area was a steaming hotbed of feminism, and that year, *It Ain't Me, Babe*, the first women's liberation newspaper in America, formed in Berkeley. By the second issue, I had found a place within the paper, drawing covers and comic strips for them.[116]

Robbins goes on to explain how this new feminist movement in comix got started and how it would affect women's and girls' comics to come. Maurice Horn, author of *Women in the Comics* (vol. 3), also points out that "the 1970s . . . witnessed the emergence of the alternative press whereby comics authors could self-publish their own creations and have them distributed through comic book shops: Wendy Pini . . . launched her long-running series of *Elfquest* comic books in just this way."[117] Women comic book writers were representing, if not more realistic characters, at least real women's thoughts by bypassing an industry that had become very closed to female writers. Offering a broad range of female perspectives, they took back an expressive art form with a revolutionary, do-it-yourself attitude that can still be found in comics today.

Comics—Now!

Comics' role in the lives of many girls—to represent the female experience and instill cultural mores—is underestimated. The object of this research is to nullify the arguments questioning the value of comics and open up a discussion of comics as a literary and artistic resource. This book approaches comics as a hybrid art form that is just emerging from a history of bias and shame to make a better name for itself and to explore what that means to female readers who have previously been marginalized by the collector industry. To better understand comics, it is important to understand how comic books are read, how they work as a composite art form, and the value of visual literacy itself. Theories of how the comic book form works—its complexity as an intricate system of symbols—will be visited, and the notion that comics are as valid an art form as the picture book, though not as widely accepted as literature, shall be explored. To borrow from opera terminology, Wagner's notion of *Gesamtkunstwerk*, which translates as "complete art work," is the word that most closely expresses the ability of comics to blend, harmoniously, literature and art—the visual with the textual—to create something that is much more than the two parts alone.

There is significant change occurring within the field of comics and in its perception by the public. The increasing popularity of the graphic novel (and the trade paperback) format, as well as the capabilities of the Internet, is generating a new wave of interest in comics. Comics and graphic novels are becoming more accessible—rising up from their underground status, moving from the small hobbyist shops and collector's arena into mainstream bookstores. Names and labels have had a significant impact on the comic book art form, and the term *graphic novel* seems to have a certain cachet that the term *comics* does not. Through their association with the literary term "novel," comics are gaining new fans. In the last decade, graphic novels have made their way into bookstores and libraries. Graphic novels are changing the female reader's appreciation of comics, as they gain their own sections in bookstores. Manga (Japanese comics) has boomed in popularity among girls and is readily available on the shelves of traditional comic book retailers and bookstores alike, introducing the comics art form to new readers. The Internet has made innovations in self-publishing possible with webcomics that are often available for free. Additionally, new technologies such as e-readers and tablet computers allow readers to follow many of their favorite comics without having to ever set foot into a brick-and-mortar store. This is an exciting time for girls and their comics as the rise in the mainstream acceptance of graphic novels and manga may be affecting the way that the comic book field is perceived, and recent media interest in the art form and newly available technology may be helping to lift comics from out of their pulp reputation.

This book also attempts to explain what it might mean to grow up with comics and explores how comics themselves are growing up. The field of comics is on an exciting journey; female roles in comics are continuing to mature, and the mainstream is starting to take the field seriously. It is an interesting time for comics and their female readers, as the feminine in comics is becoming more established in what has been considered a male art form. Comics are gaining an esteemed place upon the bookshelves of girls and young women, and this is an adventure that certainly deserves to be chronicled.

Notes

1. Scott McCloud, *Understanding Comics: The Invisible Art* (New York: Paradox Press, 1993, 2000), 10.

2. Mario Saraceni, *The Language of Comics* (London: Routledge, 2003), 1.

3. McCloud, *Understanding Comics*, 12.

4. Will Eisner, *Comics and Sequential Art: Principles and Practices from the Legendary Cartoonist* (New York: Norton, 1985, 2008), 8.

5. Saraceni, *The Language of Comics*, 1.

6. Saraceni, *The Language of Comics*, 2.

7. McCloud, *Understanding Comics*, 16.

8. Saraceni, *The Language of Comics*, 4.

9. Saraceni, *The Language of Comics*, 2.

10. Saraceni, *The Language of Comics*, 2.

11. Saraceni, *The Language of Comics*, 2.

12. Trina Robbins, *From Girls to Grrrlz: A History of Female Comics from Teens to Zines* (San Francisco: Chronicle Books, 1999), 8.

13. Saraceni, *The Language of Comics*, 2.

14. Chris Baldick, *The Concise Oxford Dictionary of Literary Terms*, s.v. "chapbook" (Oxford: Oxford University Press, 1990), 33.

15. Peter Haining, ed., *The Penny Dreadful Or, Strange, Horrid & Sensational Tales!* (London: Victor Gollancz, 1976), 24.

16. Haining, *Penny Dreadful*, 15.

17. Haining, *Penny Dreadful*, 15–16.

18. Haining, *Penny Dreadful*, 16.

19. Haining, *Penny Dreadful,* 16.

20. John Springhall, *Youth, Popular Culture and Moral Panics: Penny Gaffs to Gangsta-Rap, 1830–1996* (London: Macmillan, 1998), 39.

21. Stephen Humphries, *Hooligans or Rebels? An Oral History of Working-Class Childhood and Youth, 1889–1939* (Oxford: Blackwell, 1995), 6.

22. Springhall, *Moral Panics,* 71.

23. Springhall, *Moral Panics,* 72.

24. Michael Denning, *Mechanic Accents: Dime Novels and Working-Class Culture in America* (London: Verso, 1998), 10.

25. Denning, *Mechanic Accents,* 11.

26. Merle Curti, *Probing Our Past* (New York: Harper, 1955), 173–74.

27. Amy Kiste Nyberg, *Seal of Approval: The History of the Comics Code* (Jackson: University Press of Mississippi, 1998), 2.

28. Nyberg, *Seal of Approval,* 2.

29. Nyberg, *Seal of Approval,* 2.

30. Nyberg, *Seal of Approval,* 2.

31. Nyberg, *Seal of Approval,* 2–3.

32. Nyberg, *Seal of Approval,* 3–4.

33. Humphries, *Hooligans or Rebels?,* 9.

34. McCloud, *Understanding Comics,* 18.

35. Kimberley Reynolds, *Girls Only? Gender and Popular Children's Fiction in Britain, 1880–1910* (New York: Harvester Wheatsheaf, 1990), 92–93.

36. Haining, *Penny Dreadful,* 25.

37. Haining, *Penny Dreadful,* 26.

38. Martin Barker, *Comics: Ideology, Power and the Critics* (Manchester: Manchester University Press, 1989), 9.

39. Curti, *Probing Our Past,* 178.

40. Robert S. Petersen, *Comics, Manga, and Graphic Novels: A History of Graphic Narratives* (Santa Barbara, CA: Praeger, 2011), 144.

41. Steven E. de Souza, "Annotations," in *The Best of the Golden Age Sheena, Queen of the Jungle, Vol. 1.,* ed. Stephen Christy (Chicago: Devil's Due Publishing, 2008).

42. Petersen, *Comics, Manga, and Graphic Novels,* 144.

43. Petersen, *Comics, Manga, and Graphic Novels,* 144.

44. Petersen, *Comics, Manga, and Graphic Novels,* 144–45.

45. Les Daniels, *Wonder Woman: The Life and Times of the Amazon Princess; The Complete History* (San Francisco: Chronicle Books, 2000), 20.

46. Petersen, *Comics, Manga, and Graphic Novels,* 144.

47. "Elizabeth H. Marston, Inspiration for Wonder Woman, 100" (obituary), *New York Times,* April 3, 1993, Late Edition, Section 1, 11.

48. Mila Bongco, *Reading Comics: Language, Culture, and the Concept of the Superhero in Comic Books* (New York: Garland, 2000), 98.

49. Robbins, *From Girls to Grrrlz*, 8.

50. Robbins, *From Girls to Grrrlz*, 9, 11.

51. Robbins, *From Girls to Grrrlz*, 12.

52. Robbins, *From Girls to Grrrlz*, 15, 30.

53. Robbins, *From Girls to Grrrlz*, 15.

54. Robbins, *From Girls to Grrrlz*, 15–16.

55. Robbins, *From Girls to Grrrlz*, 12.

56. Robbins, *From Girls to Grrrlz*, 16.

57. Robbins, *From Girls to Grrrlz*, 45.

58. David Hajdu, *The Ten-Cent Plague: The Great Comic-Book Scare and How It Changed America* (New York: Farrar, Straus and Giroux, 2008), 6.

59. Nyberg, *Seal of Approval*, 53.

60. Nyberg, *Seal of Approval*, 53, 56, 59.

61. Nyberg, *Seal of Approval*, 59–60.

62. Nyberg, *Seal of Approval*, 61.

63. Nyberg, *Seal of Approval*, 61.

64. Nyberg, *Seal of Approval*, 62–63.

65. Nyberg, *Seal of Approval*, 64.

66. Nyberg, *Seal of Approval*, 83.

67. Nyberg, *Seal of Approval*, 79.

68. Trina Robbins, *Great Women Cartoonists* (New York: Watson-Guptill, 2001), 102.

69. Robbins, *Great Women Cartoonists*, 102.

70. Hajdu, *The Ten-Cent Plague*, 337 (50–51).

71. Robbins, *The Great Women Cartoonists*, 102.

72. Barker, *Comics: Ideology, Power*, 9.

73. Hajdu, *The Ten-Cent Plague*, 161.

74. John Stanley and Irving Tripp, "A Note about Lulu," in *Little Lulu: Lulu Goes Shopping* (Milwaukie, OR: Dark Horse Books, 2004).

75. Stanley and Tripp, "A Note about Lulu."

76. Robbins, *From Girls to Grrrlz*, 20.

77. Robbins, *From Girls to Grrrlz*, 20.

78. Stanley and Tripp, *Little Lulu*, 82.

79. Stanley and Tripp, *Little Lulu*, 84.

80. Stanley and Tripp, *Little Lulu*, 86.

81. Stanley and Tripp, *Little Lulu*, 86.

82. Stanley and Tripp, *Little Lulu*, 86–87.

83. Stanley and Tripp, *Little Lulu*, 87.

84. Stanley and Tripp, *Little Lulu*, 100.

85. Stanley and Tripp, *Little Lulu*, 100.

86. Stanley and Tripp, *Little Lulu*, 100.

87. Stanley and Tripp, *Little Lulu*, 100.

88. Stanley and Tripp, *Little Lulu*, 100.

89. Stanley and Tripp, *Little Lulu*, 100.

90. Stanley and Tripp, *Little Lulu*, 102.

91. Stanley and Tripp, *Little Lulu*, 103.

92. Stanley and Tripp, *Little Lulu*, 104.

93. Stanley and Tripp, *Little Lulu*, 105.

94. Stanley and Tripp, *Little Lulu*, 106.

95. Stanley and Tripp, *Little Lulu*, 107.

96. Stanley and Tripp, *Little Lulu*, 108.

97. Stanley and Tripp, *Little Lulu*, 109.

98. Robbins, *From Girls to Grrrlz*, 23.

99. Robbins, *From Girls to Grrrlz*, 24.

100. *Calling All Girls* (magazine), September 1942, 3–5, 45–47.

101. *Calling All Girls*, 54–58.

102. *Calling All Girls*, 9–13.

103. *Calling All Girls*, 19.

104. *Calling All Girls*, 19.

105. *Calling All Girls*, 19.

106. *Miss America* (comic book), 1, no. 92 (September 1958), cover.

107. *Miss America* 1, 92 (September 1947), 17.

108. *Miss America* (September 1947), 18.

109. Max Allan Collins, "Introduction," in *Patriotic Pin-Ups* (Portland: Collector's Press, 2002).

110. "Tizzie's Private Practice Session," in *Calling All Girls* (magazine), April 1959, 17.

111. "Tizzie's Private Practice Session," 21.

112. Haenigsen (cartoonist), *Calling All Girls*, October 1957, 74.

113. Haenigsen, *Calling All Girls*, 74.

114. Judith Hemming and Jane Legget, *Comics and Magazines* (Exeter: The English Centre, 1984), 56.

115. Hemming and Legget, *Comics and Magazines*, 56.

116. Robbins, *From Girls to Grrrlz*, 85.

117. Maurice Horn, *Women in the Comics; Revised and Updated, Vol. 3* (Broomall: Chelsea House Publishers, 2001), 221, 244.

COMICS AS A HYBRID ART FORM, OR THE MYSTERIOUS CASE OF THE PICTURE BOOK

As mentioned before, Wagner's concept of the *Gesamtkunstwerk* or "complete art work" aptly describes the scope of the comics field. It is a hybrid art form made from the harmonious marriage of visual and textual narratives. The way in which comics work is not unlike how picture books function. Both picture books and comics challenge how we view the reading experience as well as our concepts of literacy. The picture book has garnered esteem from teachers, critics, and the general public, whereas comics have never gained that degree of respectability. This has much to do with the history of cultural bias and the stigma attached to comic books discussed in chapter 1. In order to dispel the notion that comics are inferior to the picture book, we must examine both the differences and the similarities between the two art forms.

Defining the Picture Book

Picture books are generally created for a child readership, while comics are written for many different age groups. Picture books are defined by the heavy use of images that are often accompanied by text that ranges from very simple and often elegantly minimalist prose to a greater volume of words with more textual sophistication. However, some picture books have no words at all and rely on visual storytelling alone to convey their meaning. Therefore, the images in picture books are never merely illustrative, but play an active role in storytelling. Picture books are quite versatile, as they can be read to the youngest children as well as read by beginning readers. However, even though they are generally geared toward younger readers, there is also an abundance of material well suited for older children. Many picture books deal with complex subject matters that can be enjoyed by all ages. Books such as Shaun Tan's *The Red Tree* (2001), and *Michael Rosen's Sad Book* (by Michael Rosen and illustrated by Quentin Blake, 2005) discuss such mature topics as depression and loss. They are meant for a wider readership, yet do not rely any more on textual narrative than many other picture books that are written with younger readers in mind. The storytelling in both of these books relies heavily on visual narrative, making them examples of what some critics may deem "true" picture books because they both contain minimal prose and often rely on images to convey narrative. Some scholars of children's literature even suggest that the picture book is distinct from the "illustrated story." In *Only Connect: Readings on Children's Literature*, Uri Shulevitz insists that there is a big difference between an illustrated story (or "storybook," to use Shulevitz's term) and a picture book. Though the physical format may appear similar, the former merely illustrates a story, having an aesthetic function rather than contributing narrative itself.[1] Shulevitz elaborates:

> In a true picture book, words cannot stand on their own; without pictures, the meaning of the story will be unclear. The pictures contain information not contained in the words. Furthermore, picture books rely on pictures not only to supplement but to clarify or to take the place of words. In a picture book both the words and the pictures are read. Naturally, such an approach leads to using fewer words or none at all.[2]

Therefore, the hallmark of a picture book is narrative that relies, at least in part, on visual storytelling. If the images were omitted, then the meaning of the tale would be significantly diminished, if not lost altogether. If we compare picture books and comics at this point, it is easy to see that visual narrative is relied upon in a similar manner, though comics often (but not always) have a larger quantity of complicated textual narrative as well.

The Graphic Text and Reader-Response Theory

The similarity between comics and picture books is highlighted by the way in which they demand the reader's interaction with both image and text.

In both comics and picture books, the reader must negotiate between what the written text is saying and what the picture is showing, as well as grapple with the concept of time and movement represented in the visual narrative. Picture books and comics both allow the reader to interact with the text creatively; the combination of pictures and words allows for great variation in interpreting the meaning of these works. Although Wolfgang Iser was referring to textual narrative when he wrote *The Implied Reader: Patterns of Communication in Prose Fiction from Bunyan to Beckett* (1990), his notion of the reader "filling the gap" resonates with how the reader must interpret meaning while negotiating between textual and visual narrative. [3] Iser revises Ingarden's theory of the interruption of the flow of *Satzdenken* (sentence-thought), suggesting that the unanticipated direction of thought that literature often takes is not necessarily disruptive to the reader, as Ingarden suggests, but instead offers an opportunity for the reader to *collaborate* with the text in order to create meaning.[4] Iser states:

> Even in the simplest story there is bound to be some kind of blockage, if only because no tale can ever be told in its entirety. Indeed, it is only through inevitable omissions that a story gains its dynamism. Thus, whenever the flow is interrupted and we are led off in unexpected directions, the opportunity is given to us to bring into play our own faculty for establishing connection—for filling in the gaps left by the text itself.[5]

By "filling the gap," Iser means that it is up to the reader to imagine what is taking place in the narrative when the text is unpredictable and information is omitted. In short, Iser suggests that the reader actually "reads between the lines" and in doing so discovers a unique meaning (because no text is complete without the reader-deriving meaning from the work). Iser asserts that "one text is potentially capable of several different realizations, and no reading can ever exhaust the full potential, for each individual reader will fill in the gaps in his own way."[6] In fact, Iser refers to the interaction between the reader and the work of literature as the creation of the "virtual dimension" of the text.[7] He remarks, "This virtual dimension is not the text itself, nor is it the imagination of the reader: it is the coming together of text and imagination."[8]

As with purely textual narrative, there is also a gap that the reader actively fills in while looking at images, and the idea of the reader being involved in the making of the "virtual dimension" of the text certainly applies to picture books and comics as well.[9] In these art forms the flow of traditional reading (Ingarden's sentence-thought) is constantly interrupted by images as well as by the pauses or omissions in textual narrative common to any work of literature. When there are few or no words present to imply meaning directly, and especially when images pose a narrative *contradictory* to the text (which shall be discussed later in this chapter), the reader naturally fills this space with her own unique inferences. In the gap between image and word, there is interplay not only between what the author and artist have produced but also between the work and the individual interpretation of the reader. These themes are part of the main concerns of reader-response theory, which considers the individual reader as a co-contributor to the work of literature that is being read.

Iser's ideas are not entirely new. Thirty-four years before Iser wrote *The Implied Reader*, Louise Rosenblatt wrote *Literature as Exploration* (1938). In this seminal book, she states: "The reader brings to the work personality traits, memories of past events, present needs and preoccupations, a particular mood of the moment, and a particular physical condition. . . . These, and many other elements, interacting with the particular contribution of the work of art, produce a unique experience."[10] In the late 1930s this was a groundbreaking concept in a time when theorists took a formalist (particularly New Critical) approach to literature. Formalist critics emphasize that the meaning of the text alone is all that matters. This school of thought isolates the work of literature, insisting that the text itself transcends the biographical background of the author. Furthermore, formalism completely ignores the role that the reader plays in deriving meaning from a work of literature. Although her theory went against the grain of the popular literary criticism of the time, Rosenblatt's claim that the reader contributes a unique meaning to a text (the development of what she calls transactional theory) endured and is still considered relevant today.

The Dynamic Interaction of Image and Text

In picture books, it is understood by scholars that the transmission of narrative happens in a range of different ways. Nikolajeva and Scott identify several specific modes of picture book narrative, the most simple of which they refer to as "symmetrical interaction."[11] In symmetrical interaction, "words and pictures tell the same story"; therefore the text and the images simply mirror one another.[12] As the illustrations in a picture book begin to add to or deviate from the textual narrative, a dynamic relationship occurs between the words and the images. Nikolajeva and Scott refer to this phenomenon as "enhancing interaction," where the images don't merely echo the words but *enhance* their meaning.[13] In an enhancing interaction, images support the text in a manner that goes beyond basic illustration. While the text could possibly stand alone in these cases, the pictures add nuances that are not explained by the words. Nikolajeva and Scott use a close reading of Beatrix Potter's *The Tale of Peter Rabbit* as an example of this situation:

> The opening doublespread presents some apparent contradictions, some devices to keep the reader alert and involved. The verbal text tells us that there are four little rabbits but the picture shows only three. . . . Closer attention reveals that the hind legs and tail on the left belong to a rabbit whose head is underneath the tree root, rather than to the rabbit whose head appears the other side of the root. This little puzzle immediately sets up a tension between picture and text.[14]

The fine balance of image and word allows for subtleties in narrative. While the text of books such as *The Tale of Peter Rabbit* could, in theory, stand alone, the images offer depth and detail that is not present verbally. The pictures not only lend character to a story in the case of the enhancing narrative but provide details and narrative hints as well. From this close reading of Beatrix Potter's book, we can tell something about the main character straightaway—Peter is a mischievous rabbit, which foreshadows the pickle he gets himself into later on in the book.

As the relationship between text and image becomes more enhanced or even divergent, distinct forms of narrative become apparent. Nikolajeva and Scott refer to these different narrative styles as *complementary*, *contrapuntal* (sometimes called *counterpointing*), and *contradictory* relationships, depending upon the degree of enhancement.[15] These terms describe the variations in the types of interactions that exist between word and image. Although other scholars may have different names for these kinds of narrative relationships, and Nikolajeva and Scott themselves admit that "these terms are not absolute," for the purposes of this book their terms shall be usd as a guide.[16] It must also be noted that there are picture books with varying degrees of *integrated text*—from words that are overlaid on the image to text that is inseparable from the art.[17] There are also books that contain wordless narratives that demand that the reader interpret the full meaning of the "text," without the aid of words. Much has been written on the subject of how different types of narrative function in the picture book, but this book shall argue that comics convey narrative in the very same ways.

Complementary Narrative

The term *complementary narrative* describes a relationship between text and image in which the image both supports and *complements* the text. The complementary dynamic often occurs throughout comic book narrative. In Mariko Tamaki and Steve Rolston's *Emiko Superstar* (2008), the main character Emiko, or Emi, has a job babysitting for the Cutheberts. However, as Emi soon discovers, the Cutheberts' marriage is rapidly deteriorating. The once perfect suburban home appears to fall apart as the couple drift away from each other. As soon as Emi approached the house, she knew that something was wrong: "I could feel something was up. For one the car was gone."[18] The picture accompanying this statement complements Emi's observation; not only does this image corroborate the fact that the car is gone, but also the door is shown ajar—an element of the narrative that is not mentioned textually (see fig. 2.1). In subsequent panels on this page, Emi says that "inside . . . things looked . . . bad."[19] As Emi engages in a dialog with Mr. Cuthebert, the panel displays a scene of utter disarray. Toys and dishware are littered everywhere and, in the background, a mysterious wet substance has been left on the kitchen floor. Even baby Sam is suffering from the chaos that the failing relationship has caused. When Mr. Cuthebert hands Sam over to Emi, there are wavy lines radiating from the infant, suggesting that the baby smells and is in need of a bath or a diaper change.

In examples of complementary narrative such as this one, not only do the images illustrate what the verbal narrative suggests but they also enhance the text, contributing a depth to the story that is not always found in the words alone. Nikolajeva and Scott assert that "when enhancing interaction becomes very significant, the dynamic becomes truly complementary," as it does in figure 2.1.[20] However, the relationship between word and image

Figure 2.1. *Emiko Superstar*, 2008, page 122. **The images enhance and complement the text.**
Used with Permission of DC Comics.

can develop even more complex or divergent meanings, crossing over into a place of deepening sophistication, where the pictures can carry a narrative independent of the text.

Contrapuntal Narrative

In some picture books, the narrative conveyed by the image may be vastly different from that told by the text. In fact, there are cases in which the picture is so integral to the storytelling that, if you took away the images, the book would tell a completely different tale, if it made sense at all. Nikolajeva and Scott describe this technique by using another term borrowed from music: "counterpoint." They say, "Dependent on the degree of different information presented, a *counterpointing* dynamic may develop where words and images collaborate to communicate meanings beyond the scope of either one alone."[21] As previously discussed, images in a complementary narrative may add depth to the text, but these pictures tend to *support* what the text is saying (albeit in often exceptional and startling ways) instead of contributing a wholly unique narrative. Consequently, the more divergent the images are from the textual narrative, the closer they come to being in counterpoint with the words. In contrast to the symmetrical relationship, the counterpointing dynamic allows the images to be an equal player in the transmission of narrative. Therefore, in this type of storytelling, the words work in counterpoint with the pictures, providing harmony between word and image and forming a narrative depth that the words or pictures alone could not convey.

Picture books such as Pat Hutchins's *Rosie's Walk* (1968) or Peggy Rathmann's *Goodnight, Gorilla* (1994) make use of narrative in counterpoint, which imbues these stories with a richly humorous and even ironic twist. *Rosie's Walk* textually describes a hen named Rosie's amble around the farmyard. The twist comes as the visual narrative shows that Rosie is not alone on her walk. Following her is a hungry fox. The reader may assume that Rosie has absolutely no clue that this predator is behind her, and the irony comes when, seemingly unbeknownst to her, she thwarts the fox at every step. Rosie inadvertently leads the fox on a merry chase: first, the fox steps on a rake, then falls into a pond, then gets buried in a haystack, then covered with flour, and finally winds up in a runaway cart that knocks into bee hives. The poor fox gets chased away by a swarm of enraged bees, while our impervious chicken struts on. At the end of the book, Rosie makes it home in time for dinner, but the fox is out of luck in acquiring hers, and the reader is left delighted by the joke.

Similarly, in *Good Night, Gorilla*, a zookeeper locks up the zoo for the night to go home to sleep. In the verbal narrative, the zookeeper wishes all of the animals of the zoo a good night, but the pictures show another story unfolding. A playful, young gorilla stealthily filches the zookeeper's keys, and systematically lets all of his fellow animals out. The animals, large to small, from a tall giraffe to a little mouse, all proceed to follow the zookeeper home and to bed. The zookeeper doesn't seem to notice at all, but when the zookeeper's wife says, "Good night, dear," all of the animals say good night in reply.[22] The punch line of this sequence occurs across three successive double-page spreads. The page is almost completely black with only an air frame around it, and all that can be seen in the darkness of the zookeeper and his wife's bedroom are speech balloons (also referred to as word balloons or speech bubbles and, interestingly, a convention of the comics field). The speech balloons all contain the words "Good night" in different font sizes, suggesting the different sizes of the beasts that these disembodied voices belong to.[23] The following double-page spread is even more minimalist, yet the impact is strongly humorous; the only objects shown on the dark pages are two eyes, wide with surprise. The next double-page spread sees the zoo-keeper's wife turning the lights back on and the cheeky gorilla grinning at her from under the covers as she finds that she is surrounded by the zoo animals. She ends up leading all of the animals back to the zoo.

Textually, the story closes with the zookeeper's wife saying good night to the zoo, and then good night again to her husband as she gets into bed. However, the visual narrative shows that the sneaky gorilla and the mouse have absconded once more from the zoo and slipped into the zookeeper's bed where they go unnoticed. It is the gorilla and the mouse who have the final words in the book as they say goodnight to each other and make themselves quite comfortable in the zookeeper's bed. In books such as these, the visual narrative is just as valuable as the text. Without these images, the story of Rosie the hen would be an utterly untroubled and boring account of a hen's stroll around the farmyard, and *Good Night, Gorilla* would make no sense at all.

The use of counterpoint is not limited to picture books. Comics, be-ing an art form that employs both words and images to tell what are often complex stories, use contrapuntal narrative extensively. Holly Black and

Ted Naifeh's graphic fantasy series *The Good Neighbors, Book Two: Kith* (2009) is a prime example of a contrapuntal dynamic. The main character, a teenage girl named Rue Silver, comments on the deterioration of her parents' marriage. She notes that situations and emotions change; her father, recently widowed, has moved on and is dating again. However, Rue suspects that her mother is not really deceased. In fact, her mother is not human at all, but a faerie, and Rue believes her mother or her mother's family must have used magic to make everyone believe that she has died. In panel 4 (fig. 2.2) Rue narrates, "I like Amanda. Really, I do."[24] The image in panel 4 shows Rue's dad helping Amanda, his girlfriend, into the car as they leave for a date. It is nighttime, and their figures throw heavy shadows on the wall behind them. An observant reader will notice that there is one more shadow than there ought to be, cast blurry and indistinct upon the wall. The next panel (fig. 2.2, panel 5) shows Rue's father tenderly kissing his date on the cheek, unaware of anything nefarious at work around them. However, the disembodied shadow that was present in the last panel has now become more defined—a humanoid form that looms over Rue's dad and Amanda. The reader can now clearly see the shape of a face in silhouette and the thin shadow of an arm reaching over the couple, with its sharp, claw-like hand hovering right above Amanda's head. Rue's narrative simply reads, "But Mom's not gone. I know she's not."[25]

If it weren't for the visual narrative, Rue's statement that her mother is not gone might seem like the wishful thinking of a troubled young woman. However, the sinister shadowlike image on the wall in panels 4 and 5 suggests to the reader that perhaps Rue is right. Something supernatural is at work here. In panels 1–5 Rue's words alone do little to support the supernatural element in the story. Conversely, the images divorced from their words express an ambivalent narrative; there is no implication of what the shadow is, or what it might represent. However, together, the combination of verbal and visual narrative tells a far more complex story.

Contradictory Narrative

Sometimes the visual narrative of a book adds to the story provided by the text by *contradicting* it. Nikolajeva and Scott explain that "an extreme form of counterpointing is *contradictory* interaction, where words and pictures seem to be in opposition to one another."[26] For example, in John Burningham's *Aldo* (1991), a little girl describes her relationship with her

Figure 2.2. *The Good Neighbors, Book Two: Kith*, **2009, page 34.**

imaginary friend, an anthropomorphic rabbit she calls Aldo. The book as a whole provides perfect examples of *contrapuntal* narrative, as the text never directly states that Aldo is imaginary or that he is a rabbit; yet the images imply that Aldo is imaginary. Aldo is never shown together in an image with anyone other than the narrator. Furthermore, the narrative (both textual and visual) describes extremely mundane settings and realist episodes, whereas Aldo himself is depicted fancifully as a bipedal, grey rabbit with a striped scarf. Only the images make it obvious that the girl is not describing a relationship with another human being. Even when the little girl explains that "Aldo is only friends with me, and he's a secret. I know that he will always come to me when things get really bad," the text is ambiguous and does not directly state that Aldo is imaginary.[27] However, this text coupled with the depiction of Aldo as a huge rabbit suggests that he is only real in the narrator's mind.

At the bottom of the same page, the book reads, "Like when they were horrible to me the other day."[28] Here, the text alone offers no specific clues as to whom the narrator says was mistreating her, but the image on the next page says it all. The following page displays a scene in which two girls are bullying the narrator in what appears to be the school bathroom. The picture does not have any accompanying text, but it is obvious from the images that the narrator is having a hard time socially at school. The image shows one girl pulling the narrator's hair, while another girl simultaneously pushes and kicks her. The protagonist's school supplies go flying. From the ambiguity of the text on the preceding page, the reader may even get the sense that this is only one unhappy vignette from a day full of horrors. The next page shows the little girl crying, but Aldo has picked up her school supplies and has his arm around her shoulders, comforting her. The narrator comments, "I'm sure they went away because Aldo came."[29]

At another point in the book, the narrator appears to acknowledge the fact that Aldo is unreal or otherwise ineffectual. She says of Aldo: "Sometimes I wish he could help, but he's only my special friend."[30] The page shows the little girl in profile, standing alone in a passive stance, hunched over, her hands clasped together in front of her. The opposite page depicts two adults in profile, facing each other, their angry expressions frozen in a snapshot of conflict; mouths open wide, teeth exposed, and accusing fingers pointed at one another. There is no verbal narrative here, but the reader does not require words in order to interpret this page. The drawing is made up of simple lines and is colored in a pastel-like blush of livid, ruddy pigment, not unlike how a child might draw a scene between two arguing parents.

One of the book's most subtle and emotionally telling episodes occurs when the narrator explains that, although she is often alone, she does have her books and toys and television to keep her busy.[31] On one page in particular she states, "Sometimes we go to the park, and occasionally we go out to eat," while over on the next page the thought is continued, saying, "which is nice."[32] Burningham's choice to break up this statement by placing the words, "which is nice" on a separate page, creates an interruption in the pacing of this statement, giving the effect of a slight pause.[33] However, the images on these two pages offer more information than the text provides. Here, a careful reader will note that the images *contradict* the text. While the narrator says that going to the park and out to eat is "nice," the pictures show a little girl who is not smiling, but is always looking longingly at groups of children having fun together. On the left-hand page, a woman whom the reader may assume is the narrator's mother leads her by the hand through the park, past the swing sets where other children are playing. The mother looks straight ahead while the little girl turns her head to gaze upon the children having fun. On the next page, the little girl has an ice cream sundae in front of her, yet again she peers over her shoulder at children sitting together, enjoying not only the food but also companionship. The images contradict the information that the narrator has given us; perhaps the ice cream is nice, but there is sadness here as well. The narrator has a need for society that has gone unfulfilled, although she does not express this directly.

While Nikolajeva and Scott specifically discuss how picture books use contradictory narrative (as well as other sophisticated forms of storytelling) through images and words, this complicated literary technique extends to the art of comics as well. Shannon and Dean Hale and Nathan Hale's graphic novel *Rapunzel's Revenge* displays a perfect example of the contradictory relationship between text and image. This graphic novel is a feminist twist on the well-known fairy tale, which re-imagines Rapunzel's story, giving it a Wild West spin. This Rapunzel is more Annie Oakley than helpless maiden awaiting her liberation by a prince. In fact, she uses her wit and her hair to free herself from her tower prison (which, in this tale, comes in the form of an enchanted treetop cell) without the aid of anyone else. In the episodes detailing her escape, Rapunzel uses her hair as a lasso to rope a nearby treetop (fig. 2.3). The verbal narrative is in first person and Rapunzel explains how, after some failed attempts, she succeeds in using her hair as the means of her escape: "And then at last . . . / . . . I managed to lasso the tree . . . / . . . swing gracefully from my prison . . . / climb down the tree's branches . . . / . . . and land triumphantly on the forest floor."[34]

Figure 2.3a. *Rapunzel's Revenge*, 2008, page 35. **Rapunzel's escape is not as graceful as she would like the reader to believe.**

Meanwhile, the images tell a very different story. Rapunzel's escape from her jail is nothing close to graceful, nor does she appear as confident as her words would have the reader believe. The images show Rapunzel's eyes wide with terror as she flies through the air, swinging by one of her lengthy braids as if it were a jungle vine. And she doesn't climb down the tree as much as fall through it, snapping branches as she plummets. As for her "triumphant landing," she is shown falling into a shallow forest pool. The next panel displays our hero looking defeated, pained, and sodden as she sits awkwardly in the water, sticks and leaves in her long, bedraggled tresses.

Figure 2.3b. *Continued*

What the narrator would have us believe is in acute contrast with the images, and the reader can easily infer that Rapunzel may be sugar-coating some of the events in her story—the overall effect of which is both comedic and ironic. This episode also suggests that Rapunzel is an unreliable narrator—a technique often used in literature—creating an ambiguous story with more than one possible interpretation. According to Nikolajeva and Scott, the contradictory relationship "challenges the reader to mediate between the words and pictures to establish a true understanding of what is being depicted."[35] Once again, here is an example from the comics field where complex narrative style and literary devices are used to tell a story.

In works like *Rapunzel's Revenge*, the interaction between the narrative of the text and the narrative of the image encourages the reader to become an accomplice in the creation of meaning: what is actually going on in the story is up to the reader to decide. How the reader interprets this interaction between image and word may vary from reader to reader, with nuances in meaning influenced by the reader's own personal experiences and cultural background. Rosenblatt (1938) touches on this essential point in her classic of transactional theory, *Literature as Exploration*, when she acknowledges that the reader contributes an original point of view when interpreting the text: "The content of the reader's past life and present concerns plays an equally important part . . . in enabling him to have a rich and balanced response to a given literary work."[36] While Rosenblatt may have been referring, specifically, to the relationship between the reader and the *written* text, the same applies to visual narrative. In her book *Looking at Pictures in Picture Books* (1993), Doonan describes the picture book as a "composite text" referring to the blending of textual and visual narratives to form a whole.[37] She comments: "The emotional tone of the composite text emerges from the interaction of the two sources of information—words that tell and pictures that show," while the reader, herself, is influenced by her own "expectations and assumptions," which results in a unique reading.[38] Doonan states that when interpreting picture book images, "there is no single right answer" when considering what the pictorial symbols exemplify.[39] Furthermore, Nikolajeva and Scott assert that "as soon as words and images provide alternative information or contradict each other in some way, we have a variety of readings and interpretations."[40] As with written narrative, nonverbal narrative is found in the "gaps" between the interaction of images and words and leaves room for the reader's personal experiences and imagination. This, essentially, allows the reader to collaborate with the author and illustrator in the making of meaning.

Integrated Text

In some picture books, there are instances where the lines between textual and visual narrative blur and the words may become a part of the image itself. Doonan (1993) discusses how the incorporation of text within the image ranges from "partly integrated," which includes examples where the words may appear overlaid on the image as well as examples where the text appears next to an image in different parts of a book, to what Doonan defines as a "wholly integrated layout," where the text is part of the image and takes on characteristics of the style of the art.[41] Examples of this phenomenon can be seen in James Stimson's *Thirteen O'clock* (2005), the story of a little girl who is not afraid of ghosts and things that go bump in the night, or even a clock that strikes thirteen, for that matter. Many of the words that punctuate this spooky little tale are rendered in furry, rough-edged charcoals, merging with the shadows of the illustrations.

In *The Stinky Cheese Man and Other Fairly Stupid Tales* (1992), Scieszka and Smith play with the idea of storytelling and toy, metafictively, with the traditional book format itself. In this book, the words do not reflect the style of the art as much as they are an *inseparable part* of the visual storytelling, investing the book with a richness and personality that standard typesetting cannot convey. The book contains text in different font sizes to emphasize importance—or even false importance—of the subject matter, thereby playing with publishing conventions. This is apparent in the "Title Page" where the words "Title Page" are in bold and take up two-thirds of the layout, while the actual title of the book is in parentheses and in a much smaller font size. When the Little Red Hen speaks, her dialog is coded in red, unlike Jack, the narrator, whose words appear in plain black. The dedication is printed upside down and lilts at a jaunty angle, as Jack appears to "drag" it into its place. Frustrated with his task, Jack addresses the audience as in a Shakespearian aside saying, "I know. I know. The page is upside down. I meant to do that. Who ever looks at that dedication stuff anyhow?"[42] The acerbic Jack suggests to us readers that if we would like to read the dedication, we could stand on our heads.[43] Even the text of the "Table of Contents," which cascades willy-nilly across the page, conveys the chaos of these demented re-imaginings of well-known tales. *The Stinky Cheese Man and Other Fairly Stupid Tales* is just one of many examples of storytelling that demonstrates how the interaction between text and art is virtually limitless.

This artful play between words and images is not confined to picture books. Comic books also employ various methods of conveying narrative through the imaginatively blurred relationship between words and art. Castellucci and Rugg's two-part graphic novel series, *The Plain Janes* (2007) and *Janes in Love* (2008), contains a multitude of instances of partially to wholly integrated text. The books focus on a girl named Jane who makes art with a group of friends, most of whom have some variant of the name "Jane." Jane's need to create art stems from her experience of being the victim in an unexplained bomb attack in "Metro City." Directly after the attack, when Jane regains consciousness, she awakes to panic, with bodies lying everywhere. Next to the form of an unconscious young man, she finds a notebook that says "ART SAVES" across the cover. Jane fixates on this notebook, its unidentified owner, and the notion that art can provide her with hope and healing.

When she has physically recovered from the attack, Jane begins to add to the notebook and ends up keeping it. However, she continues to visit the notebook's owner who is in a coma and is only known as John Doe. While Jane sits by John's bedside, she confides her most personal feelings about her life, art, and how everything has changed for her since the attack. When her family moves to a suburb as a result of the family trauma incurred by the attack in Metro City, many of Jane's thoughts are construed in letters that she writes to the unidentified young man. Panels 1 and 2 (fig. 2.4) display the blending of text with visual narrative. Panel 1 features a close-up of Jane's hands, with pen poised over a letter to John. The author and artist's choice to show the letter itself, with its flowery handwriting, rather than using another method of conveying this narrative (as in the subsequent panel) lends authenticity to Jane's situation, flavoring the narrative with a tone of intimacy. In the next panel John is depicted lying unconscious in his hospital bed while the text appears in a thought bubble modified to look like a torn piece of paper that says "Love, Jane." Other mail, which the reader may also assume is from Jane, adorns

Figure 2.4. _The Plain Janes,_ 2007.
Used with Permission of DC Comics.

John's hospital room wall and bedside table. It also serves to remind the reader that, although this "John Doe" is a complete stranger, he shares an experience with Jane that those close to her cannot fully understand; Jane and the unconscious boy have shared the same ordeal, and he becomes her unwitting confidant in dealing with this trauma.

The unexplained attack on the generically named "Metro City" is evocative of the September 11 attacks on the United States. The wake of fear, distress, and paranoia in Jane's world after the Metro City attack acts as a commentary on the September 11 attacks' lasting effects. Yet the tone of the series suggests a hopeful future and the discovery of inner strength and the ability to heal. Even though the books focus on a girl who has survived a traumatic event, Castellucci and Rugg's Jane does not dwell on horror and self-pity. Jane reinvents herself in order to survive and finds a positive outlet in creating art as a method of transforming her fears and isolation into beauty. Jane explains that during the attack, when she was thrown down, she noticed a dandelion growing in a crack in the pavement. She marvels that, through all of the chaos and violence, this flower remained alive and untouched. Jane comments, "I knew that if that dandelion could survive . . . so could I. But everything would have to be different. _I_ would have to be different."[44]

The accompanying images display several examples of text integrated into the art. The first panel shows Jane putting up missing-person flyers for John Doe while, in the foreground, a newspaper vending machine displays the headline "orange alert"; this panel uses wholly integrated text to set the anxious tone of the scene without superfluous expository text. The second panel reveals to the reader the moment that Jane decided to keep John Doe's notebook, with its poignant "ART SAVES" cover, and the last panel shows Jane filling a page in John's notebook with a drawing of a dandelion. These images, combined with the text, suggest that Jane's interest in art is kindled as she takes the message on the cover of John Doe's notebook to heart.

Even though Jane has found solace in art, she begins to feel set apart from her friends and even her family. Her popular friends suddenly seem shallow, and she can't seem to relate to them any longer. Jane's home life is also affected by the aftermath of the attack. Her parents decide to move away from Metro City, away from what they now consider to be an increasingly dangerous environment. When Jane moves to the suburban town of Kent Waters, her transition is a tough one until she meets a group of outsiders: another Jane, who loves the dramatic arts; "Brain Jayne," who is a science whiz; and Polly Jane, who loves sports. Even though this unlikely crew doesn't warm to her at first, Jane manages to win them over with her scheme of developing a secret art group called People Loving Art in Neighborhoods. This organization, P.L.A.I.N., takes public art to a new level, employing nighttime guerilla tactics to fabricate their whimsical and often thought-provoking installations. Castellucci and Rugg cunningly use the graphic medium in order to reveal P.L.A.I.N.'s art projects to the reader. In P.L.A.I.N.'s first "art attack," they construct large pyramids out of the rubble at the building site of what is scheduled to become a new strip mall. On the chain link fence surrounding the site, P.L.A.I.N. painted over the signs that formerly read, "Coming soon! New Strip Mall" to say, "The Pyramids lasted for thousands of years. Do you think this strip mall will?"[45] Castellucci and Rugg's choice to use wholly integrated text appears to comment on the nature of art itself, where text is combined with visual art in order to increase the impact of the work. In their next escapade, P.L.A.I.N. beautifies the neighborhood by pouring detergent into a public fountain. On the street, in bubbly letters that echo the foamy prank, is written, "Bubbles are Plain."[46] The only other text on this page comes from a police officer, who muses to himself in wonderment, "Bubbles. Crazy."[47] In both of these scenes, and in many more throughout the two-book series, the text is heavily integrated into the images, thereby making lengthy exposition unnecessary—in other words, Castellucci and Rugg allow P.L.A.I.N.'s art to speak for itself.

Art helps Jane to survive and adapt to the changes and trauma in her life. However, not everyone sees P.L.A.I.N. as a positive force. The local police, newspaper, and even the high school view the art installations, not as fun or beautiful, but as a threat. The concern of the people of Kent Waters over these displays of public art may seem extreme, but when put in the context of a post–September 11 world, the situation and its insanity seems plausible. In the first book, *The Plain Janes*, even Jane's mother feels threatened by the P.L.A.I.N. installations. The attack on Metro City, which had put Jane in the hospital, has made her mother fearful and overly protective of her daughter.

The anxiety and paranoia that Jane's mother experiences is only hinted at but these become prominent in the second graphic novel. In this book, *Janes in Love*, another terrorist attack occurs in Metro City, and this time a friend of Jane's mother is killed when she receives anthrax-laced mail.[48] After the terrible news, Jane's mother refuses to come out of the house and even makes the mailman leave the mail on the front lawn.[49] Jane also mentions that her mother is taking medication, which the reader may assume is for anxiety or perhaps depression.[50] Her mother's fear and anguish only further propel Jane in her creative pursuits. Jane believes that if she makes the world beautiful enough with her art, perhaps it will help her to rejoin society. Jane says, "One of the reasons I want to make the world beautiful is so that my mom can remember it is."[51] However, Jane and P.L.A.I.N. come up against major obstacles in their mission: a lack of funding, and the way in which the community perceives the art collective.

Continuing the theme of art as a healer, in *Janes in Love* John Doe wakes up from his coma. He turns out to be one Miroslaw Raminski of Krakow, Poland. Perhaps the series' best use of wholly integrated text is when Jane receives a package from Miroslaw containing a notebook that Jane had sent him. Jane opens the notebook to find it filled. A double-page spread (fig. 2.5) featuring pages of the notebook reveals that Miroslaw is a budding poet, not primarily a visual artist, as Jane had previously assumed. "Photographs" combined with collage and hand-written words intimately share with Jane (and the reader) Miroslaw's slow, bittersweet recovery process. Even though Jane finds out that Miroslaw has a girlfriend, there is an indelible bond between the two pen pals. In fact, it is Jane's continued

Figure 2.5. *Janes in Love*, **2008, pages 32–33.**
Used with Permission of DC Comics.

communications with Miroslaw that galvanize her drive to create art when she is in doubt; a letter from Miroslaw helps to spark an idea that has the potential to solve P.L.A.I.N.'s problems. Jane decides to apply for an arts grant for P.L.A.I.N., legitimizing it as an art collective and securing money that will help the friends to continue producing art for the benefit of the Kent Waters community. Through perseverance and tenacity, P.L.A.I.N. wins the grant. The award of the art grant does, indeed, cultivate a feeling of community that chips away at the paranoia of a post–terrorist attack climate. It also strengthens the bond between Jane and her friends as well as her parents. Near the end of the series, Jane's mother finally returns to society and enjoys P.L.A.I.N.'s public art installation, "The Universe Is a Garden,"[52] which turns a derelict city lot into a beautiful, recreational space.

From its whimsical and humorous usage in *The Stinky Cheese Man* to sophisticated comics and graphic novels such as the *Janes* series, examples of partially to wholly integrated text in comics and picture books abound. The varied range of how text and art in picture books and comics can work together to relate a story displays the reflexivity of image and word, not only in their ability to complement each other but in how they dynamically convey narrative as a unit.

Wordless Narrative

Another technique that is used by both picture books and comics is the *absence* of words. This has been well documented in picture books where the images stand alone without any text. In books like these, the images themselves must be "read." To illuminate this point, Doonan refers to a two-page spread in John Burningham's sparsely worded picture book, *Granpa* (1985), as an example of how the reader interprets images when text is absent. She says,

> We recognize a display of open hostility in the page opening in *Granpa* where the little girl and the old man have turned their backs on each other, and we are tempted to verbalize what each is thinking, feeling, and saying, from the facial expressions, poses, and the relationship between the position of each figure on the picture plane.[53]

The only text that appears on these two pages is, "That was not a nice thing to say to Granpa."[54] Since this picture book functions as a series of vignettes displaying different interactions between the little girl and her "Granpa," the circumstances surrounding this tiff are left completely up to the reader's imagination. Doonan goes on to discuss the ways in which we interpret images such as these, noting that it depends on how we read them culturally. For example, in Sendak's picture book, *Outside Over There* (1981), Ida reaches out toward her baby sister in a pose that Doonan interprets as reminiscent of the Virgin Mary.[55] Comics are no different in this sense. Eisner comments:

> Comprehension of an image requires a commonality of experience. This demands of the sequential artist an understanding of the reader's life experience if his message is to be understood. An interaction has to develop because the artist is evoking images stored in the minds of both parties.[56]

When icons and symbols are created to invoke meaning or emotion, there is communion between the artist and the "reader," who must have worldly experience to be able to make these connections. Moreover, images allow us as individuals to construct unique readings of the narrative through our own cultures and personal experiences. Rosenblatt asserts: "Every personality which reacts to the work of art has incorporated a fund of attitudes and interests deposited by former interactions with the environment."[57] Therefore, all of the reader's combined experiences contribute to the way in which they perceive narrative, whether textual, visual, or a combination of the two. The particular culture that the reader is exposed to influences how the reader assigns meaning to words and pictures; what one reader may find visually symbolic may have little meaning to another reader who comes from a different cultural background. Rosenblatt states that the reader "will bring to his reading the moral and religious code and social philosophy assimilated from his family and community background."[58] Therefore, when looking at picture books, multiple readings are possible due to the influence of the particular reader's social and cultural environment. In wordless picture books, the ambiguity of the "text" is even more prominent, since there are no words to act as guidelines for interpretation. The reader's own experiences and personality as well as cultural influence have an enormous impact on how meaning is extrapolated from the images.

However, it must be noted that images, even more so than words, often have a universal meaning. It is not surprising that, according to the back flap copy of *Granpa*, Burningham's books have been translated into at least eleven different languages, including Finnish and Zulu. No matter what culture you come from, the concepts found in many of his books, such as those of familial love and loss explored in *Granpa*, are easy to understand. Though Burningham's book displays a relationship in a culturally Western context, the bond between grandfather and granddaughter is universal, as is the concept of loss. At the end of the book, the author chooses not to include a verbal narrative; Granpa's empty, overstuffed armchair needs no words to convey its meaning.

Images, free from words, can liberate the narrative. However ambiguous some word combinations may be, images can provide more freedom of expression than the text because words may limit interpretation. Even though images work in their own "language" of semiotics, wordless narratives may make more room for the personal and cultural connections that a reader attaches to an image.

Quentin Blake's *Clown* displays an effective use of visual narrative to tell a story without the aid of words. In this picture book, a toy clown, along with some other old toys, gets thrown out with the trash. However, Clown manages to free himself. He dusts himself off, and after finding a pair of tiny sneakers, takes off on an adventure to find a new home for himself and the other discarded toys. First, through the unconventional use of the speech balloon, Clown "talks" to a toddler on reins. The image that appears within the speech balloon displays the trash can full of homeless toys, but the toddler has no time to reply. Adults who do not seem to notice that she is interacting with Clown quickly pull the child away. She comically gets pulled upward by her reins and is carried away in suspension by adults, who don't even look her way. Even though Blake's cartoon style can be light-hearted, the scene in which the child is yanked away by her reins has an underlying disturbing quality. The child's needs are being ignored while the grownups go about their business of talking and shopping (both of the adult figures are shown carrying large, heavily laden shopping bags). And the child is depicted wearing reins as though she were some small animal or merely an accessory to the garrulous, materialist adults. The little girl waves goodbye awkwardly as she dangles from her bonds, and Clown stares on, dejectedly.

Clearly, there is something wrong here in the way that adults relate to children in this tale. As Clown continues to go through various trials, Blake uses wordless narrative to explore societal problems such as the contrasts of excess and poverty, while also dealing with the concept of children's efficacy: he juxtaposes scenes in which children are powerless, with empowering scenes showing that a child can effect change. In the next vignette, Clown is mistaken for a child and placed in a group of children in costumes. However, he manages to tell a little girl about the problem of the toys that were thrown away (again, through the wordless speech balloon). When her nanny takes her home, the little girl brings Clown with her. They arrive at a well-appointed home; even with Blake's minimalist style, it is obvious that this mother and daughter are well to do. The purple drapes are lavish, there are potted plants, and fancy mirrors hang on the wall. A big wooden table set for a party with wine glasses, bottles, an ice bucket, and sundry other articles dominates the scene. The child's mother is also bedecked in jewelry. When the mother examines the toy, which her daughter has brought into the house, the reader can see that she is appalled. With a look of disgust, she tosses the toy clown out of the window. Once more, Blake invites the reader into a scene where the needs of a child are being ignored. Furthermore, whatever sort of party it is that the table in the little girl's house has been set for, it is obviously not an event planned for children. Blake shows the reader children who are impoverished of love or attention, though they live in households where there is plenty, in the material sense.

In successive adventures, Clown suffers further indignities by being chased by an angry dog and hurled into the air by a brutish-looking skinhead. However, his luck changes when he lands inside of the one-room apartment of a little girl and her baby brother. The reader can assume that the inhabitants of the apartment are poor; the paint is peeling on the wall and there is one bare light bulb and only one bed and table. The apartment is a mess. There are dirty dishes on the table, and the baby is crying. However, when Clown arrives, he dances for the children and juggles and this makes them happy. Through the wordless speech balloon, Clown again tells his tale about the toys that had been thrown away. The girl "replies" with her own speech balloon that shows us an adult woman wiping sweat from her brow and a clock behind her on the wall. From this the reader can deduce that the children's mother has been at work. Clown is then shown holding his chin, as if in thought. The next image of Clown shows him sticking his finger in the air as if to say, "I have an idea." The next two pages display a series of images showing the clown helping the little girl to clean and straighten the house; he even changes the baby. Afterward, they venture outside to save the other toys from the trash. The little girl piles all of the toys into the perambulator with the infant, and they head back home together. Clown has even found a ribbon for the little girl's hair and a bouquet of flowers among other people's waste. At home, the apartment looks tidy and inviting, and the toys spruce up what was previously a very empty living space. When the mother comes home she kisses the little girl and sheds a tear of joy. In the penultimate image, the mother is shown sitting on the bed, holding the baby aloft and smiling, perhaps talking. The little girl stands nearby holding out a mug for her mother while glancing knowingly and happily behind her shoulder at Clown and the other new toys.

Although this family and their living situation may be far from ideal, Blake clearly depicts them as a loving trio, and theirs is the only child-adult relationship in this book that presents a grownup who is happily and lovingly engaged with a child. Though the tale is wordless, the reader can understand that, in a plea to save them, the clown is "speaking" to every child that he meets on the street about the toys that remain in the garbage can. This is achieved through the use of a speech balloon—a common feature in comics storytelling. What is strikingly original in this book is that, where the speech balloon would normally contain text, instead there is an image of the sad-looking toys in a trashcan. The convention of a speech balloon usually signifies spoken content. But Blake's proves this mechanism to be an effective way of communicating without the use of words.

Blake often utilizes the comics style. As well as employing speech balloons, he sometimes uses multiple panels to tell a story. However, he also blends this with the use of images that are not as structured; many are frameless, and some even take up the entire page. Blake's style itself is messy, with wavering pen and ink lines that are softened by his use of watercolors, often in pastel or muted hues. His characters often appear whimsical, yet rumpled and full of nervous energy, due to this painterly style. Blake also utilizes white space, and oftentimes his characters seem to float on the white background. Through this seemingly simplistic tale, Quentin Blake manages to say a lot without a single word.

Wordless picture books are able to conduct their narratives visually, using such techniques as the careful utilization of space, color, and perspective to tell a story. They prove that successful narratives do not have to be verbal. Just as most people are able to communicate with body language, the artist is able to create images with expressive and emotional depth in order to structure the narrative. Furthermore, the wordless narrative is the perfect medium in which to explore themes that are, at times, difficult to express in words.

Perhaps one of the most well-known and convincing examples of how a wordless narrative manages to express the inexpressible to children of a wide age range and beyond is Raymond Briggs's *The Snowman* (1978). While *The Snowman* is a much-celebrated picture book, it is clearly composed in the style of comics, where many of the pages are filled with different panels framing action. *The Snowman*, though containing no words, conveys the feeling of loss with poignancy. A boy spends the day building a snowman. That evening he goes to sleep, but awakens in the night to find that his snowman has come alive. Adventure ensues, and it is apparent that a bond of friendship has been made between the two. As the pair move from the boy's home to the outdoors, the number of panels decrease while the size of the panels increase until the image expands across a double-page spread.

The book contains only two double-page spreads that nearly run to the edge of the page; there is only a slip of blank, white space remaining around the edges of the frames that surround these images as the duo fly together in the wintery night sky. As dawn arrives, they fly back home and the frames recede into small panels again. The opening up of the frames suggests a feeling of freedom and fantasy, as the boy and snowman are airborne. However, this joy cannot last. The boy must go back to bed, and the snowman must stay outdoors. When the boy wakes in the morning and runs outside, there is only a puddle and clothing where the snowman once stood. Briggs chooses to leave this picture small, but boldly framed by the blankness of the white paper, which gently speaks of the loneliness of loss. Graham suggests: "What seems to happen is that because there is no printed verbal story children feel active and powerful in their role of finding words to shape the story."[59] Briggs's decision to omit text from this book gives the reader control and allows them to put their own words to the feeling of loss.

Not only is *The Snowman* a distinguished work of children's fiction, but it is also an example of comics. The presentation of this story in book form is perhaps what validates it as a piece of literature and explains why it has not been stigmatized as the rest of comic book art and literature often has been. Even though the picture book is lauded for its ability to combine textual and visual narrative, comics are left behind.

Comics' Influence on the Picture Book

It is clear that many picture books owe much to their cousin, comics. The use of panels and speech bubbles run throughout the field. David Lewis comments: "The technique of caricature and of storytelling in words and pictures came to have an influence on the picture book through the comic strip."[60] The influence of comics is obvious in picture books like Sendak's *In the Night Kitchen*. *In the Night Kitchen* begins with the narrative being related in panel form—the art style most typically associated with comics— across a double-page spread. A boy named Mickey is shown tucked into his bed, yet unable to sleep. Here, the verbal narrative is three-fold: the narration starts off in a caption, which spans the width of three distinct panels of action, that reads: "Did you ever hear of Mickey, how he heard a racket in the night and shouted . . ."[61] Here the caption terminates and Mickey's word balloon erupts across the page, crowding out of the fourth panel, saying "Quiet down there!" in large, bold lettering, which cues the reader into understanding that these words have been yelled.[62] The first three panels contain word balloons that do not represent speech but rather *sound*. They read, "Thump/dump clump lump/bump," indicating the racket that keeps Mickey awake.[63] The first panel depicts, in Sendak's usual subdued tones, a little boy in his bed being roused by a "thump." In the second panel he sits almost fully upright, and his facial expression with brow turned down and chin protruding suggests annoyance. In the third panel he is standing on his bed, completely out from under the covers, bent double with the effort of shouting; his eyes are scrunched up and his mouth wide open, right fist clenched. On the following page is another four panels featuring the narration in captions and small speech balloons issuing forth Mickey's exclamations of awe and joy as he sails through the air on his adventure to the Night Kitchen. By the time he arrives in this fantastic new world, which includes three giant bakers and a cityscape full of baking ingredients and kitchen implements, the panels have widened into one image per page, resembling a more traditional picture book style. As the panels enlarge and broaden (similar to the previously discussed Briggs book, *The Snowman*, which was published eight years after *In the Night Kitchen*, and echoing Max's psychodrama in *Where the Wild Things Are*), so is Mickey's world "opened up" to the incredible sensory experience of tumbling naked into cake batter, and being clad in a suit of the same, flying around in a airplane made of bread dough, and swimming in an enormous bottle of milk. As the story continues, Mickey is returned from his fantasy back into his bed, and the four symmetrical panels return, closing snug and safe around him.

Sendak was deeply influenced by comics. According to John Cech, Sendak

> became a fervent fan of not only the Mickey Mouse cartoons but the Mickey Mouse comics and the Disney big-little books, along with other comic books. . . . These objects, images, and media strongly shaped Sendak's early imaginative life . . . and Sendak, like so many others, continues to be under their potent pull, much as he tried to counter it with more sophisticated influences.[64]

Classic works of "high" art and literature have, of course, had a strong influence on Sendak's art and method of storytelling, but the popular culture of Sendak's childhood also left an indelible impression on the man and his work—a fact that is celebrated in *In the Night Kitchen*. Cech calls *In the Night Kitchen* a turning point, commenting that "Sendak shocked elitist defenders of high culture in children's book illustration with his newest book [*In the Night Kitchen*]."[65] Cech also notes that the influence of comics on Sendak's work extends so far that "Sendak was simply borrowing from and expanding upon the graphic and thematic elements of Winsor McCay in his comic strip 'Little Nemo in Slumberland.'"[66]

Cech's statement may not be entirely true; it could be argued that Sendak takes the basic themes of "Nemo" and makes them his own. In his book *Caldecott & Co.: Notes on Books and Pictures* (1988), Sendak himself describes his affinity for Winsor McCay when he says, "McCay and I serve the same master, our child selves. We both draw not on the literal memory of childhood but on the emotional memory of its stress and urgency. And neither of us forgot our childhood dreams."[67] Therefore, Sendak utilizes and expands upon the themes found in "Little Nemo in Slumberland." When his agitation is quelled and his quest is fulfilled, Mickey comes back from his dream and finds himself safely tucked in his bed and content. This again draws comparisons with the themes found in *Where the Wild Things Are* where Max, after having been sent to his room and subsequently embarking on a dream-like journey to the land of the Wild Things, returns to his bedroom and finds a hot meal awaiting him. Both characters, Mickey and Max, return to a reassuring environment, while McCay's Nemo doesn't always return to comfort. Sendak's love affair with comics is also expressed in 1993's *We Are All in the Dumps with Jack and Guy*, where Sendak again utilizes speech balloons. The speech balloons in this book not only give a voice to his characters, but are the tools that Sendak uses to draw two separate nursery rhymes together.

Just as comics have had an important influence on picture books, so have picture books, due to the reflexive nature of art, influenced comics. There are some books that are very difficult to classify, as Raymond Briggs's *The Snowman* (not to mention his other notable works, such as *When the Wind Blows* and *Gentleman Jim*, both of which are intended for older readers). Is it a picture book, or a comic book? There is a lot of crossover between the two fields and these graphic works can be claimed by both of them. Shaun Tan's delicate, wordless story *The Arrival* (2006) exemplifies just how much hybridization has come forth from these two art forms. *The Arrival* contains no words and therefore no difficult vocabulary, but the visual and cultural references are complex. *The Arrival* is not *strictly* wordless, because it contains a fantastical alien script that neither the reader, nor the protagonist of the story, can read. The theme of this book is the immigrant experience, and the confusion of living in an alien land with its new customs and cultures. Even the disorientation of not understanding the language and writing of one's adopted country are aptly expressed.

Without words, Tan is able to convey a complicated tale. In one scene the protagonist goes shopping at what appears to be a market. Baffled by how the market works and the unfamiliar food, he is approached by a man and his son who help him to select his groceries. A friendship is kindled. In panels 3 through 11, the protagonist "tells" the man the story behind his emigration to this new, strange country. His new friend does not speak his native language, so, in order to elucidate his story, he draws a picture. The drawing displays what appears to be a monstrous tail looming over a group of houses. Whether the monster represents war, famine, or some other strife does not matter. The huge monster is symbolic of the many reasons why people leave their native lands in search of a better life. The other man's reaction to the protagonist's tale is to reach out and touch him on the shoulder (panel 7, fig. 2.6). The next panel (panel 8) shows the other man leaning forward, lips parted, and fingers splayed upon his chest as he gestures toward himself. It is as if he is saying, "Something like this has happened to me, too." The subsequent panels show the man gesticulating with his hands in the air, and the next panel presents a close-up view of his face. He has a faraway look, as he appears to recall past memories. The last panel shows a close-up of the man's eye; a careful "reader" will note that the man's iris reflects an image of flames. The next page is a double-spread featuring a scene of holocaust. Masked giants in exterminator's uniforms raze a city to the ground as tiny humans flee or are sucked into the air by some vacuum-like apparatuses that the giants carry with them. Flames shoot out of the back of each of the giants' vacuum-pack canisters, evoking thoughts of crematoria. Great search lights beam across the destroyed land through each giant's single eye. It is no accident that these monsters are depicted as Cyclopes. Their view is narrow, and they only see the world in one way—their own. Without words Tan is able to convey heartbreaking narrative through the elegant

Figure 2.6. *The Arrival*, 2006, panels 1–11.
From *The Arrival* by Shaun Tan. Copyright © 2006 by Shaun Tan. Reprinted by permission of Scholastic Inc.

use of sequential art. Much like *The Snowman, The Arrival* is constructed in panel format and sits just on the cusp of what is considered comics and what is considered a picture book.

Distinctions between Comics and Picture Books

Comics, like picture books, often contain images that must be read. They also contain examples of artistic ambiguity, where it is difficult to tell where the art ends and the text begins, where the text is inseparable from the art. The text and image may complement each other or contradict one another. Nevertheless, comics, while employing the same storytelling techniques as picture books, are not commonly viewed as being of equal literary value.

Of course, comics also function in ways distinct from the average picture book. Since comics are not usually created and marketed toward the youngest readers, the subject matter and language are often (but not always) more mature and complex. Comics typically convey visual narrative across panels, and verbal narrative usually occurs in thought bubbles, speech balloons, and captions, which shall all be further discussed in the next chapter.

Though picture books have borrowed many of comics' techniques of blending visual and textual narrative, picture books currently enjoy a status that comics do not. Lewis notes this sad fact as he states, "The comic has never been entirely respectable and has remained outside the mainstream of publishing for most of its life."[68] This is unfortunate. Comic book narrative can be just as complex and literary in technique as picture book narrative and is deserving of equal esteem. They offer a wonderful and unique literary experience and also require advanced skills in the *visual literacy* of readers. The next chapter shall examine the importance of visual literacy, as well as how comics are a unique form of art with their own distinct capabilities.

Notes

1. Uri Shulevitz, "What Is a Picture Book?" in *Only Connect: Readings on Children's Literature*, 3rd ed., ed. Sheila Egoff, Gordon Stubbs, Ralph Ashley, and Wendy Sutton (Toronto: Oxford University Press, 1996), 238.
2. Shulevitz, "What Is a Picture Book?" 239.

3. Wolfgang Iser, *The Implied Reader: Patterns of Communication in Prose Fiction from Bunyan to Beckett* (Baltimore: The Johns Hopkins University Press, 1990), 280.

4. Iser, *The Implied Reader,* 280.

5. Iser, *The Implied Reader,* 279, 280.

6. Iser, *The Implied Reader,* 280.

7. Iser, *The Implied Reader,* 279.

8. Iser, *The Implied Reader,* 279.

9. Iser, *The Implied Reader,* 279.

10. Louise M. Rosenblatt, *Literature as Exploration* (New York: D. Appleton-Century-Crofts, 1938), 37.

11. Maria Nikolajeva and Carole Scott, "The Dynamics of Picturebook Communication," *Children's Literature in Education* 31, no. 4 (2000): 225.

12. Nikolajeva and Scott, "Dynamics of Picturebook Communication," 225.

13. Nikolajeva and Scott, "Dynamics of Picturebook Communication," 225.

14. Nikolajeva and Scott, "Dynamics of Picturebook Communication," 230.

15. Nikolajeva and Scott, "Dynamics of Picturebook Communication," 226.

16. Nikolajeva and Scott, "Dynamics of Picturebook Communication," 226.

17. Jane Doonan, *Looking at Pictures in Picture Books* (Stroud: The Thimble Press, 1993), 85.

18. Mariko Tamaki and Steve Rolston, *Emiko Superstar* (New York: Minx, 2008), 122.

19. Tamaki and Rolston, *Emiko Superstar,* 122.

20. Nikolajeva and Scott, "Dynamics of Picturebook Communication," 225–26.

21. Nikolajeva and Scott, "Dynamics of Picturebook Communication," 226.

22. Peggy Rathmann, "Good Night, Dear," in *Good Night, Gorilla* (New York: G. P. Putnam's, 1994).

23. Rathmann, "Good Night, Dear."

24. Holly Black and Ted Naifeh, *The Good Neighbors, Book Two: Kith* (New York: Graphix, 2009), 34.

25. Black and Naifeh, *Good Neighbors,* 34.

26. Nikolajeva and Scott, "Dynamics of Picturebook Communication," 226.

27. John Burningham, *Aldo* (New York: Crown, 1991), "Aldo is only friends with me, and he's a secret. I know that he will always come to me when things get really bad."

28. Burningham, *Aldo,* "Like when they were horrible to me the other day."

29. Burningham, *Aldo,* "I'm sure they went away because Aldo came."

30. Burningham, *Aldo,* "Sometimes I wish he could help, but he's only my special friend."

31. Burningham, *Aldo*, "Of course I watch television, and I have lots of toys and books and things."

32. Burningham, *Aldo*, "Sometimes we go to the park, and occasionally we go out to eat, which is nice."

33. Burningham, *Aldo*.

34. Shannon Hale, Dean Hale, and Nathan Hale, *Rapunzel's Revenge* (New York: Bloomsbury, 2008), 34–35.

35. Nikolajeva and Scott, "Dynamics of Picturebook Communication," 226.

36. Rosenblatt, *Literature as Exploration*, 95.

37. Doonan, *Looking at Pictures*, 18.

38. Doonan, *Looking at Pictures*, 18, 15.

39. Doonan, *Looking at Pictures*, 15.

40. Nikolajeva and Scott, "Dynamics of Picturebook Communication," 232.

41. Doonan, *Looking at Pictures*, 85.

42. Jon Scieszka and Lane Smith, *The Stinky Cheese Man and Other Fairly Stupid Tales* (New York: Viking, 1992).

43. Scieszka and Smith, *The Stinky Cheese Man*.

44. Cecil Castellucci and Jim Rugg, *The Plain Janes* (New York: Minx, 2007), "I knew that if that dandelion could survive."

45. Castellucci and Rugg, *The Plain Janes*, "The Pyramids."

46. Castellucci and Rugg, *The Plain Janes*, "Bubbles are plain."

47. Castellucci and Rugg, *The Plain Janes*, "Bubbles are plain."

48. Cecil Castellucci and Jim Rugg, *Janes in Love* (New York: Minx, 2008), 24.

49. Castellucci and Rugg, *Janes in Love*, 25, 28–29.

50. Castellucci and Rugg, *Janes in Love*, 28.

51. Castellucci and Rugg, *Janes in Love*, 63.

52. Castellucci and Rugg, *Janes in Love*, 98.

53. Doonan, *Looking at Pictures*, 17.

54. John Burningham, *Granpa* (New York: Crown, 1985), "That was not a nice thing to say to Granpa."

55. Doonan, *Looking at Pictures*, 17.

56. Will Eisner, *Comics and Sequential Art: Principles and Practices from the Legendary Cartoonist* (New York: Norton, 2008), 7.

57. Rosenblatt, *Literature as Exploration*, 95.

58. Rosenblatt, *Literature as Exploration*, 110.

59. Judith Graham, "Texts That Teach: Wordless Picture Books," *Language Matters*, no. 1 (1987): 22.

60. David Lewis, "The Jolly Postman's Long Ride, or, Sketching a Picture-Book History," *Signal*, no. 78 (September 1995): 109, 191.

61. Maurice Sendak, *In the Night Kitchen* (New York: Harper & Row, 1970), "Did you ever hear of Mickey, how he heard a racket in the night and shouted."

62. Sendak, *In the Night Kitchen*, "Quiet down there!"

63. Sendak, *In the Night Kitchen*, "Quiet down there!"

64. John Cech, *Angels and Wild Things: The Archetypal Poetics of Maurice Sendak* (University Park: The Pennsylvania State University Press, 1995), 188.

65. Cech, *Angels and Wild Things*, 188.

66. Cech, *Angels and Wild Things*, 190.

67. Maurice Sendak, *Caldecott & Co.: Noted on Books and Pictures* (New York: Farrar, Straus and Giroux, 1988), 78.

68. Lewis, "Jolly Postman's Long Ride," 191.

CHAPTER THREE
THE POWER OF
VISUAL NARRATIVE

Visual literacy is a skill that is necessary for everyone to learn but is highly underappreciated and mostly misunderstood. It is the skill that allows us to navigate our world, from our interpretation of street signs to our understanding of art and even advertising as well as the deciphering of emotional cues and body language. It is what enables us to construe the meaning of symbols that we encounter in everyday life. According to the International Visual Literacy Association (IVLA) the term originated in 1969 with John Debes when he stated that

> Visual Literacy refers to a group of vision-competencies a human being can develop by seeing and at the same time having and integrating other sensory experiences. The development of these competencies is fundamental to normal human learning. When developed, they enable a visually literate person to discriminate and interpret the visible actions, objects, symbols, natural or man-made, that he encounters in his environment. Through the creative use of these competencies, he is able to communicate with others. Through the appreciative use of these competencies, he is able to comprehend and enjoy the masterworks of visual communication.[1]

In the years since Debes introduced the term, the definition of visual literacy has evolved to encompass rapidly developing technology in an ever-changing world. Now, the term *visual literacy* may be used in different ways. The IVLA website acknowledges this fact:

> However, there are many more definitions of the term. In fact, each visual literacist has produced his/her own! Understandably, the coexistence of so many disciplines that lie at the foundation of the concept of Visual Literacy, thus causing and at the same time emphasizing the eclectic nature of it, is the major obstacle toward a unanimously agreed [upon] definition of the term.[2]

This book will use Debes's original meaning for the term but will also take into consideration that the definition of visual literacy can be broad and is certainly mutable, due to constant changes in technology. Nevertheless, whether we are navigating a world of books made of paper, or a world of bits and circuits, visual literacy is essential to the success of human development.

Why Visual Literacy Is Important

Linda Cooper paraphrases Randhawa and Coffman's 1978 findings when she states that "the way we understand images is a cultural convention that is learned."[3] It is not a skill that comes to us naturally; just as we are not born knowing how to read, we must also learn how to interpret visual information, such as signs and symbols. Our interpretation of visual information is also influenced by our culture. In fact, interpretation of an image may vary within any particular culture. As Cooper puts it, "Meaning may not be the same from person to person or from one group to another."[4] Cooper gives an astute example of this phenomenon:

> For example, in addition to conveying the concept of "house," a picture of a house might also mean "home for a family" to one person or "real estate" to another. A picture of a middle class home in the United States may be "read" as an upper class home in another country.[5]

Understanding the implied meaning of visual information within its context can be an understandably difficult task. Children, without worldly experience, may be able to understand the basic or literal meanings of symbols. However, the nuances of images may go misunderstood if they are not taught how to develop their skills in visual literacy. Cooper suggests that we must work with children to help them decode our world and the complexities of its visual signs and symbols. She goes on to say, "While a child may note the literal meaning of a graphic representation, he or she may lack the experience to immediately grasp meaning that is implied or abstract . . . [he or she] may need support to move to a more sophisticated level of visual understanding."[6] One might think that we just acquire the ability to distinguish the implied meaning of visual information through experience and development; but, while it is true that a young person is exposed to visual information through their own life experiences, the development of a more sophisticated understanding of visual input can be strengthened through instruction.[7] According to Cooper, "We can teach children to read visual information in a manner similar to that which we use to teach them to read textual information."[8]

Cooper draws upon Piaget's theory of cognitive development to explain how children "read" images at different stages of developmental growth.[9] In Piaget's theory, there are four major cognitive phases: the sensory-motor period, which ranges from zero to two years of age; the period of preoperational thought, which takes place between (approximately) the age of two to seven years; the period of concrete operations, which develops around age seven and concludes at about eleven or twelve years of age; and the last stage, referred to as the period of formal operations, which begins around eleven or twelve years of age.[10] Cooper applies this theory to how children read images during different stages of their cognitive development. She suggests that in the preoperational stage children are still egocentric; thus "they are unlikely to interpret implied meaning in visual information."[11] Children in this stage of development tend to interpret images in a literal way since the competency for abstract thought (inference) has not yet developed.[12]

Interestingly, Cooper demonstrates how a child on the cusp of the preoperational and the concrete operations stage can be coached toward improved visual literacy. She describes a vignette from her experiences in a school library where she talks to a first grade girl who is doing a report on a country.[13] The little girl had been looking at a book above her reading level, and she was having difficulty finding information about the country that she was researching. However, the book contained pictures, and Cooper asked the child "if there was any information in the pictures."[14] At first, the little girl said that there was not any information. Cooper then prompted the girl to look at the picture again and describe what she saw.

The first grader then described a mountain capped with snow.[15] Then the little girl was asked to think about what it must be like on the top of that mountain. From this prompt, the girl was able to interpret that it must be a cold place, judging from what the visual information in her picture implied.[16] In this scenario, the little girl is at the cognitive stage where images are read literally, but Cooper demonstrates that children at this stage can be guided toward an understanding of more abstract information contained in images.[17] This shows how visual literacy can be taught and developed by teachers and guides.

The teaching of visual literacy also has implications for improved understanding of the rapidly changing world of technology. Harris states:

> In classrooms that are increasingly electronic and arguably "virtual," scholars like Jay David Bolter (1998) have concluded that "literacy in electronic environments may have more to do with the production and consumption of images than the reading and writing of either hypertextual or linear prose."[18]

Harris goes on to stress the importance of visual literacy in the everyday lives of university students:

> Visual research and the use of images in scholarly communities and discourses is no longer the province of specialists, but a common activity in the lives of students that connects their "school life" and their "real life" away from school. In a world raining with images, where an abundance of visual texts acts as naturalized and peripheral parts of every waking moment, it is reasonable to expect that many of our students may not be critical readers of images and visual information.[19]

Harris suggests that "as faculty members, librarians, students—as all of us—become more active seekers, users, and creators of images, it is increasingly vital that we work to connect information literacy, with the visual literacy initiatives."[20] Although Harris is referring to university students and he discusses his theory of preparing these students through the combined teaching of visual and information literacy, the message remains clear: in their everyday lives, and certainly when dealing with technology, people must be able to interpret images. In order to advance academically, even the youngest students will benefit from being taught and encouraged to be fluent readers of visual information.

Doonan also makes the point that visual narratives can improve literacy and may be used for "raising visual awareness."[21] She remarks: "Looking at pictures is a pleasurable activity, not regarded as work by pupils, and pictures make satisfying subjects for investigation."[22] If picture books are helpful in the acquisition of visual literacy, then comics can be equally valuable in building the visual literacy of young people. Doonan states that "reading words and looking at pictures are very complex activities."[23] Visual literacy is underestimated in its complexity and its importance. It gives us the tools that we need in order to decode symbol systems in the world around us. It enables us to interpret cultural and emotional images, body language, and facial expression. The implements of visual literacy are essential to people in a modern society that increasingly communicates in symbols and icons. We encounter symbols on a daily basis, forcing us to make many visual negotiations without even realizing it. Comics can encourage visual literacy, which helps young people to navigate a world that is full of symbols. Picture books, of course, foster this ability, but comics can also have equal value. When a young person's reading level encourages them to pursue more challenging texts, and picture books are out of fashion with their age peers, comics may have a significant role to play in the cultivation of visual literacy.

The Value of the Visual Text

The promotion of visual literacy is not the only virtue of comics; they also contain deceptively complex narratives. In her book *How Texts Teach What Readers Learn* (1988), Meek acknowledges the importance of comics:

> Outside the classroom, the library, the bookish [children] find the popular culture of childhood in comics. Looking back at the debates that have arranged around these productions I'm surprised that we have ignored for so long the reading skills they taught our readers. The classic comic demands that two interpretations be made together, of pictures and text. Balloon dialog, inset sketches, drawing "asides," together with the reader's impulse to keep the story going while taking all this in, should have alerted us sooner to the ways by which the young reader becomes both the teller and the told, what Bakhtin calls "the dialogic imagination."[24]

Meek understands that reading comics is a complicated skill that can assist young people in becoming more effective readers. A piece of literature that includes pictures in its narrative strategy is not necessarily unworthy of older readers. Meek asserts that the devaluation of visual narrative had its genesis in the rigidness of the educational system—an education system that places great value on the written word alone works against itself, shutting out other forms of narrative. Meek comments on this pressure in schools to "put away childish things":

> It's schooling, and the teaching of reading as a concern with words alone, that puts into our heads the notion that books with pictures are a preliterate form of storytelling, while all the time the very force of television shows us this is not the case.[25]

Even though picture books are lauded for their storytelling and aesthetics while comics are generally not, there is still a bias present in Western culture that assumes that stories containing pictures are, as Meek says, "preliterate." Children are usually encouraged to move beyond picture books toward "chapter books." It is, of course, considered a natural progression in a text-driven society, yet the value of visual narrative is overlooked. Typically, once the literacy milestone of having read a book without pictures has been reached, the reader may view stories that contain pictures as "babyish." Of course, gaining advanced, sustained reading skills is a triumph for any young reader. Children usually look forward to being considered "big kids," but perhaps part of a child's newly found disdain for books with accompanying images is also influenced by societal pressures.

Julie Bosman's 2010 article in the *New York Times* stirred up quite the fuss about the supposed decline of picture books. The article boldly claims that, aside from the classics, picture books are "fading," stating that "publishers have scaled back the number of titles they have released in the last several years, and booksellers across the country say sales have been suffering."[26] Many refute this claim. In their article for *The Horn Book Magazine*, Vice President and publisher of Beach Lane Books, Allyn Johnston, and picture book author-illustrator and Caldecott Honor recipient, Marla Frazee, assert that the question "are picture books dead?" seems "absurd" to them.[27] Karen Springen, writing for *Publishers Weekly*, also refutes Bosman's claim, pointing out that children's book publishers and booksellers tell a different story: they are not seeing the remarkable decline in picture book sales that Bosman is so concerned with.[28] Springen stresses: "The true story is more complicated, involving the cyclical nature of the economy, the strong interest in picture books in public libraries, and the changing retail market."[29] When taking into consideration periodic dips in the economy, it does indeed seem absurd to make any predictions about the continuing popularity or relevance of an entire art form—especially an art form that has a long tradition of being instrumental in teaching literacy skills to children.

While Bosman's article might be a premature prediction of things to come for the children's book market, and may even be considered alarmist, she does raise an interesting point:

> The economic downturn is certainly a major factor, but many in the industry see an additional reason for the slump. Parents have begun pressing their kindergartners and first graders to leave the picture book behind and move on to more text-heavy chapter books. Publishers cite pressures from parents who are mindful of increasingly rigorous standardized testing in schools.[30]

Bosman's charge that children are increasingly pushed toward text-based books remains open for further examination. However, there is no denying that visual storytelling is seriously undervalued. This is no new phenomenon. Meek points out that this prioritizing of written narrative is a great flaw in our educational system: "The ousting of images by text has not been an unmitigated gain in the teaching of literacy, as we are only now beginning to realize."[31] The reevaluation of works like comics could be the key in reintroducing the concept of visual literacy and furthering the understanding of complex narratives for our youths, who have been taught for so long that there is shame in reading a work of literature that includes pictures.

If we are to believe that picture books are considered a "preliterate form of storytelling,"[32] then it is safe to assume that the literary qualities of comics are often terribly misunderstood. On top of a history of negative associations with delinquency and a general assumption that comics are a degenerate art form, parents and other figures of authority may be under the impression that comics are childish or have no literary value. Many still believe that comics can even stunt the literacy of young people. In *Seduction of the Innocent*, Wertham calls his research in classrooms for children with developmental and learning disabilities "conclusive proof that severe reading difficulties and maximum comic-book reading go hand in hand, and that far from being a help to reading, comic books are a causal and reinforcing factor in children's reading disorders."[33] It is a logical fallacy to conclude that, because young people with learning disabilities or mental delay may enjoy comics, comics stunt literacy.

Wertham's unsubstantiated claims did great damage to public opinion of the art form. But new researchers are finding counter-evidence to Wertham's claims. Krashen cites several studies that prove that comics are harmless and may even be beneficial for young readers. He states: "A number of studies confirm that long-term comic book readers, those who continue to read comics after the early grades, are at least equal to non-comic book readers in reading, language development, and overall school achievement."[34] Krashen implies that long-term comic book readers are on par with their non–comic book–reading peers, possibly even surpassing them in literacy and language arts skills. In his survey of the results of studies in the field, Krashen even appears to find evidence indicating that long-term comic book readers may even read *more* conventional books than their peers who do not read comics.[35] This also raises the question of why these advanced readers continue to read comics, if comics have been deemed to be of little literary worth or, at best, valuable only as a stepping-stone toward advanced literacy. This is because comics offer a unique literary experience and may often convey sophisticated subject matters and narratives.

The graphic novel collecting the mini-series *Ojo* (2004, 2005), by Sam Kieth, Alex Pardee, and Chris Wisnia, is a prime example of how comics are able to transmit complex narratives that engage the reader. *Ojo* tells the story of an eleven-year-old girl named Annie whose mother is recently deceased. Annie feels that somehow it is her fault that her mother died, a feeling that is reinforced by her lack of success in keeping her pets alive. Her lizard, Phred, dies first, and then a hamster named Molly. She even feels responsible for the death of an insect that she accidentally squishes. Finally, she finds an injured little creature named Ojo whom she nurses back to health and is able to care for properly (although through dubious means, as she also has to feed its mother—a full grown monster). At the end of the tale, Annie releases Ojo to its mother, thus letting go of her own "monsters," which relate to her inner feelings about her mother's death.

The last page (fig. 3.1) is narrated by Annie as an adult, and we realize that this event happened in the distant past. Annie is shown as a girl burying her mother's things: a tape, a jacket, and Polaroid pictures that Annie took during her mourning period. She is shown laying out little "headstones" for her pets. The text reads, "I was eleven years old and had already caused three deaths. But *only* three."[36] Annie writes the name of

Figure 3.1. *Ojo*, 2005, page 124. The complementary image adds depth, allowing the visual narrative to speak for Annie, illustrating her acceptance of the loss of her mother.

her pet monster on a new stone, but then rubs it out and writes "Mom" in its place, finally laying her guilt to rest and saying goodbye to her mother. The text is minimal and relies on the image to carry the emotional weight of the situation. The text in the last six panels directly discusses the death of her pets. But the *images* show that Annie is letting go of her unnecessary guilt over the death of her mother. The panels that display Annie rewriting "Ojo" on the stone to read "Mom" instead convey the transfer of feelings about her mother onto her pet and her acceptance of the loss. Without these images, the text would not have depth, and there would be no sense of closure to the story. David Lewis makes the observation that

> [p]ictures can illustrate words—that is, they can show in iconic form something of what the words say—but they can also show something different. Newspaper cartoons have always exploited this gap, allowing the spark of meaning to jump between the picture and the caption.[37]

This is one of the most important concepts that comics employ in terms of narrative: comics rely heavily on counterpoint and complementary narratives, just as some of the best picture books do. This is precisely what is misunderstood about the two fields: reading text is not always easy, but reading a *picture* is a complex and sophisticated skill.

Comics and picture books have much in common, as discussed in chapter 2. But they differ significantly as well. Comics often contain complicated narrative structures, such as juxtaposed inner and outer dialog, represented by captions and "thought bubbles" (which show interior thoughts) and "word balloons" and exclamations (which show exterior dialog). The joining of visual and textual narrative also often creates polyphony or dialogism as different narratives or voices interact with one another. The comic book form also enables multiple characters to have different voices, both outwardly and inwardly as thoughts and statements within the same panel. This marks comics as a unique and complex literary medium that should not only be respected for its contribution to the literacy of children and teens but for the unique and visionary qualities of the art form itself.

The Mechanics of Comics

One of the defining characteristics of the comic book form is the visualization of narrative in the form of word balloons, thought bubbles, dialog boxes, captions, and the like. Some of these devices, such as the voice-over style of caption, have been borrowed from theater and film. In comics, a caption may be defined as text that typically appears in a box above, below, or in the middle of the image in a cartoon panel (though, sometimes, there is no box and the caption appears as floating text). This text functions as expository narrative by an omniscient narrator or may serve as interior monologue for a character. However, the caption distinguishes itself as having a separate function than the ubiquitous thought bubble. Thought bubbles give the reader a window into a character's personal thoughts, whereas the caption allows the narrator to knowingly impart information to the reader, not unlike a Shakespearean aside. Captions may also indicate temporal dislocation between the action shown in the image and the caption's narration. Many motion pictures from the film noir genre have what is known as a *voice-over*. For instance, the protagonist or an unknown character (in film noir detective dramas it is often the detective) narrates a back-story or expresses the inner thoughts of a character—a technique that has become a convention of mainstream cinema today, as well as many comics and graphic novels.

In Ted Naifeh's comic book series, *Courtney Crumrin and the Night Things* (2002), the comic book convention of the voice-over caption is used throughout the story. The implied narrator is unknown to us and open for speculation. At first, it appears to be Butterworm, the goblin, as he introduces himself and the neighborhood, saying, "Name's Butterworm. I saw Crumrin house built. It were the first house in 'illsborough, before it become a posh neighborhood full 'a spoilt little brats."[38] However, the style of narration shifts out of Butterworm's vernacular speech to an omniscient authorial voice. This displays the dialogic complexity of narrative style in comics (see fig. 3.2 for an illustration of the voice-over phenomenon). In this example, the protagonist, young Courtney Crumrin, has come to live in her uncle's old, creepy mansion in Hillsborough. She has trouble adjusting to her new life—especially to school and her new home. In these two panels, Courtney is shown wandering through the darkened house at night because she cannot sleep. The caption tells us what Courtney discovers: "A warm inviting light came from under the door."[39] A second caption tells us about the emotional conflict occurring in Courtney's own mind, as it explains the

Figure 3.2. *Courtney Crumrin and the Night Things,* 2002, panels 1–4. The caption narrates the story and adds a sense of drama to the image.

little girl's struggle between her fear of her elderly uncle and the need to feel secure in the unfamiliar surroundings of the house at night. In panel 1, Courtney is shown facing the door with her back to us. The stillness of this moment is captured as a pause. We are told what she is thinking, and we can assume that this frame represents a mental and physical pause, as Courtney is not shown in motion. Nor is there any indicative line art such as motion lines to suggest movement. The picture captures a moment of indecision as she stands outside the door, the image of the door being the center of the panel, at the heart of the matter. This moment builds visual tension, but as the caption is read, the reader becomes aware that Courtney has made a decision. The caption reads: "Her dread of the lonely house was much more powerful";[40] thus the reader is able to predict that this tempting door will be opened, against all other judgment. What the caption does not say, the image itself expresses: the next frame displays a timid-looking Courtney gazing upward, as a little child to an adult person, as she calls her uncle's name, as if to see if he is there. Half of her face is hiding behind the door, awkwardly, as she is not sure whether she should be there. The drawn-out moment of indecision adds drama to this turning point in the plot through the interplay of visual and verbal narratives, the combination of caption and image heightening the experience of suspense for the reader.

Saraceni concurs that the caption is a technique unique to the comics narrative. He looks at an example where the caption functions as a voice-over, yet within the same frame, two characters engage in dialog that is quite separate from the narration. Saraceni comments, "This seems to be different from conventional literature, where . . . the narrator's voice is much more intrusive and often merges with the character's speech."[41] Another function of the caption, according to Saraceni, is to "[fill] the gap represented by the gutter."[42] The gutter is "the blank space that separates each panel from the others,"[43] the panel being the frame in which the action and the text usually take place. Saraceni defines it as "a rectangular frame that contains pictures and, usually, speech balloons depicting a single scene within a narrative in comics."[44]

While this description is accurate, it must be mentioned that not all comics adhere to the traditional, six-panel rectangular format. Some images "break" the frame or are depicted as frameless. The panel, however, not only serves as the transmitter of narrative information, but is also another device that marks the passage of time in the comics narrative. Just as a picture book may use the strategic placement of text in order to create a dramatic pause (for example, text that continues after a page turn), comics use visual cues to suggest a sense of time being paused as well as time elapsing or even stretching. Aside from the image itself, the concept of timing has much to do with the paneling of the story: how it is broken up into frames and the way in which this is presented on the page.

McCloud explains the visual construction of time when he depicts how something that he calls "the pause panel" works. McCloud offers three effective solutions to lengthening a pause: multiply the number of panels for the "silent" panel, widen the gutter between panels, or change the shape of the panel (see fig. 3.3). McCloud also explains how a borderless (or frameless) panel can also affect the reader's perception of time (see fig. 3.4). A panel can also bleed to the edge of the page, which is another device used by comic artists to denote a concept of time.[45] In figure 3.2 from *Courtney Crumrin and the Night Things*, there is an evident use of the panel to create a sense of elapsed time. In another example from *Courtney Crumrin and the Coven of Mystics* (fig. 3.5), there is an example of time slowed down, before an arrow pierces its mark, the night thing, Skarrow.[46] The panel, depicting Skarrow reaching out to his mother, is bisected by an image of an arrow in flight—an arrow that literally and visually comes between them, preventing the reunion of mother and son. In this example, the breaking up of the panel shows us *simultaneous* action of the doomed embrace and the arrow's flight.

There are many techniques that can be used in comics to imply the passage of time, and just as many, if not more, to construct emotion. Often, the style of the text itself is expressive of emotion or situation, as in figure 3.6. If the text had been lettered in a normal font, the impact would not be as great as in this handwritten exclamation, offset in negative within a black balloon. The black balloon that it sits in cannot contain the emotion of the word as the letters themselves bleed beyond its borders. Text can also be used to convey an idea, when it merges with the art itself

BUT IF THE CREATOR OF THIS SCENE WANTED TO *LENGTHEN* THAT PAUSE, HOW COULD HE OR SHE DO SO? ONE OBVIOUS SOLUTION WOULD BE TO ADD MORE PANELS, BUT IS THAT THE ONLY WAY?

D'YA THINK THE SOX COULD FINALLY *DO IT* THIS YEAR?

I GUESS.

IS THERE ANY WAY TO MAKE A SINGLE SILENT PANEL LIKE THIS ONE SEEM *LONGER?* HOW ABOUT WIDENING THE SPACE *BETWEEN PANELS?* ANY *DIFFERENCE?*

WE'VE SEEN HOW TIME CAN BE CONTROLLED THROUGH THE *CONTENT* OF PANELS, THE *NUMBER* OF PANELS AND CLOSURE *BETWEEN* PANELS, BUT THERE'S STILL *ONE MORE.*

HEY, I *DESERVE* A BETTER JOB! I COULD BE A BRAIN SURGEON!

I GUESS.

AS UNLIKELY AS IT SOUNDS, THE PANEL *SHAPE* CAN ACTUALLY MAKE A *DIFFERENCE* IN OUR *PERCEPTION* OF TIME. EVEN THOUGH THIS LONG PANEL HAS THE SAME BASIC "MEANING" AS ITS SHORTER VERSIONS, STILL IT HAS THE *FEELING* OF GREATER LENGTH!

THAT *MADONNA,* MAN, SHE'S ONE *HOT BABE!*

I GUESS.

Figure 3.3. *Understanding Comics: The Invisible Art,* **2000, page 101. Panel shape can dramatically change the perception of time.**
Pages 1 (entire) and 103 (one panel) from *Understanding Comics* by Scott Mccloud. Copyright © 1993, 1994 by Scott McCloud. Reprinted by permission of HarperCollins Publishers.

Figure 3.4. *Understanding Comics: The Invisible Art*, 2000, page 103. **The frameless panel seems suspended in time.**

Pages 1 (entire) and 103 (one panel) from *Understanding Comics* by Scott Mccloud. Copyright © 1993, 1994 by Scott McCloud. Reprinted by permission of HarperCollins Publishers.

Figure 3.5. *Courtney Crumrin and the Coven of Mystics, 2003.* Simultaneous action—the panel is utilized to slow down perceived time.

Courtney Crumrin and The Coven of Mystics is ™ and © 2003 Ted Naifeh. Unless otherwise specified, all other material © 2002 Oni Press, Inc.

Figure 3.6. *Courtney Crumrin and the Coven of Mystics*, 2003. Emotion is expressed through the graphic emphasis of the text.

Courtney Crumrin and the Coven of Mystics is ™ and © 2003 Ted Naifeh. Unless otherwise specified, all other material © 2002 Oni Press, Inc.

to contain an expression that the word alone does not say. Eisner gives his own example of this phenomena (see fig. 3.7), as he cites the Hebraic lettering from the title page of his influential graphic novel, *A Contract with God and Other Tenement Stories* (1978). Eisner says of his own use of the technique,

> Lettering (hand-drawn or created with type), treated "graphically" and in the service of the story, functions as an extension of the imagery. In this context it provides the mood, a narrative bridge and the implication of sound.[47]

A technique used widely in comics, the artistic enhancement of lettering can also function as image, melding with the visual narrative to create what Eisner terms a "gestalt"—the completeness of the art and literary hybrid.[48]

Saraceni examines comics in terms of semiotics (the study of signs and symbols), which breaks down images into three major categories: *icon, index,* and *symbol*.[49] An *icon* is an image that represents what it means—for instance, an image of a flower represents a flower. An *in-*

Figure 3.7. *Comics and Sequential Art: Principles and Practices from the Legendary Cartoonist,* **1985, 2008, page 4. Eisner's graphic treatment of text creates atmosphere.**
From *Comics and Sequential Art* by Will Eisner. Copyright © 1985 by Will Eisner. Copyright © 2008 by Will Eisner Studios, Inc. Used by permission of W. W. Norton & Company, Inc.

dex, however, is a sign that represents something other than what is illustrated. Saraceni gives the example: "Smoke stands for fire, because it indicates its presence."[50] A *symbol* is an image that stands for an object, and this means that a symbol can be a word. Saraceni uses the example of a dog, which can be represented by the image of the word "dog," which in English is associated with the actual animal.[51] All of these techniques and ideas come together to create the "gestalt" in comics that Eisner talks about.

Comics, though not widely recognized as a valid literary field or art form, also create the perfect space for the expression of voices that have been previously marginalized and silenced, because comics use many methods to convey narratives, including interior, silent voices. The thoughts and feelings of those who cannot speak for themselves or are otherwise ignored are given equal weight in comics' verbal narratives and in the emotional impact of the images. This includes the stories of ethnic and religious minorities, people of various sexual orientations, children, adolescents, and females. The medium's use of images creates narrative where words could not be expressed, as in the atrocities of the Holocaust, which Art Spiegelman explores in his seminal work, *Maus* (parts I and II). Giving a voice to the silent or silenced is difficult to convey successfully in prose, yet the narrative strategies of comics, in combining the textual and the visual, opens up dialogic communication. Independent comics, which are not under pressures to appeal to the mainstream and reinforce the status quo, can be even more experimental in their approach to narrative and are, therefore, the ideal media for reaching and representing marginalized people.

Comics Giving a Voice to the Underrepresented Female

The combination of comics' varied expressive techniques—the *Gesamtkunstwerk* that defines the form—makes it a unique mode of expression found in no other literary field. Though the female perspective has always found expression in politics, art, literature, and music (to name just a few outlets), the comics, as an ever-changing underground art and literary mode, has the potential to act as an open canvas on which the female point of view can be given life. However, comics that have been specifically oriented toward girls and women, have, in the past, not always been quality reading. Many have promoted stereotypical gender roles and have hawked the values and wares of a consumerist culture in their obsession with boys and makeup. Betty chased after Archie, competed with Veronica, and seemed to have nothing better to do. Nowadays, the current is shifting, and the underground has opened up new possibilities for the way in which females are represented in comic books, broadening girls' choices in what has been a male-oriented collector's market. Girls' comics are becoming experimental and literary, offering an alternative to the stereotypes typically found in mainstream comics, which often continue to objectify the female body and neglect her power as a human being.

Mariko Tamaki, author of *Emiko Superstar*, and her cousin Jillian Tamaki's Ignatz award–winning graphic novel *Skim* (2008) beautifully and delicately explores the time of flux and discovery that is adolescence in a coming-of-age tale. The story conveys the first-person narrative of the main character, Kimberly Keiko Cameron, known by her nickname, "Skim," as she writes about her feelings of otherness, alienation, and her dawning sexuality through the device of diary entries. Skim is a sixteen-year-old Japanese-Canadian girl who is at the cusp of change in her life. She is an outsider, and even her best friend (and fellow dabbler in Wicca), Lisa Soor, doesn't seem to understand her like a best friend should. In fact, Lisa's understanding of Skim's feelings is so limited that she never thinks twice about calling her by the negatively connotative nickname "Skim." She is called Skim because she is slightly overweight, and as she explains to her parochial school English teacher, Ms. Archer, the name is ironic. Ms. Archer broaches the subject, saying, "May I ask you something? Why do the students call you Skim?" and Skim replies, "Because I'm not."[52] However, Skim accepts this as her name, and even identifies herself as "a bit of a freak,"[53] which is at once something that she is proud of (an expression of uniqueness), yet at the same time is self-degrading. Skim's home life is also not ideal: her parents are separated and she lives with her mother,[54] who does not seem to be very warm or in touch with her daughter. Her father, who has recently suffered two heart attacks, appears mostly absent from her life. On top of these complications, Skim finds herself attracted to Ms. Archer.

In many instances throughout this graphic novel, the reader is privy to Skim's thought process as she writes down her musings, often striking them out, and revising them, although, in the way that the artist has rendered this, the scratched-out words are always visible. The act of writing aids Skim in clarifying her thoughts, distilling them into a deeper meaning. At other times, the act of crossing out what she has previously written appears to be an act of self-censorship or self-denial; it is as if Skim is too embarrassed to commit her feelings to paper or not yet ready to admit them to herself. Even when Skim is not writing them down, the reader is privy to her inner thoughts. Sometimes this internal dialog is shown to be at odds with what she says aloud; even when she talks to her best friend, Lisa, she

Figure 3.8a. *Skim*, **2008 page 28. Skim withholds her true thoughts and feelings from her best friend. However, the reader is in the privileged position of omniscience.**
Excerpts from *Skim* text copyright © 2008 by Mariko Tamaki, and illustrations copyright © 2008 by Jillian Tamaki. Reproduced with permission from Groundwood Books, Toronto.

often cannot say how she truly feels. In real life there is often a dichotomy between what we think and what we say. The integrated text in *Skim* lends authenticity to the teenage experience that even adults will be able to relate to. Figure 3.8 shows an example of how we, as individuals, do not air our private thoughts, even to those with whom we are supposed to be closest.

Figure 3.8b. *Skim*, 2008, page 29.

Another major theme that runs throughout *Skim* is the suicide of a peripheral character, a boy named John Reddear, who had been dating Katie Matthews, one of the popular girls at Skim's school. In the wake of this incident, the school guidance counselor, Mrs. Hornet, brings each tenth grade student into her office for a counseling session. Skim feels especially picked on by Mrs. Hornet. She paraphrases Mrs. Hornet saying that the counselor is "particularly concerned about people like me, because people like me are prone to depression and depressing stimuli" and that "students who are members of the 'gothic' culture (i.e., ME) are very fragile."[55] Skim complains that her feelings are probably normal for a sixteen-year-old and that it probably has nothing to do with being "goth."[57] She suggests that the boy who killed himself was a member of the mainstream: "John Reddear was on the VOLLEYBALL TEAM, not a goth, and he KILLED HIMSELF!!!"[58] Observantly Skim muses, "How come all the girls on the soccer team aren't in counseling?"[59] Shortly after the death of John Reddear, Mrs. Hornet announces at the school prayer assembly that Katie Matthews has broken both of her arms after accidentally falling off a roof. Skim implies that Katie's fall was no accident, but a suicide attempt.[60] The entire school is affected by these tragedies. Skim writes, "Dear Diary, today in prayers Julie Peters (Katie M's best friend) announced that she is starting a new club."[61] The club is called the "GCL" or "Girls Celebrate Life club."[62] The GCL club creates a bulletin board in the school hallway where they post a newspaper clipping with an image of the dead boy and a flyer for a screening of *Dead Poets Society*.[63] Both Skim and Lisa scoff at the club's efforts, perhaps because they believe the bulletin board is in poor taste, or perhaps because they do not get along with the group of popular girls who comprise the GCL.[64]

Skim's narrative suggests that the topic of teen suicide and depression has turned into something of a farce at the school, where it becomes popular to talk about depression or suicide. Because Skim is an outsider, she is approached by the leader of the GCL, Julie Peters, who gives her a hug after class one day and invites her to the GCL movie screening. Lisa later informs Skim about rumors involving her. She says, "Julie Peters is telling people that you are showing classic signs of someone who is suicidal."[65] This displays a rare moment where Lisa Soor, who is generally depicted as a rude and selfish girl, shows concern for Skim, all the while not realizing what is truly bothering her. Skim is actually discovering deepening feelings for Ms. Archer, the English teacher, which she keeps secret, even from Lisa. She is unable to talk to Lisa about her personal feelings and as the story advances, Skim and Lisa appear to understand each other less and less.

On the other hand, Ms. Archer seems to pay an unhealthy amount of attention to Skim. At first, the interest that the English teacher takes in Skim seems innocent, but this quickly changes. Page 39 displays a white page, free of panels, with a very simple, yet elegant drawing suggesting birds flying through the tops of trees. The top right of the page says, "Dear Diary," and in the lower right hand corner of the page Skim's entry reads:

> For the record, not all Wicca books are boring. This is what I found in my new book: "The 'Charge' comes to each of us in a different manner. It is that moment in our lives when we feel the Magick of the Universe coursing through us for the very first time, and we know beyond all real and imagined shadows that this calling to the mysteries is indeed there. Silver RavenWolf, *To Ride a Silver Broomstick.*"[66]

The next two pages display a double-spread. In contrast to the previous page, the image is busy, filling the entire space. It reveals Skim and Ms. Archer seated in Skim's favorite thinking spot—a wooded ravine near the school—kissing. There are no words; Skim does not describe this tryst. The images juxtaposed with the text of the previous page suggest that Skim feels that this is that powerful moment that RavenWolf describes as the "Charge."[67] Skim appears to view this as a spiritual turning point. However, this may be the moment when Skim realizes her own sexuality, as well. Nevertheless, the kiss and the attention that Ms. Archer lavishes upon Skim are wrong, and it is questionable whether or not Skim realizes how inappropriate a relationship between a teacher and a student is. Soon after this incident, Ms. Archer is absent from teaching. It is not long before she leaves the school for good.

After Ms. Archer's departure, Skim feels a confused mixture of rage, sadness, and self-pity. On page 89 (see fig. 3.9), Skim's diary entry begins in the book's usual small lettering, with the typical mode of address, "Dear Diary."[68] However, this orderly thought is interrupted by words that explode across the page. The image shows a birds-eye view of an outdoor scene. The setting is stark; the landscape is bare, but for a huge snow-laden tree in an expanse of white ground, and a few more skeletal trees off in the distance. A solitary bird flies by. In a landscape that speaks of loneliness is the small, dark figure of Skim dressed in her parka. She is shown dragging her feet through the snow to make out block capital letters that spell the words, "I hate."[69] The word "you," follows, but is crossed out. Skim has corrected her message to read, "everything."[70] That the letter "G" is missing tells the reader that this

Figure 3.9. *Skim*, 2008, page 89.

Excerpts from *Skim* text copyright © 2008 by Mariko Tamaki, and illustrations copyright © 2008 by Jillian Tamaki. Reproduced with permission from Groundwood Books, Toronto.

statement is a work in progress. She is still trudging through the fallen snow in order to express herself. In this artistic rendering of the text, Skim's words dwarf her. Her feelings could be understood to be bigger and more oppressive than can be contained by her diary, as Skim appears to be bursting with sadness and anger. Further down the page, the orderly lettering returns, stating, "It's snowing."[71] The message in the snow has become ambiguous; the reader cannot be sure who is being referred to as the "you" in her unrevised statement. Since the text starts off saying, "Dear Diary," the reader may assume that Skim is referring to the diary or, more specifically, to her own personal life and thoughts. In essence, it could be determined that she is externalizing her own self-loathing. However, the addition of the more conventional text stating, "It's snowing,"[72] conflicts with the suggestion that the words written in the snow are a part of her diary entry at all. The reader could interpret the writing in the snow as an omission from her diary—a raw statement of Skim's feelings that she cannot bear to commit to paper, therefore she lets her emotions out in a more ephemeral medium, writing them in the snow. The word "you" that has been crossed out could also be in reference to Lisa, from whom Skim is drifting apart, or perhaps Ms. Archer, who she feels has abandoned her following their inappropriate and clandestine meetings. Conceivably, Skim herself doesn't know to whom she is referring, or perhaps she means that she hates all of these people, together, including herself.

Furthermore, in the lower right hand corner of the page (see fig. 3.9), there is an inset image bearing the photograph from the GCL corkboard of the local boy who had recently committed suicide. The epithet "fag" has been scrawled across the forehead of the dead boy in the picture.[73] There is no expository text explaining the inclusion of this image, leaving the interpretation up to the reader. One gets the feeling that Skim had seen the graffiti marring the boy's photograph and that she is now reflecting on the discovery of her own sexual orientation and how the school and society at large may perceive her. It is also possible that Skim, although she does not acknowledge it in words, is having suicidal thoughts as her world destabilizes around her.

Resolution of Skim's feelings of abandonment and isolation comes in an unexpected form. After her supposed "accident" Katie Matthews finds that she can no longer abide her old clique of friends. Skim observes Katie's unhappiness when the popular girl returns to school. She notes that, on Katie's first day back, "a bunch of students followed her around all day carrying her things."[74] The opposite page features a group of five happy-looking girls clustered around the hunched form of Katie who appears miserable.[75] When Lisa makes a particularly insensitive comment about Katie comparing her deceased ex-boyfriend, John Reddear, and her to the tragic deaths of Romeo and Juliet but "on a delay," a panel shows Skim with her brow furrowed in annoyance as she reminds Lisa that Katie *didn't* die.[76] She then comments, "Everything Lisa says drives me crazy these days."[77] Soon after this conversation, Skim starts avoiding Lisa.[78]

In the book's subtle conclusion, Skim ends up finding a friend in Katie Matthews and begins to let go of her attachment to Lisa. Katie turns out to be a deceptively deep and respectful friend, the type of friend that Lisa never was. At the very end of this graphic novel, Skim remains friends with Lisa, but there is a distance between them. They have both grown and changed. Lisa, who, according to Skim, had previously said that she didn't believe in love, falls for a boy named Sam who goes to St. John's Collegiate school.[79] Lisa, who never realized that Skim had experienced her first stirrings of love and as well as heartbreak, says to Skim, "Being in love changes you, you know? . . . I can't explain it, obviously. I mean, it's very complex. No one can put it in words. . . . It's just . . . it makes things different, you know? It's like you turn a corner . . . it's kind of amazing."[80] Skim listens to Lisa and agrees with her, saying, "It is," with a small, sweet, and knowing smile on her face.[81] The subtlety of Skim's reaction to this talk about love shows that Skim has already turned that corner; she has found love and confusion, sadness and wonder, but, above all, she has found herself.

On the final page of the graphic novel, Skim is shown walking around the school to the nearby ravine where she likes to sit and think. A careful reader will notice that Skim is not the only figure on the page; Katie Matthews's beret peeks out from the edge of the ravine where she presumably sits awaiting Skim's arrival. This is a loaded image, considering that this spot is always shown to be Skim's private thinking space. Moreover, this is the place where Skim and Ms. Archer kissed. Whether or not Katie is just Skim's new best friend, or more than that, is up to the reader to decide.

The graphic novel *Ghost World* by Daniel Clowes is a story that originally appeared in the comics series *Eightball*, between the years 1993 and 1997. Like *Skim*, it explores themes of growth, change, and interpersonal relationships between teenage girls. *Ghost World* is often considered a controversial book for young adult readers, as it contains some material that may be deemed inappropriate; yet it is obvious that young people often "read up" and select reading material that may confound some adults. Keeping titles such as *Ghost World* off YA bookshelves does not mean that teens will not find these titles and read them, anyway.

For all of its brashness and open sexuality, at its core, *Ghost World* is a collection of realist vignettes exploring the themes of female adolescence, in particular the very last remainder of childhood before a young woman is thrust into adulthood. It offers a "slice of life" in all of its beauty and ugliness. It follows the pranks and mundane life of best friends Enid and Rebecca, through their drifting apart as they emerge out of adolescence into an uncertain and bittersweet womanhood. However commonplace their lives are, the story of Enid and Rebecca is engaging and surprisingly touching. In a neighborhood that remains comfortingly the same, the girls are changing. A rift develops between the best friends when Rebecca finds out that Enid is taking the entry test to get into Strathmore. Becky (as she is nicknamed) feels betrayed by Enid, who never told her that she had any intention of applying to college. In front of Becky, Enid casually mentions to an acquaintance that she might be attending Strathmore in the following year.[82] Becky reacts to this with surprise, but they do not speak of it again until much later when Becky overhears Enid's father mention that he talked to the staff at Strathmore and that Enid would have to take the entrance exam (see fig. 3.10, panels 1–6).[83] Enid's father appears to have no clue that his daughter has withheld this information from her best friend. In panel 2 Becky's face shows confusion after hearing this news. Her brow is furrowed as she looks at Enid's father, with whom she is apparently close enough to call "Pops" (panel one). However, Enid ignores her father, refusing to engage in any dialog with him and instead tries to distract Rebecca, calling attention away from this important revelation, joking, "C'mon, let's go in my room and abuse drugs and stuff!"[84] It is unclear whether or not Enid really wants Becky to know about Strathmore at this point in the story, or whether she really wants to avoid thinking of

Figure 3.10. *Ghost World*, 2001, page 50, panels 1–6. Clowes utilizes the visual form of comics to portray the increasing distance between Enid and Becky.
Courtesy of Fantagraphics Books, Inc., copyright 2001 Daniel Clowes.

college herself and the changes that it would bring to her life. However, the sidelong glance in panel 2 may be an admission of guilt, as it becomes more and more apparent throughout the rest of the story that Enid is severing her ties, slowly, with Becky.

Rebecca is much affronted by Enid's lie-by-omission, and we see a darker side to her—the clingy, selfish, and jealous side that fears abandonment. Rebecca says to Enid, "You're not really going to go are you?," shortly followed in the next panel by "It's like *impossible* to get into Strathmore! There's *no way* you'll ever be accepted. . . ."[85] The body language in these five panels says just as much as the words do. Not once do they face each other, and Rebecca is featured as small and crumpled in the background, while Enid is dominantly featured in the foreground. This is significant, as Doonan finds that there is much psychological inference in the positioning of an object in the picture plane. She paraphrases Rudolph Arnheim, when she says, "perceptual forces cause us to see pushes and pulls in visual patterns as genuine properties of the perceived objects themselves."[86] Enid is therefore given importance and psychological weight by being placed in the foreground, as opposed to Becky, who is small and in the background. This underlines the drifting apart of Enid and Rebecca, manifested in a physical sense. This distance, however, is foreshadowed by Becky's disappointment that Enid went to an adult store, Adam's II, with a boy named Josh, instead of her.[87] Going into the controversial store may be interpreted as being a rite of passage into adulthood, from which Enid excludes Rebecca.

Ghost World highlights the quirks of same-sex friendships among adolescent girls. This offers a realistic view of teenage relationships—one that mirrors issues adolescent readers are going through, feelings that they, too, have had. It may help teenage girls negotiate tough periods through the catharsis of relating to the story. In *Becoming a Reader: The Experience of Fiction from Childhood to Adulthood* (1994), J. A. Appleyard discusses the difference in the reading habits of teenage girls and boys, asserting:

> Sex differences are more marked here than any other age . . . the formation of a self-conscious sense of identity, a central theme of adolescence, is heavily influenced by the bodily changes of puberty and by the need to imagine acceptable versions of adult maleness and femaleness . . . show[s] up in the books adolescents voluntarily read.[88]

Comics like *Ghost World* may suit the female adolescent's need to read material that is relative to her own transition into womanhood and her desire for realism in her reading diet. Appleyard comments on the benefits of realism in young adult literature when he states:

> The adolescents' books deal with sex, death, sin, and prejudice, and good and evil are not neatly separated but mixed up in the confused and often turbulent emotions of the central characters themselves.[89]

According to Appleyard, this shift from fantasy and simple good versus evil stories comes from the developmental change that occurs at adolescence—"the discovery of the subjective self."[90] This means that adolescents become aware of their inner selves and inner lives, viewing the inner self as more "authentic" than their public lives.[91] However, Appleyard's hypothesis may not be accurate. In recent years, there has been an upsurge in adolescents preferring fantasy to realism in literature. Perhaps Appleyard dismisses fantasy too easily as a genre that can convey what it means to be a teenager. Good fantasy can discuss very serious topics through the veil of the fantastic. Whether the comic book or graphic novel tends toward realism or fantasy, the dialogic possibilities of the comics form allow adolescents to get that view-through-the-keyhole into the minds of the characters. Reader trends may come and go, but *Ghost World* is a peepshow into the inner lives of adolescents, particularly female relationships, providing the gravity that adolescent readers crave.

The gender-nonspecific *Optic Nerve*, by Adrian Tomine, is similar in its realistic exposure of the lives of everyday people. Each issue typically introduces several unrelated stories or sometimes follows the story of one character, usually resolving in a cynical and unfinished way that imitates real life. Issue no. 3, August 1996, contains the story titled "Dylan and Donovan," featuring twin sisters who are very different in their demeanor. Tomine often uses interior monolog, and "Dylan and Donovan" is no exception. The narrator, Dylan, presents herself as the well-adjusted twin, explaining the differences between her sibling and herself.

Dylan gives the reader a quick debriefing on her and her sister's background, subconsciously, perhaps, setting up the reason why there is such a disparity in their popularity and personality. She muses, "When we were growing up, Mom called Donovan my 'little sister.'"[92] As an aside she adds, "(Sorry if this is totally scatter-brained, but sometimes stuff just pops into my head. I can't help it)."[93] This side-note creates a realistic tone and also suggests that she is not as confident in herself as she claims to be. Visually, Tomine employs the technique of illustrating the caption with a "snapshot" of the twins as toddlers, to give the reader a sense of the history of the girls. It can be assumed that it is Donovan who is drawn smaller. Tomine uses form to comment on the psychological state of the twins; even though Donovan is standing in front of her sister, there is a noticeable size difference. This visual reference helps to reinforce the idea of a discrepancy, early on, between the twins' personalities, whether biological or through the different treatment of the children by their parents.

The story revolves around a summer vacation that the girls are spending with their hippie father (their parents are divorced, and they live predominantly with their mother). Their father decides to take them on a trip to a comic book convention, hoping to get a withdrawn Donovan interested in a family activity. Dylan expresses her frustration that Donovan acts uninterested, though she knows how much Donovan enjoys comics. During the entire car trip, Donovan is silent, staying in the back seat with her headphones on, covered up in the hot summer heat with her ratty sweater. Page 3 shows Dylan looking out the window of the car. Her caption reads: "A lot of the time, I feel like it's up to me to cheer her up 'cause I'm so close with her and everything, but I don't really know what else I can do. I can tell she just wants to be left alone, y'know?"[94] Dylan expresses her surprise that Donovan hasn't lightened up at all, even being on a trip and out of school—a place where she is taunted and ridiculed daily. Dylan is resentful that Donovan doesn't appear to be responding to her and her father's efforts to please her.

Dylan finds it very difficult to cope with Donovan's silence, and she finally does something about it: she reads her sister's diary. This metafictive device serves to let the reader in on Donovan's point of view, and it also possibly exposes Dylan's unreliability as a narrator, as Donovan expresses her excitement over the trip to the comic convention, which Dylan assumed that her sister didn't care about. Through Dylan's narrative, Tomine misleads the reader into believing that Dylan is telling the "true" story, when it is actually a one-sided representation of the situation. When Dylan reads the diary, she realizes that her twin sister has thoughts and secrets that she hides from her. Here, among the daily disappointments in Donovan's school life, is a revelation as to what is happening to Donovan, and why she is even more withdrawn on a trip that was planned with her interests in mind. The diary reads:

3/12—That guy Brian invited me over to his dorm room. Weird being on the campus. We sat around, listened to records, made fun of his roommate's soccer and swimsuit posters. He kept asking me stuff about school, then he'd say something like, "Yeah, I remember that . . ."[95]

In the subsequent panel, the bomb drops: "We started making out a little, then had sex on the linoleum floor. Guess I really didn't like it."[96] Dylan expresses her hurt that her twin never told her about her "first time." She appears more upset that Donovan withheld details of her private life from her than she is concerned for her sister and what might have been a very negative experience for her. Only one panel indicates that the sexual encounter may have been more wounding than what Donovan describes in her diary, the contrapuntal image adding polyphonic depth when coupled with the text. Tomine decides to show a suggestive scene: a close up of Donovan's hand, palm up, restrained at the wrist by Brian on the background of the linoleum floor. The issue of consent is brought up by this subtle image implying restraint, dominance, and possibly even rape. Surely, the reader may also assume that, at the very least, Donovan is under the age of legal consent. This is hinted at by the birth date that Dylan gives for the twins at the beginning of the tale and the date of the time of publishing of this comic book, which, assuming that this is in realistic chronological order, means that the twins would be no older than seventeen. The main drive of this tale is what is not said by the text or the image alone, but in the gaps in between that the reader must fill.

"Dylan and Donovan" is a study in alienation. Within adolescent fiction, there are plenty of books that deal with tough issues such as teenage drug abuse and sexuality, though there are many parents who would be even more uncomfortable with their children and teens reading comics that express these matters in visual form (at some stores the buyer must be eighteen or over to purchase a copy of certain comics). There is something about the visual expression of these topics that makes it more palpable; perhaps because it is so difficult for the reader to avoid such an image when confronted with it in such a direct manner. Parents' and educators' squeamishness about visual representations of these subject matters is compounded by comics' reputation as "pulp," which can lead to censorship.

However, even in pulp there are valuable lessons for the female reader. In Imelda Whelehan's essay "Feminism and Trash: Destabilising the Reader," she states:

[T]he time for feminist critics to reenergize their activities and look at the popular is well overdue. I do not make this assertion simply because trash is trendy: if "the personal is political," then so are our private pleasures.[97]

Whelehan is adamant that popular modes of fiction deserve to be examined closely, even though they contain negative portrayals of the feminine. She insists that popular fiction "often find[s] 'ordinary' women's lives the centre of narrative attention, a position that may be interpreted as one of strength."[98] However, comics like *Optic Nerve* are not portraying females negatively but rather giving them a voice, allowing the young reader, as a critic, to examine images of females and female issues.

Courtney Crumrin, written and drawn by Ted Naifeh, is an example of a story from the fantasy genre, but it also has its roots in the tradition of the school story. In fact, the cover of the trade paperback bears a rating that reads "Youth: seven and up."[99] Although the age rating is dubiously liberal (age seven might be developmentally too young for this sophisticated comic), the series has the wonderful potential to appeal to children, teens, and adults alike. While it is a spooky but endearing tale, combining elements of mystery and uncanny horror with the fantasy of fairies, witchcraft, and talking animals, at its heart is the familiar story of a little girl who doesn't quite fit in with the crowd. Courtney comes from a different socioeconomic background than her schoolmates, and because of her name and her shabby clothes, she is mostly ignored and even abused by her peers. In figure 3.11 the caption reads: "Courtney had come from a relatively modest neighborhood in the city, and stood out among her privileged classmates."[100]

Although the story involves the fantastic and supernatural, the reality of inequality of status, whether it be monetary or social, is a problem that many children have to face in the harsh battleground of peer politics at school. Naifeh champions the underdog, the unpopular and the underprivileged, in his establishment of Courtney as the protagonist of the story. Though Naifeh invites the reader to buy into the idea of Courtney as decidedly "uncool," he places the reader in the position of siding with her as the key character. The "popular crowd" is depicted negatively, while the reader is urged to identify with the visually appealing Courtney as above average and *peerless*. Her classmates treat her like a loser, but it is apparent that she is smarter than they are. Besides, she is more interesting because she practices witchcraft. By questioning the equation of popularity with self-worth, the series sends a

Figure 3.11. *Courtney Crumrin and the Night Things*, 2002. Courtney is surrounded by the disapproval of her new classmates.

Courtney Crumrin and the Night Things is ™ and © 2002 Ted Naifeh. Unless otherwise specified, all other material © 2002 Oni Press, Inc.

message that young people do not have to follow the crowd and be a pawn to the peer-circus at school. However, this series makes it clear that school is an integral part of growing up. Even though Courtney may not like school and does not always get along with her classmates, or even the teachers, she eventually finds that knowledge is the power that will set her free.

In issue no. 1, Courtney is afraid of her uncle, Professor Aloysius Crumrin, who is described as having "terrible eyes" in "a face that would curdle new milk."[101] Courtney does not look forward to the prospect of living under his roof. However, she soon discovers that she has a kinship with the old man. She is besieged by night terrors made corporeal (little daemons referred to as "night things") and seeks out her uncle in her loneliness and fear of the night (fig. 3.2). Mr. Crumrin comforts her, and Courtney realizes that she has misjudged her uncle. She discovers that he is a warlock, and he becomes her closest friend and ally. On one of her sleepless nights she seeks out her "Uncle A.," as she affectionately calls him, but discovers one of his magic books instead (figs. 3.12a and 3.12b).

The visual narrative contained in panels 1 through 8 shows the point at which Courtney's life is forever changed. She bangs on the door to the office, which Naifeh displays with a graphically enhanced "Bang, Bang, Bang" (panel 1, fig. 3.12a).[102] Naifeh also uses action lines to signify the impact of her fists on the door. When no one answers, she enters the room to find his office empty. Courtney immediately begins poking around like any curious and bright young person might (panels 1–5, fig. 3.12a). Panels 1–4 depict Courtney as small; the door of the office dwarfs her, as does the desk. Once in the office, she discovers a book containing a spell on how to capture a goblin in order to make him do the sorcerer's bidding (panel 5, fig. 3.12a). She takes the book off its podium (panel 6, fig. 3.12b), and through the cinematic technique of the close-up shot, the reader is able to read the title of the tome over Courtney's shoulder: "A Bestiary of Night Things Great and Small" (panel 7, fig. 3.12b).[103] After panel 3 there is no text; the narrative is delivered visually with one exception: the title of the book. A careful reader can deduce that the author of this book, "A. Crumrin," is none other than her own uncle Aloysius.

In panel 8, Courtney is shown in her uncle's great chair, which might be symbolic of taking up his mantle, as she sits and reads the huge book. We are reminded of Courtney's youth and size again as Naifeh illustrates her sitting in an overly large chair with a book that seems to be half her size. She may be taking up her uncle's path, but this suggests that she is also taking on tasks that are too big for her as yet. Whatever Naifeh's intention, it is obvious that panel 8 (fig. 3.12b) shows the beginnings of a new Courtney, invested with the power of knowledge. Naifeh adds to the drama by his use of contrast of shadow and light, obscuring Courtney's face as she reads. It is then that Courtney begins her magical journey toward learning and self-discovery. She finds that she is able to master

Figure 3.12a. *Courtney Crumrin and the Night Things*, 2002, Panels 1–5.
Courtney Crumrin and the Night Things is ™ and © 2002 Ted Naifeh. Unless otherwise specified, all other
material © 2002 Oni Press, Inc.

Figure 3.12b. *Courtney Crumrin and the Night Things*, 2002, **Panels 6–8.**

and control the night things (see fig. 3.13) and that she is well on her way to becoming a powerful witch. She is able to perform the spell on Butterworm, the resident goblin, and strikes a bargain with him to send some of his night thing pals over to the house of the girl who had beaten her up and stolen her lunch money earlier in the story. The utilization of magic gives Courtney a sense of control over her life that she did not have before. However, Courtney soon finds out that using magic to get what

Figure 3.13. *Courtney Crumrin and the Night Things*, 2002. **Courtney subdues the goblin Butterworm with magic, thus demonstrating her capabilities.**
Courtney Crumrin and the Night Things is ™ and © 2002 Ted Naifeh. Unless otherwise specified, all other material © 2002 Oni Press, Inc.

she wants may have ramifications over which she has no control. In issue no. 2, Courtney casts a "glamour spell" on herself that only causes her trouble, and her uncle has to come to her rescue.

The series is an adventure, but it has a strong didactic tone. In subsequent tales, Courtney's penchant for getting revenge against those who hurt her backfires, and she learns some sobering lessons. She discovers that she is capable, but with capability she must also learn responsibility and restraint. Even though the didactic message is apparent, it is not an example of a strong-willed female being "put in her place," a theme that appears in many works of children's fiction (however, not as often in young adult novels). She is not discouraged from learning magic, but she is encouraged to learn temperance in order to cope with a world that *would* like to "put her in her place."

In the second series, *Courtney Crumrin and the Coven of Mystics* (2003), Courtney learns that school is important, though she may not like it. With her newly acquired powers she has bewitched one of the top students in her class to do her homework for her. Courtney soon finds out that cheating does not pay off, when she is caught and humiliated with a "zero" mark for her efforts (or lack thereof), bringing the reader back to the didactic core of the series. Courtney is mistaken when she thinks that school is not relevant to her life and that she can get away with not doing her lessons. A new teacher, Ms. Calpurnia Crisp, is introduced in *The Coven of Mystics*. Ms. Crisp holds Courtney back after class to speak with her about her school performance, and Courtney is stunned to find out that her new teacher is much more than she appears. Ms. Crisp is quite familiar with how Courtney acquired the answers to the homework assignment. She confronts Courtney, saying,

> Courtney, I happen to know you're getting an excellent education from your uncle. However, there are certain things you're not going to learn from him, and you'll need them to live in the ordinary world. Do you understand?[104]

Until this point in the series, Courtney had not met any other witches or wizards, aside from her uncle. In fact, there have been no strong female role models for Courtney at all. She is resistant to the idea of being bested and her secret shared. Courtney is also ignorant of her own need for female society and solidarity and responds to her teacher in a confrontational manner. In figure 3.14, panels 2–6, there is an exchange of looks between Ms. Crisp and Courtney that speaks more powerfully than words alone; it is a mental showdown. In panel 2 Courtney is defiant and cocky, until Ms. Crisp casually informs her that she knows about witchcraft, and her feline face (the feline being a construct of female power that Naifeh toys with throughout the series) holds a casual, but cool, attentive expression. This is juxtaposed with the headshot of Courtney shocked and speechless, as denoted by her tiny, nearly empty speech balloon. Panel 5 (fig. 3.14) cuts to a close-up of Ms. Crisp's face, suddenly not so placid. Her eyes and nose are scrunched up, and

Figure 3.14. *Courtney Crumrin and the Coven of Mystics,* **2003, panels 1–6.**
Courtney Crumrin and the Coven of Mystics is ™ and © 2003 Ted Naifeh. Unless otherwise specified, all other material © 2002 Oni Press, Inc.

she peers at Courtney harshly, as if in warning, an expression to which the reader is tempted to put words, such as "Don't test me. I know how to deal with you." In panel 6 (fig. 3.14) Courtney appears crestfallen, as she answers in the manner of a perfectly trained student, "Yes, Ms. Crisp."[105]

Courtney submits to Ms. Crisp this time, but she is not deterred from doing the things that come to her naturally—being defiant and experimenting with magic. In time, Courtney gains from having a shared female experience with Ms. Crisp, though it takes her a while to see it in this way. In *The Second Wave: A Reader in Feminist Theory* (1997), Radicalesbians write:

> It is the primacy of women relating to women, of women creating a new consciousness with each other, which is at the heart of women's liberation. . . . Together we must find, reinforce, and validate our authentic selves. As we do this, we confirm in each other that struggling, incipient sense of pride and strength, the divisive barriers begin to melt, we feel this growing solidarity with our sisters.[106]

Although the article is addressing sex roles and sexual orientation, this passage describes the importance of solidarity among females. For Courtney, Ms. Crisp offers a role of sisterhood and guidance, not just as a teacher but also as a witch in a male-dominated coven. Ms. Crisp encourages Courtney's magical talents while pushing her toward personal and academic excellence. When Courtney comes up with a scheme to get Ms. Crisp to take her on a field trip to the "Hall of Wonders" at Radley Hall, Ms. Crisp demands that Courtney make a pact to complete her creative writing assignment for class, using the project as a bargaining chip to get Courtney to apply her intelligence to her education in the ordinary world.[107] Ms. Crisp's concern that Courtney should learn to integrate in that world, and not become an outsider like her uncle,[108] is in response to Courtney's male-identification and fixation on Uncle Aloysius. She advises Courtney, "It's not wise to turn your back on the world."[109] In *The Kristeva Reader* (1986), Toril Moi condenses Kristeva's theory of male identification and rejection of femininity and feminine power when she states:

> If women refuse this role, as the unconscious truth of patriarchy, they are forced instead to identify with the father, thus turning themselves into supporters of the very same patriarchal order.[110]

According to Moi and Kristeva's theories, Courtney's isolation as a female and attachment to her uncle may hamper her development as a woman, subjecting her to rejection and oppression by the patriarchy later.

Ms. Crisp's insistence on Courtney completing the writing assignment becomes another turning point in her story, as it allows Courtney to get in touch with her feelings and her own femininity. It becomes an enriching experience for her when she writes a poem about her first crush (fig. 3.15). The poem itself is simple, yet the images illuminate the conviction behind those words. The visual narrative conveys the emotion and electricity of her writing, as the classroom darkens and we see the inhabitants of the room in silhouette, while outside the window a storm is shown brewing. Lightning flashes, and when the poem reaches its emotional apex the windowpane cracks, punctuating the intensity of her words. Panel 6 (fig. 3.15) features Courtney in a position of dominance as she looks down at her audience. It is as though Courtney is ascendant in power through the reading of her poem, coming into her own as a female. The storm rolls away as soon as she finishes her recitation. Naifeh chooses to convey a complementary narrative with images that show Courtney's puissance and act as a visual validation of her feelings and creativity.

The character of Ms. Crisp is interesting, as she subverts accepted gender roles. She is a grade school teacher, a career traditionally filled by women, yet she is also a powerful witch, who, later in the series, is elected a council member of the Coven of Mystics. Her benevolent presence as a teacher is underscored by her power to mold her students, even taking on the difficult Courtney. Spatially, Naifeh often represents Ms. Crisp as a dominant figure, which reinforces her importance as a character. She is almost always shown wearing white or light tones, which may imply her role as a positive figure, even though most of the positive characters often wear dark clothing in the Crumrin series. This is not simply a reference to the familiar cinematic influence of Westerns where the "good guys" wear white hats. Ms. Crisp represents a positive guide, or shining light for Courtney, and also a voice of reason; Courtney's Uncle Aloysius is a good character, but he has turned his back on the world, and Courtney seems ready to follow the same path. Ms. Crisp is there to remind Courtney to not give up on the mundane world around her and not give into the same bitterness and solitude into which her uncle has retreated. Additionally, Naifeh frequently manipulates perspective in a way that demands the

Figure 3.15. *Courtney Crumrin and the Coven of Mystics*, 2003, panels 1–6. Courtney's emotions are literally "electric" during the reading of her poem.

reader to "look up" at Ms. Crisp, underlining the fact that Ms. Crisp is not just a schoolteacher but a dangerous and powerful woman.

Throughout the *Courtney* series, Naifeh reinforces the importance of learning. Through the acquisition of knowledge, Courtney is on the path to becoming a peer in the "mystical community" as well as joining the society of womanhood. She is taught the value of paying attention to lessons in issue no. 2 of *The Coven of Mystics* when she follows the cats Boo and Quick into the forest to learn the cats' "wisdom of the night"[111] by transforming into a cat herself. The transformation into cat-form is, again, suggestive of feminine power and even sexuality; by becoming a cat, Courtney gains knowledge and also meets the "night thing," Skarrow, her first crush, for whom she wrote her poem.

The *Courtney Crumrin* comic books deal with themes of change and learning to like oneself as well as embracing difference, which are important ideas that girls often lose sight of in a world that deifies competitiveness. More importantly for female readers, it has a bold, feminist message that portrays girlhood femininity as vital for girls to embrace, for in it they cultivate their own power.

Go Girl! by Trina Robbins and Anne Timmons is an upbeat, perky, yet subversive feminist reclaiming of the superhero genre. With a big helping of humor, Robbins and Timmons portray a normal girl as a protagonist with some not so normal superpowers. She can fly, and she is strong enough both physically and mentally to thwart the evil plots of villains. *Go Girl!* is filled with feminist concerns, such as equal rights for women and the importance of learning self-defense; yet it is not so heavy-handedly didactic that these messages spoil the fun. A younger reader may relish the adventures of a girl hero on a surface level, while a more mature reader may appreciate the strong messages of feminism and equal rights (as well as the sardonic humor and the kitsch factor of *Go Girl!*'s vintage comics flavor). Figure 3.16 shows that mothers can be good role models for teenage girls and even (gasp!) "cool." In the first panel of *Go Girl!* issue no. 1, the reader is shown a newspaper clipping marked 1973, in which a flying female superhero has apprehended two criminals. A speech balloon appears with the remark "Way cool!"[112]

The perspective then zooms out in the following two frames where it becomes obvious that two friends, Lindsay Goldman and Haseena Ross, are going through Lindsay's family scrapbook. Haseena remarks, "I can't believe

Figure 3.16. *Go Girl!*, 2001, 2002. Robbins and Timmons demonstrate that mothers can be superheroes, too. "Way cool!"
Go Girl™ © 2012 Trina Robbins and Anne Timmons.

your mom was a superhero, Lindsay! That is *soooo* cool! I wish my dad was a superhero instead of an—ugh!—lawyer!"[113] The two girls view the fact that Lindsay's mom was a superhero as if it weren't anything strange in this world—a little bit unusual, but not unheard of. Lindsay's mom is like any other strong woman who works miracles, like a single parent or an activist in the women's rights movement. The mother figure in this story is not an oddity, but someone her daughter can be proud of. Instead of featuring the conventional hero archetype of the father figure, it is the mother who consistently bails Go Girl out of trouble and comes to the rescue when she is needed. In *Go Girl!* the only father figures are Haseena's lawyer father (whose professional life Haseena obviously disdains) and Lindsay's father, who is absent from Lindsay's life, as her mother is raising Lindsay by herself.

The emotional aspect of the family situation, however, is not discussed. *Go Girl!*, though exploring some serious issues within its pages, has a light-hearted tone. Sometimes the humor is bittersweet—when Mrs. Goldman discovers that the two girls have been looking through her scrapbook she sits down with them to have a flip-though history. Haseena asks her why she quit being Go-Go Girl (her groovy superhero alter ego); she remarks, "How could I hope to compete with that?" as she holds up a picture of a scantily clad woman with the words "Lady Badd" printed on it (fig. 3.17) and adds, "and I wouldn't be caught dead in that outfit."[114] This comment and the expression on Mrs. Goldman's face point toward the unfortunate detail that many comic books in the past, continuing into the present, have objectified women's bodies with costumes that are not fit for anything except for the bedroom—certainly not for fighting crime. In mainstream comics, women's bodies have often been drawn unrealistically, with impossible waist to hip ratios and even more impossible breasts rivaling the size of their speech balloons (although it would be unfair not to mention that superhero comics have traditionally created male superheroes with unrealistic body proportions as well, though they typically seem to wear more clothing). *Go Girl!* subtly and humorously points out these sad and embarrassing facts and ultimately subverts them.

Nonetheless, it must be noted that Robbins and Timmons fail in their attempt to completely abandon the sexism of the superhero genre. Enlightened as Mrs. Goldman is, her alter ego, Go-Go Girl, is still a sexualized figure, though not as brazenly obvious as "Lady Badd." However,

Figure 3.17. *Go Girl!*, 2001, 2002. **Lady Badd is dressed "baddly" for a crime-fighting occasion.**
Go Girl!™ © 2012 Trina Robbins and Anne Timmons.

the depiction of Go-Go Girl could be interpreted as a nod to the earlier female superheroes who may have been portrayed as glamorous or even sexualized, but were also strong, fierce, and inspiring for a new generation of girls (many of whom would grow up to see or take part in great changes in women's rights). There is no doubt that Robbins and Timmons were inspired by such female superheroes. Nonetheless, though *Go Girl!* is both homage and satire of the superhero genre, it bears mentioning that both mother and daughter in this comics series are examples of popular beauty: they are both slender, blonde, and their crime-fighting uniforms accentuate their "ideal figures." Also, when Lindsay and her mother go to visit her mother's old crime-fighting partner, "Right-On Sister," mother and daughter find that Right-On Sister has gained a lot of weight (apparently due to her addiction to her "prize-winning pecan pie").[115] When Lindsay gets into trouble in this episode, her mother is slow in coming to the rescue because she can't fit into her costume and fly.[116] At the end of the story Lindsay reprimands her mother, exclaiming, "You won't get off the ground until you lose ten pounds!"[117] These image-conscious factors are strangely incongruous to the feminist ideology the series tries to promote.

Negative aspects aside, *Go Girl!* portrays a young woman as superhero and a competent mother who dons her uniform and go-go boots when a situation gets too rough for her daughter to handle, which (for the most part) subverts the superhero genre and defies ageism and sexism. When Mrs. Goldman first finds out that Lindsay has inherited her bravery and her ability to fly and fight crime, it appears that Go Girl is going to get a scolding and be told that she should not be fighting bad guys. The reader might expect that Lindsay will be told that a teen girl has no right to interfere with adult issues, causing her to have to lead a double life and serve justice behind her mother's back. But *Go Girl!* does not cling to the old clichés. Instead, her mother briefly admonishes her, saying, "As for you, young lady, you could've been killed in there!" but quickly follows this comment with, "You have to know how to fight! Being a superheroine takes more than just the ability to fly."[118] On the next page, mother and daughter are shown in a full-page panel flying side by side, making plans for Lindsay's bright future as a crime fighter (fig. 3.18). Mrs. Goldman does not stifle her daughter's imagination and power but wants to encourage and support Lindsay's ambitions. The transition of names from Go-Go Girl to Go Girl, from mother to daughter is itself significant. This change is empowering because of the insinuation that go-gos are a form of entertainment, while "Go Girl" is a positive and active statement.

Go Girl! does not buy into the idea that traditional superhero comics promote—the notion that a male can complete a female or that the female is weak (such as Superman continually rescuing Lois Lane and Lana Lang while the two women compete for his affections). When Lindsay asks her mother why she really gave up crime fighting, Mrs. Goldman remarks, "Well honey, your dad was kinda threatened by having a wife who could fly."[119] The complexity of contemporary womanhood—the precarious balance of being a mother and having a career—is underlined here. Through this superhero fantasy, *Go Girl!* reflects the

Figure 3.18. *Go Girl!*, 2001, 2002. Mother and daughter fly side-by-side, breaking barriers of sexism and ageism, though their outfits still appear to sexualize them.

Go Girl!™ © 2012 Trina Robbins and Anne Timmons.

very real issues of our own world. After the second wave of feminism when women began to pursue careers, many men did not know how to handle the new image of womanhood, and many felt that their role was usurped. Now that women could have the children *and* have a career, the male seemed superfluous. Lindsay's mother continues her story as she says, ". . . and I had to get a real job, because you can't feed a child on what a freelance superheroine makes."[120] She adds, "Probably couldn't fly now if I wanted to,"[121] which she later proves wrong, defying the age stereotype of the female superhero.

The Robbins and Timmons team are aware of the history of girls' comics that presumably inspired their careers. They lovingly pay homage to the comics of the past with paper doll designs like *Katy Keene* comics (a serial that Robbins marks as influential), proving that a girl can be powerful, a girl can be the hero, but she can also still be a girl and wear a floral dress or jeans. While much of what is popularly considered "feminine" is no more than a social construct, Robbins and Timmons appear to buy into the feminist theory of "difference," seeing the female as biologically different from the male. According to Allwood, the theory of difference means that because they are born different from men, "women should have the space necessary to develop their femininity, attaining equality while remaining different."[122] Progress to this subtle level of feminism in a comic book written with young women in mind has been made possible by the feminist movement in comix (and their descendants), which has allowed not only women's narratives to be explored in this medium but girls' experiences as well.

The only drawback of this new wave in girls' comics is that it is only a small cross-section of young females that have had exposure to the field—particularly those who have had access to and have felt comfortable with shopping at comics specialty stores (which are typically geared toward males). However, the tide may be turning. The explosion in the popularity of manga (Japanese comics) in America has contributed to recent changes in the reception and accessibility of comics. Interest in manga, as well as an improvement in the general reception of the graphic novel format, is bringing comics into the literary market of major booksellers, as well as the acquisition lists of librarians. This is encouraging because comics have so much to offer to a female readership. Through its unique form, comics are in a special position to give a voice to the repressed female and present positive role models for girls and young women.

Notes

1. John Debes, quoted in Maria Avgerinou, "What Is 'Visual Literacy?'" *International Visual Literacy Association (IVLA)*, accessed January 29, 2011, http://www.ivla.org/org_what_vis_lit.htm.

2. Avgerinou, "What Is 'Visual Literacy?'"

3. Linda Z. Cooper, "Supporting Visual Literacy in the School Library Media Center: Developmental, Socio-cultural, and Experiential Considerations and Scenarios," *Knowledge Quest* 36, no. 3 (January/February 2008): 15.

4. Cooper, "Supporting Visual Literacy," 15.

5. Cooper, "Supporting Visual Literacy," 15.

6. Cooper, "Supporting Visual Literacy," 15.

7. Cooper, "Supporting Visual Literacy," 15.

8. Cooper, "Supporting Visual Literacy," 15.

9. Cooper, "Supporting Visual Literacy," 16.

10. Mary Ann Spenser Pulaski, *Understanding Piaget: An Introduction to Children's Cognitive Development* (New York: Harper & Row, 1971), 24–27.

11. Cooper, "Supporting Visual Literacy," 16.

12. Cooper, "Supporting Visual Literacy," 16.

13. Cooper, "Supporting Visual Literacy," 16.

14. Cooper, "Supporting Visual Literacy," 16.

15. Cooper, "Supporting Visual Literacy," 16.

16. Cooper, "Supporting Visual Literacy," 17.

17. Cooper, "Supporting Visual Literacy," 16.

18. Benjamin Harris, "Blurring Borders, Visualizing Connections: Aligning Information and Visual Literacy Learning Outcomes," *Reference Services Review* 38, no. 4 (2010): 523.

19. Harris, "Blurring Borders," 523.

20. Harris, "Blurring Borders," 523.

21. Jane Doonan, *Looking at Pictures in Picture Books* (Stroud: The Thimble Press, 1993), 49.

22. Doonan, *Looking at Pictures,* 49.

23. Doonan, *Looking at Pictures,* 58.

24. Margaret Meek, *How Texts Teach What Readers Learn* (Stroud: The Thimble Press, 1988), 25.

25. Meek, *How Texts Teach,* 25.

26. Julie Bosman, "Picture Books No Longer a Staple for Children," *New York Times*, October 7, 2010, http://www.nytimes.com/2010/10/08/us/08picture.html?pagewanted=1.

27. Allyn Johnston and Marla Frazee, "Why We're Still in Love with Picture Books (Even Though They're Supposed to Be Dead)," *The Horn Book Magazine*, May/June 2011, 16.

28. Karen Springen, "Don't Write the Obit For Picture Books Yet," *Publishers Weekly* 257, no. 49 (2010): 15.

29. Springen, "Don't Write the Obit," 15.

30. Bosman, "Picture Books No Longer."

31. Meek, *How Texts Teach*, 28.

32. Meek, *How Texts Teach*, 25.

33. Frederic Wertham, *Seduction of the Innocent* (New York: Rinehart, 1954), 130.

34. Stephen D. Krashen, *The Power of Reading: Insights from the Research*, 2nd ed. (Westport, CT: Libraries Unlimited, 2004), 101.

35. Krashen, *Power of Reading*, 102.

36. Sam Kieth, Alex Pardee, and Chris Wisnia, *Ojo* (Portland: Oni Press, 2005), 124.

37. David Lewis, "The Jolly Postman's Long Ride, or, Sketching a Picture-Book History," *Signal*, no. 78 (September 1995): 190.

38. Ted Naifeh, *Courtney Crumrin and the Night Things* (Portland: Oni Press, 2002), "It were the first house in 'Illsborough, before it became a posh neighborhood. . . ."

39. Naifeh, *Courtney Crumrin*, "A warm, inviting light came from under the door."

40. Naifeh, *Courtney Crumrin*, "A warm, inviting light came from under the door."

41. Mario Saraceni, *The Language of Comics* (London: Routledge, 2003), 63.

42. Saraceni, *The Language of Comics*, 10.

43. Saraceni, *The Language of Comics*, 28.

44. Saraceni, *The Language of Comics*, 109.

45. Scott McCloud, *Understanding Comics: The Invisible Art* (New York: Paradox Press, 2000), 103.

46. Ted Naifeh, *Courtney Crumrin and the Coven of Mystics*, 1st ed. trade paperback (Portland, OR: Oni Press, 2003), "Go on! Just go!"

47. Will Eisner, *Comics and Sequential Art: Principles and Practices from the Legendary Cartoonist* (New York: Norton, 2008), 2, 4.

48. Eisner, *Comics*, 7.

49. Saraceni, *The Language of Comics*, 15.

50. Saraceni, *The Language of Comics*, 15.

51. Saraceni, *The Language of Comics*, 15.

52. Mariko Tamaki and Jillian Tamaki, *Skim* (Toronto: Goundwood Books, 2008), 27.

53. Tamaki and Tamaki, *Skim*, 13.

54. Tamaki and Tamaki, *Skim*, 9.

55. Tamaki and Tamaki, *Skim*, 22.

56. Tamaki and Tamaki, *Skim*, 22.

57. Tamaki and Tamaki, *Skim*, 22.

58. Tamaki and Tamaki, *Skim*, 22.

59. Tamaki and Tamaki, *Skim*, 22.

60. Tamaki and Tamaki, *Skim*, 45.

61. Tamaki and Tamaki, *Skim*, 52.

62. Tamaki and Tamaki, *Skim*, 52.

63. Tamaki and Tamaki, *Skim*, 52.

64. Tamaki and Tamaki, *Skim*, 53–54.

65. Tamaki and Tamaki, *Skim*, 62.

66. Tamaki and Tamaki, *Skim*, 39.

67. Tamaki and Tamaki, *Skim*, 39.

68. Tamaki and Tamaki, *Skim*, 89.

69. Tamaki and Tamaki, *Skim*, 89.

70. Tamaki and Tamaki, *Skim*, 89.

71. Tamaki and Tamaki, *Skim*, 89.

72. Tamaki and Tamaki, *Skim*, 89.

73. Tamaki and Tamaki, *Skim*, 89.

74. Tamaki and Tamaki, *Skim*, 68.

75. Tamaki and Tamaki, *Skim*, 69.

76. Tamaki and Tamaki, *Skim*, 71.

77. Tamaki and Tamaki, *Skim*, 71.

78. Tamaki and Tamaki, *Skim*, 100.

79. Tamaki and Tamaki, *Skim*, 64, 139–40.

80. Tamaki and Tamaki, *Skim*, 141.

81. Tamaki and Tamaki, *Skim*, 141.

82. Daniel Clowes, *Ghost World*, 6th softcover ed. (Seattle: Fantagraphics Books, 2001), 24.

83. Clowes, *Ghost World*, 50.

84. Clowes, *Ghost World*, 50.

85. Clowes, *Ghost World*, 50.

86. Doonan, *Looking at Pictures*, 27–28.

87. Clowes, *Ghost World*, 33–35, 38.

88. J. A. Appleyard, *Becoming a Reader: The Experience of Fiction from Childhood to Adulthood* (Cambridge: Cambridge University Press, 1994), 99.

89. Appleyard, *Becoming a Reader*, 100.

90. Appleyard, *Becoming a Reader*, 96.

91. Appleyard, *Becoming a Reader*, 97.

92. Adrian Tomine, *Optic Nerve,* no. 3, August (Montreal: Drawn and Quarterly Publications, 1996), 1.

93. Tomine, *Optic Nerve*, 1.

94. Tomine, *Optic Nerve*, 3.

95. Tomine, *Optic Nerve*, 7.

96. Tomine, *Optic Nerve*, 7.

97. Imelda Whelehan, "Feminism and Trash: Destabilising 'The Reader,'" in *Gendering the Reader*, ed. Sara Mills (New York: Harvester Wheatsheaf, 1994), 233.

98. Whelehan, "Feminism and Trash," 222.

99. Naifeh, *Night Things*, back cover.

100. Naifeh, *Night Things,* "Courtney had come from a relatively modest neighborhood in the city, and stood out among her privileged classmates."

101. Naifeh, *Night Things*, "He shot her a withering gaze with his terrible eyes," and "Uncle Aloysius was even nastier than she remembered him, with a face that would curdle new milk."

102. Naifeh, *Night Things*, "Bang, Bang, Bang."

103. Naifeh, *Night Things*, "A Bestiary of Night Things Great and Small."

104. Naifeh, *Coven of Mystics*, "Courtney, I happen to know you're getting an excellent education from your uncle."

105. Naifeh, *Coven of Mystics*.

106. Radicalesbians, "The Woman Identified Woman," in *The Second Wave: A Reader in Feminist Theory*, ed. Linda Nicholson (New York: Routledge, 1997), 157.

107. Naifeh, *Coven of Mystics*, "A field trip?" and "Radley Hall was one of those big blank buildings. . ."

108. Naifeh, *Coven of Mystics*.

109. Naifeh, *Coven of Mystics*, "It's not wise to turn your back on the world."

110. Toril Moi, *The Kristeva Reader* (Oxford: Blackwell, 1986), 139.

111. Naifeh, *Coven of Mystics*, "Boo, are the eyes of mortal children meant for our private affairs?"

112. Trina Robbins and Anne Timmons, *Go Girl!* 1st ed. trade paperback (Milwaukie, OR: Dark Horse Comics, 2002), "Way cool!"

113. Robbins and Timmons, *Go Girl!*

114. Robbins and Timmons, *Go Girl!* "How could I hope to compete with that?"

115. Robbins and Timmons, *Go Girl!* "My prize-winning pecan pie."

116. Robbins and Timmons, *Go Girl!* "It doesn't fit!"

117. Robbins and Timmons, *Go Girl!* "You won't get off the ground until you lose ten pounds!"

118. Robbins and Timmons, *Go Girl!*, "As for you, young lady, you could've been killed in there!"

119. Robbins and Timmons, *Go Girl!* "Well honey, your dad was kinda threatened by having a wife who could fly."

120. Robbins and Timmons, *Go Girl!*

121. Robbins and Timmons, *Go Girl!*

122. Gill Allwood, *French Feminisms: Gender and Violence in Contemporary Theory* (London: UCL Press, 1998), 12.

CHAPTER FOUR
THE APPEAL OF MANGA

U p until recently, comics have been marginalized—relegated to hobbyist and specialty stores. However, there has been a general shift toward the comics field receiving the recognition it deserves within literary and artistic spheres. Perhaps the most interesting evidence of this change is the upsurge in the female readership of comics and graphic novels, thanks in large part to the rising popularity of Japanese comics, known as *manga*.

In the foreword to Stephen Weiner's book *Faster than a Speeding Bullet: The Rise of the Graphic Novel* (2003), Will Eisner says: "Japanese manga, with their animation related artwork, are finding a huge following among American teenage readers."[1] Even though there have been many wonderful and innovative Western comics released before the widespread introduction of manga in America, the number of female readers had largely dwindled since the boom in girls' and women's comics of the mid-twentieth century, as explained in chapter 1. Mila Bongco discusses this decline:

> Up until 1944, the number of girls reading comicbooks was almost the same as boys, especially between the ages of 6 to 11. From this year on, however, there has been a steady decline in comicbook readership among girls, particularly in the superhero comicbooks. . . . Although girls continued to patronize funny animals and romance comics, in total numbers, there were noticeably more boys steadily reading comicbooks, coinciding with the persistent popularity of superhero comicbooks relative to general comicbook sales.[2]

Unfortunately, the American comic book industry catered to a male readership for many years. As discussed earlier, the culling of comics talent that occurred after the introduction of the Comics Code created a dearth of female authors and artists. As a consequence, there was a marked decrease in comics for females. Even though the 1960s and 1970s brought forth a whole new generation of female comic book authors and illustrators, and therefore comics written for females, these works remained, for the most part, underground. Even when comics for females began to increase, the damage had been done; the popular perception that comics were all about superheroes, and catered to boys, was solidified.

In the 1990s, manga was just beginning to emerge as popular reading fare for teens. In particular, many teenage girls latched on to manga, as Japanese comics, not bearing the stigma attached to American comics, often feature female-centric story lines. Unlike American comics, manga is readily available in a variety of genres and topics created to suit the needs of a diverse readership. Some main types of manga are *shōnen*, comics for boys that may be generalized by being action-oriented and often feature a boy as the lead character; *seinen*, which is aimed toward a more mature male audience, can involve more sophisticated subjects, and may be often risqué; *josei*, oriented toward women, which is similar to *seinen* in that they often portray more sophisticated subject matters and may also contain more examples of explicit sexuality; and *shōjo*, which is intended for younger female readers and is characterized by a focus on emotions and relationships. In the foreword to *Japanese Visual Culture*, Schodt remarks that "Japan is today one of the only countries in the world where 'comic books' have become a full-fledged medium of expression, on par with novels and films, and read by what often seems to be everyone."[3] This is in stark contrast to the American tendency to focus on the superhero genre, which narrows comics' readership in the United States. This by no means implies that Western comics lack variety—on the contrary, American comics are as diverse as their readership. However, the majority of material published by major comics publishers are superhero comics, and the image representing comics in the popular imagination of the average American is that of the superhero.

Due to this perceived lack of diversity in Western comics, it is not surprising that girls gravitate toward manga, which offers distinct reading material for girls and young women. Fourteen-year-old Davi Gabriel, who has been enjoying manga since about the third grade, comments that, although she occasionally reads them, she finds that it is generally harder for her to "get into [Western] comics" and that "superheroes are kind of a turn-off."[4] Gabriel explains that one of the reasons why manga appeals to her is that she is able to find a wealth of stories that feature "younger people doing less mature things."[5] Echoing Schodt's comments, Gabriel suggests that many young women read manga and that there is manga "for literally everyone, instead of [being primarily for] twenty [or] thirty-something men."[6] Gabriel also comments that selecting Western comics can be "really daunting because some of the comics have been around for forty-plus years."[7] She pointed out that this makes it difficult to know where to start in such long-running series.[8] However, Gabriel does confess that "some people may feel the same way about manga,"[9] referring to some of the longer-running manga series. Nonetheless, the fact that manga does have genres intended specifically for girls (although females will also consume manga meant for males and vice versa) makes manga an attractive choice for the female reader.

In the United States, comics' association with a male readership is beginning to erode thanks in part to manga's popularity with female readers. In order to explain how this phenomenon has arisen, we must first explore the history of manga in Japan and how it arrived in America and became overwhelmingly popular among American girls.

Manga's History

To understand the popularity of manga in the United States, and its special appeal to a female readership, it is important to appreciate its separate history. The term "manga" means "'sketches made for fun or out of a sudden inspiration.'"[10] Some attribute the term to Katsushika Hokusai, master *ukiyo-e* artist.[11] *Ukiyo-e* is a genre of woodblock art and means "images of the floating world."[12] The *ukiyo-e* style often depicted scenes and caricatures of celebrities from the Yoshiwara teahouse district.[13] Even though the word "manga" is generally attributed to Hokusai, who is said to have coined the term in 1814, Bouissou explains that the word "had been in use since the end of the eighteenth century."[14] According to Petersen, the term, in fact, "was based on the Chinese word *manhua*, which meant 'impromptu sketches.'"[15] Petersen also maintains that before Hokusai produced the first collection of sketches and caricatures called *Hokusai Manga*, the term was seldom used—in fact, the use of the word "manga" to describe Japanese visual narrative only came into being in the twentieth century.[16] Interestingly, the *Hokusai Manga* do not relate stories.[17]

Some of the earliest origins of manga were in Japanese caricature or *toba-e*, as well as scrolls called *emaki* that emerged in Japan in the middle of the eighth century.[18] *Emaki* were scrolls that contained both pictures and text and were used by storytellers, called *etoki hoshi*, who recited the tales that the scrolls told in order to teach Buddhist values and to encourage the audience to make donations that would be collected for charity.[19] Interestingly, these cunning storytellers would use the words on the *emaki* as a rough scaffolding to support their storytelling, as they typically changed the story slightly in order to suit the listeners.[20] Therefore, the pictures on the *emaki* were used not only as props for the audience but guides (along with the text) for the storyteller.

In 1775, a new form of popular narrative appeared that came even closer to the comic book form that is enjoyed today: the *kibyoshi* (meaning "yellow books") named for the yellow covers on these works.[21] The *kibyoshi* were aimed toward an educated readership and featured "longer original stories published in multivolume series with more closely linked sequential actions" than their predecessors.[22] Though much of the narrative was transmitted through the images, integrated text was a typical feature of *kibyoshi*. The text in a *kibyoshi* was often cleverly written and rendered. In fact, one could easily compare the *kibyoshi* to the complicated narrative forms that appear in comics today. Petersen remarks, "It is tantalizing to consider just how close the *kibyoshi* publications came to realizing the form of the modern comic book."[23] This is especially true when considering the way in which the *kibyoshi* used text on the page. Petersen describes this phenomena: "The *kibyoshi* artists also followed the *ukiyo-e* tradition by employing the Chinese idea of a balloon- or cloud-shaped form emanating from a figure to represent dreams and fantasies."[24] Though it is easy to draw comparisons between the modern speech balloon and the *kibyoshi* "clouds," the clouds are not interchangeable with the speech balloon as we know it. Instead, they were used to denote visions—not dialog.

Unfortunately, though they appeared to be ahead of their time, the *kibyoshi* eventually died out. One of the reasons for the decline of *kibyoshi* was that the intelligentsia that produced the *kibyoshi*, as well as the people for which they were written, were made up of intellectuals prone to scrutiny by the government.[25] *Kibyoshi* would be replaced with less intellectual material.[26] Peterson remarks, "Despite the ready market for popular publications in Japan, it would be almost 100 years before Western-style comics would arrive and create the impetus for a new form of graphic narrative, manga, which would rival the complexity of *kibyoshi*."[27] Although Japan had a rich tradition of pictorial storytelling and graphic arts, it wasn't until the late nineteenth century (and the transition of Japan from the feudal system to modernity in a relatively short span of time) that Japan would develop the style of sequential storytelling known today as manga.

What we now think of as manga is an amalgamation of the traditional, indigenous arts of Japan combined with a Western influence. Two men, in particular, are credited with bringing the conventions of modern comics to Japan. Their names were Charles Wirgman and George Bigot. Wirgman was an "eccentric correspondent" for the *Illustrated London News*.[28] He would be the first to introduce the concept of modern comics to Japan.[29] Wirgman ended up quitting his British employment[30] and started up his own magazine, *The Japan Punch*, in 1862, aimed at the émigré community in Yokohama.[31] Wirgman went on to live the rest of his life in his adopted country.[32] Each issue of *The Japan Punch* was ten pages long, and the illustrations used the woodblock print technique traditional to Japan.[33] Through *The Japan Punch*, Wirgman is also credited with the introduction of speech balloons to Japanese cartoons.[34] According to Petersen,

> Wirgman tailored his humor magazine to the growing expatriate audience in Yokohama by showing cartoons in a manner typical of the British satire of the time. The ethnocentric humor focused on the many weird and ironic ways Japan was adapting to modern Western culture, including, for example, Japanese who politely removed their shoes when entering a train only to learn they were left on the platform when leaving the station.[35]

As biased toward the overseas community as *The Japan Punch* was, Wirgman's style stirred the interests of the Japanese people. *The Japan Punch* was translated into Japanese, and it wasn't long before the Western style of caricature spread.[36] Petersen explains that "Wirgman so effectively established the cartoon genre in Japan that even long after *The Japan Punch* ceased publication, cartoons were called *ponchi-e* or 'punch-pictures.'"[37] To this day, Wirgman is celebrated as one of the forebears of modern comics in Japan.[38] Annually, in Yokohama, a ceremony honoring Wirgman is held at his grave.[39]

Following Wirgman, George Bigot first published his magazine, *Tôbaé*, in 1887.[40] Bigot immigrated to Japan from France in 1882, and according to Schodt, was "an even more flamboyant figure that Wirgman."[41] He also drew satirical cartoons. According to Schodt, *Tôbaé* "satirized both Japanese society and government. Bigot was constantly in trouble with the Japanese authorities, but to the Japanese artists, who had long been forbidden to criticize their government, his acts seemed bold, and worthy of emulation."[42] Elements of Bigot's style, such as the sequential arrangement of narrative, would go on to influence the structure of modern manga.[43]

Wirgman and Bigot's work inspired native Japanese artists to experiment with the newly introduced European styles. This fresh perspective, along with the introduction of Western printing methods, led to a burst of new Japanese newspapers and magazines.[44] Most notably, a magazine called *Marumaru Chimbun*, inspired by *The Japan Punch*, arrived in 1877.[45] Schodt explains how thoroughly Japanese artists incorporated Western conventions and technology into the existing national style, stating that the art and humor of *Marumaru Chimbun*

> suggests the speed with which the Japanese were absorbing Western techniques, for technically the magazine was superior to Wirgman's and closer to the original British *Punch*. The cover, drawn by Kinkichirō Honda, incorporated Japanese puns but was drawn in a distinctly British style with a pen [instead of the traditionally Japanese brushwork].[46]

It wasn't long before American cartooning would begin to capture the Japanese artistic imagination. Schodt states, "By the end of the 19th century . . ., the focus of Japanese cartoonists began to shift from Europe to the United States, where a lively, less subtle type of political cartoon was popular, and where Joseph Pulitzer's *New York World* was experimenting with color Sunday supplements and the first true comics strips—complete with sequential panels and word balloons."[47] Two Japanese cartoonists, Rakuten Kitazawa and Ippei Okamoto, were instrumental in bringing the American style of comics to Japan and, in doing so, shaped the future of modern Japanese comics.

Kitazawa began his career working for an American magazine published in Yokohama called *Box of Curios* and would go on to become a great *mangaka* (cartoonist).[48] According to Schodt, Kitazawa became

> one of the most versatile and skilled cartoonists to emerge in Japan. . . .
> When he cartooned with a pen, as was usual, his drawings had the tight lines and attention to anatomy and perspective that characterize Western cartoons. When he used a brush, he could draw in the loose, simple, and subjective style the Japanese excelled at.[49]

After having worked as assistant to the Australian artist and cartoonist Frank Nankivell, for *Box of Curios*, Kitazawa became the editor of the Sunday comics supplement of *Jijishimpo* newspaper.[50] This Sunday supplement "was the first in Japan to capitalize on the idea popularized by Pulitzer in the *New York World* six years earlier."[51] Kitazawa's *Tagosaku to Mokubē no Tōkyō Kembutsu*, which translates as "Tagosaku and Mokubē Sightseeing in Tokyo," made its appearance in 1902.[52] It would be "the first serialized Japanese comic strip with regular characters."[53] Even though this early strip did not contain speech balloons, *Tagosaku to Mokubē no Tōkyō Kembutsu* was presented in quite the same way in which American comics were featured back then and still are today—in a Sunday supplement.[54]

Ippei Okamoto was a political cartoonist for a newspaper called *Asahi*.[55] After travelling to the United States and observing the *New York World*, Okamoto fell in love with the lightheartedness of American "Sunday Funnies."[56] In 1922, he wrote to the *Asahi*, describing these cartoons.[57] On November 14, 1923, *Bringing Up Father* by American cartoonist George McManus, made its Japanese debut in the *Asahi Graph*.[58] The translation of this American comic strip was a success, and other American serials soon followed. In 1924, a comic strip called *Nonki na Tōsan* appeared in the *Hōchi* newspaper.[59] *Nonki na Tōsan* translates as "Easy-going Daddy"[60] and was obviously influenced by *Bringing Up Father*, although the stories and situations were more relevant to a Japanese audience. A national comics style soon developed out of comics and art styles both new and old, domestic and foreign.

The arrival of American "Funnies" in Japan would also become one of the influencing forces in the creation of Japanese comics for children. In the 1920s, original children's comic strips began to run in Japanese newspapers.[61] A former apprentice of Ippei Okamoto, Shigeo Miyao, would become "one of the first professional artists to specialize in children's comics."[62] His comic strip series, *Manga Tarō*, was compiled and published as a book.[63] However, the majority of these copies did not survive the Great Kantō earthquake of 1923.[64] Nevertheless, Miyao persevered in his art, and in 1924 he began to write *Dango Kushisuke Man'yūki*, which was published as a successful hardbound book.[65] The collation of these comics in a book format would set the tone for the reception of such works in future years.

From the very beginning, comics were treated differently in Japan than their American counterparts. Japanese comics did not have the baggage that Western comics had accumulated over time. It is only in recent years that American comics (especially children's comics) have found popular and critical acclaim and have been bound into books and shelved in bookstores and libraries, helping them to find an audience outside of the comics collector's market. Manga, not suffering from the early moral panics ingrained in the history of American comics, grew to be a medium for the masses that catered to adults as well as children, males as well as females.

However, like American comics, Japanese comics were also shaped by censorship. The early explosion of comics for children is owed, at least in part, to political change that occurred in the 1920s and 1930s. Many artists that focused their work on political topics found their art to be increasingly dangerous as the nation's political currents shifted. Schodt describes this changing political climate and its effect on Japanese comics: "Even as artists were being politicized, an out-of-control ultranationalistic military, bent on expansion on the continent of Asia, was taking control of the civilian government. Ideological artists . . . frequently suffered arrest, and occasionally torture."[66] Not only were individual artists attacked for their controversial work, but entire magazines were targets of the right-wing takeover. Schodt explains:

The government's new thought-police, armed with an Orwellian "Peace Preservation Law," learned to control those who harbored subversive ideas. . . . They did so by intimidating artists and their editors. More than one magazine was forced to close; most were coerced into self-censorship. Arrest was the fate of editors who did not comply, and it happened so often that some magazines designated an employee as "jail editor"—he who had the honor of taking the rap and saving the company.[67]

Fear and threat effectively stifled many cartoonists' desire to create political commentary. However, one positive change in comics occurred through this unfortunate period in Japanese history—children's comics blossomed.[68] Comics created for a youth audience became the safe choice for cartoonists. By the 1930s, magazines such as *Shōnen Club* (a monthly boys' magazine), *Shōjo Club* (a monthly girls' magazine), and *Yōnen Club* (a monthly magazine aimed at younger children) began to run longer, complete stories instead of the shorter strips that were popular earlier in the century.[69] These long-running serials would often be compiled and sold in hardcover volumes. Schodt describes these books as "beautiful, clothbound, hardback volumes of around 150 pages, printed in color and sold in fancy cardboard cases"[70]—a treatment that comics and graphic novels are only now receiving in America.

Shōjo Manga: A Tradition of Girls' Comics

World War II was a dark time for Japanese comics. The magazines that had propelled the development of children's comics in the past became more focused on wartime articles and propaganda.[71] As a result of this shift in focus, along with wartime paper shortages, the number of comics featured in these magazines dwindled. The only magazine to continue to be regularly published during the war was *Manga*.[72] *Manga* was the official magazine of *Shin Nippon Mangaka Kyōkai* (The New Cartoonists Association of Japan), a government-endorsed cartoonists' association devised to marshal Japanese cartoonists under one official political banner.[73] Schodt comments that

After Pearl Harbor . . . cartoonists who were not banned from working or off fighting on the front were active in one of three areas: producing family comic strips that were totally harmless or promoted national solidarity; drawing single-panel cartoons that vilified the enemy in *Manga* or other domestic media; and working in the government and military service creating propaganda to be used against the opposing troops.[74]

Even though cartoonists were stifled by a wartime government, and Japan ended up surrendering to the Allied forces, Japanese comics would not only survive the war but go on to thrive.

Directly after the war, censorship still existed, but as the country's politics shifted, such restrictions began to ease. Cartooning slowly began to regain its previous diversity. Comic strips of this time period were characterized by their innocuous themes typically focusing on family. They were often humorous and were just what postwar Japan needed at the time—a sense of comfort and stability.[75] One of the most popular comics of this postwar era was written by a woman named Machiko Hasegawa and featured a young woman as the protagonist. Hasegawa's *Sazae-San* comics set the tone for the new representation of the modern Japanese woman. Hashimoto writes that "Sazae—the first ever female protagonist in Japanese daily cartoons—was a cheerful, scatterbrained housewife, daughter, and mother in this family. . . . She lived in an uxorilocal household with her own parents, not her husband's—a relatively uncommon arrangement at that time which gave her comparative freedom to act unconventionally as a young woman."[76]

The postwar period was a time of reevaluation of the woman's place in society, and, as is often the case, this social change was represented in the popular media of the time. What is fascinating about Sazae is that she pushed the boundaries of the traditional roles of womanhood, yet was able to subvert cultural norms in such a way that her exploits were humorous and seemingly innocuous to the status quo. Hashimoto explains the *Sazae-San* phenomenon:

Her travails invariably ended in blunders and mishaps, but always tested the limits of the "new order" in a rapidly changing society. When she defied policemen, reprimanded burglars, and went on joy trips with women friends, readers cheered her on enthusiastically because Sazae was a trailblazer in her own way. . . . Yet, even when she spoke out for gender equality, she remained a homebound woman whose father and husband worked as breadwinners in office jobs. . . . In a fairy tale world of unrealistic happenings and absurd consequences, Sazae succeeded in exposing the contradictions of the new egalitarian and democratic values within her reach, and did so with the most heartening and reassuring naivety.[77]

Though *Sazae-San* was not created specifically for girls, it showed that female characters, even subversive ones, had an audience. This also had implications for female cartoonists; Hasegawa's achievements proved that female mangaka could find success in the field.[78] In fact, *Sazae-San* was one of Japan's longest running manga series, beginning in 1946 and ending only in 1974. And Sazae's legacy would even live on in a weekly animation series that bears the distinguished honor of being the longest-running television show in Japanese history.[79] This was only the beginning of a new era of female-centric manga.

After the war, Japan was ripe for social change. The new constitution included an equal rights clause and women were granted the right to vote.[80] Comics by and for females began to appear. However, a male cartoonist named Osamu Tezuka is widely credited with revolutionizing comics for girls, known in Japan as *shōjo* (or *shoujo*) manga.

Tezuka, born in 1928, grew up with such influences as Western comics and Disney films,[81] as well as the animation of Max Fleischer.[82] These early influences clearly had an impact on Tezuka's artistic style, and his work has been described by many as cinematic. Petersen comments that Tezuka's 1947 breakthrough success, *Shintakarazima*, or *New Treasure Island*, looked "more like a storyboard for an animated movie than a comic book."[83] It was Tezuka who was instrumental in the development of the concept of *sutorii manga* (meaning "story manga"), which consisted of lengthy stories—a departure from the old comic strip formulas.[84] Tezuka's revolution in the style and capability of Japanese comics would, in fact, earn him the moniker "God of Manga."[85] However, another undeniable influence on Tezuka's manga was his exposure to the renowned Takarazuka Revue—an all-women theater troupe. According to Phillipps, "As a boy, Tezuka went to many of their performances with his mother, and he liberally imported themes, plots, scenery, scene sequences, and characters from the stage into his manga. Thus, these had enormous influence on Tezuka's girls' manga."[86]

It was out of the feminine influence of the Takarazuka theater and the fluidity and action of the cinema that Tezuka's *Ribon no kishi* (translated as *Princess Knight*, but literally meaning "Knight with Ribbons") was born.[87] *Ribon no kishi* was a romantic saga that ran from 1953 to 1956, and took place in a European fairy tale–like setting.[88] The protagonist, Princess Sapphire, set a new standard for shōjo manga. Instead of the passive characters and story lines found in previous examples of Japanese girls' comics, the Princess took an active role. Petersen explains:

> Osamu Tezuka was instrumental in establishing *shōjo manga* stories that had more action by introducing a more dynamic leading female character . . . Tezuka was very cautious to maintain the customary gender distinctions, but he allowed Princess Sapphire a greater dramatic range by saying she was a child born with both a boy and a girl soul. Furthermore, her father raised her as a boy to ensure that she could inherit his throne, which—like the emperorship of Japan—was forbidden to women.[89]

In essence, Tezuka created manga that had all of the trappings of *shōnen* (or boys' manga—e.g., adventure and action), but instead of a male protagonist, the hero was female. This would prove to be a great success, and shōjo manga would never be the same again.

It must be noted that historians often erroneously give Tezuka credit for creating the field of shōjo manga. However, Takahashi asserts that girls' comics had "existed long before Tezuka came on the scene," and cites examples of artists such as Jun'ichi Nakahara and Makoto Takahashi as large contributors to the evolution of shōjo manga's aesthetics. But she does give Tezuka credit for major developments in the field. [90] Takahashi admits that "complex narratives such as *Ribon no kishi* did not exist in the pages of shōjo manga magazines before Tezuka successfully adapted his shōnen manga stories for girl readers; he definitely raised the narrative bar by introducing his sequential manga style."[91] It is undeniable that Osamu Tezuka's influence on Japanese comics has helped shape what has become modern shōjo manga.

Today's shōjo manga is an extensive genre with many different subgenres, yet they are united by core themes, style, and aesthetic values. No matter whether the plots are fantastic or realistic, if they are more action-oriented or are emotionally based, there is typically a focus on relationships, romance, and personal development in shōjo manga. Even the visual style of shōjo manga may be distinguished from shōnen manga. As much as Osamu Tezuka is credited with establishing the genre, the particular conventions of modern shōjo manga are owed to the legacy left behind by female mangaka. In the 1960s and 1970s changes began to take shape in shōjo manga, an era that Prough describes as "the golden years of shōjo manga."[92] By this time Japan was beginning to recover from the economic devastation wrought by the war, and this meant that manga was being published widely once more.[93] The revitalization of the publishing industry, coupled with the evolving role of women in Japanese society, led to a burst of female mangaka that would change the look and feel of shōjo manga, as well as the greater manga art form.[94] Prough elaborates:

> Women artists began to dominate the drawing/writing of shōjo manga. . . . These early women artists reinvigorated the genre as they sought to capture their protagonists' and readers' innermost feelings. Rather than the more action- and dialog-based plot construction of the standard boys' genre of the time, these female artists began to experiment with how to express emotion, inner thoughts and feelings, memories, and musings.[95]

In particular, the so-called "24 nengumi" left the greatest impression on modern shōjo manga.[96] The 24 nengumi were a "loosely knit group of shō jo manga artists that . . . received substantial popular and scholarly attention. . . . These renowned artists honed the genre through an expansion of content, a renovation of layout, and the enrichment of the characters."[97] They were referred to as 24 nengumi because of the year generally associated with their birth, Shōwa 24 (or 1949). Although some of the artists associated with the 24 nengumi were not born in that exact year, they are unified in this style movement.[98] According to Takahashi, "Motō Hagio (1949–), Riyoko Ikeda (1947–), Toshie Kihara (1948–), Keiko Takemiya (1950–), Yumiko Ōshima (1947–), and Ryōko Yamagishi (1947–) are usually included in this group,"[99] to name some of the most prominent contributors.

Prior to the arrival of the 24 nengumi artists, shōjo manga was much less explicitly romantic and sexual—Prough comments that before the 24 nengumi shook up the art form, "even kissing scenes were rare."[100] It is also important to understand that, before the inception the 24 nengumi's revolutionary work, shōjo manga was largely considered a trashy genre. Takahashi elucidates this fact, stating, "Before the 24 nen gumi appeared, shōjo manga were dismissed as the lowest form of Japanese manga. The

24 nen gumi's work changed this."[101] The manga of 24 nengumi artists gained acclaim, where the genre had previously been largely overlooked, and these mangaka were praised for their stories' narrative complexities. The reason for this shift from simple and mostly comedic stories to bold and often challenging topics is due in part to the manga that the 24 nengumi were exposed to while growing up. The work of Osamu Tezuka and his groundbreaking cinematic style and storytelling left a deep impression on these mangaka as children and young adults.[102] Takahashi remarks that the 24 nengumi, especially Motō Hagio and Keiko Takemiya, were profoundly influenced by Tezuka: "Their works, like Tezuka's, also explored bold new themes, such as science fiction, religion, sexual problems, and history, instead of the standard shōjo manga fare of school life and love stories."[103]

Although the 24 nengumi were praised by critics for their writing, their aesthetic contributions to the field were initially disregarded.[104] The 24 nengumi made great innovations in visual style that would become the hallmarks of shōjo manga today. They popularized disproportionately large, liquid eyes often marked by an extra shine, or starburst near the pupil, indicative of femininity, romance, and perhaps, innocence.[105] Takahashi points out how oversized eyes are able to convey emotions which, in turn, assist in engaging the reader with that character on an empathetic level, explaining that, in shōjo manga, the eyes are "literally windows of the soul."[106]

One of the greatest contributions of the 24 nengumi was the breaking away from the strict, rectangular panel form with the introduction of image montages to convey narrative and emotion.[107] Prough comments that

> early women artists found this [traditional] format restrictive and refashioned the page in order to better represent the more interior and emotional content of their manga. These artists experimented with the placement of panels, and the use of dialog to really capture more aesthetics of feeling than had been previously possible in the genre.[108]

The montage form was a more abstract and interpretive method of storytelling than the traditional panel style, but it also freed the artist, enabling her to set a definitive mood and feel of the manga. A reader who is unused to the conventions of shōjo manga might, at first, have a difficult time interpreting the meaning of the montage page, but once she familiarizes herself with these differences in layout, the montage style is able to engage the reader with the emotional and atmospheric aspects of the story. Prough remarks, "A montage panel format made it easier to track back and forth among characters' actions, dialog, and thoughts."[109] Common aspects of montage images are decorative motifs such as free-drifting flowers, petals and leaves, and other ornamental patterns (e.g., designs imitative of lens flares seen in cinema), as well as close-up detail of characters' faces. Montage images also typically display figures situated in the picture plane in a way that has more to do with thoughts and feelings than with action or a linear sense of time and place. The double-spread found on pages 130 and 131 of Fuyumi Soryo's *Mars, Volume 8* displays an exemplary montage image. It is replete with a lens flare pattern and close-ups of the characters' faces and eyes that combine in a special aesthetic alchemy that is illustrative of the complexity and romance of the situation. In Soryo's *Mars*, Kira, an introverted girl with great artistic talent, falls in love with Rei, an extroverted bad boy on the outside, yet terribly troubled and sensitive on the inside. Although so different in personalities and disposition, the two teenagers both have heartrending pasts. When this unlikely pair meet, they begin to tear down the emotional walls that each has built. The attuned reader will understand that the eyes, belonging to the main character, Kira, are not to be read literally as disembodied, floating eyes. They are, instead, close-up, cinematic images detailing an emotive sequence—the first set of eyes show an expression of surprise at the realization of her boyfriend, Rei's, sincerity, while the set of eyes underneath and to the left on the picture plane (remember that manga is read right to left) depicts the next moment—tears dot Kira's lower lashes as she is moved by Rei's declaration of love. The overall effect of a montage image such as this one is that of an emotional collage.

Not only did montage and the other innovations made by the 24 nengumi shape the direction of shōjo manga, but their style also had a major influence on other varieties of manga. Prough explains, "Gradually, the montage style of shōjo manga has influenced shōnen manga as well."[110] However, shōnen manga is not the only genre that has benefitted from the shōjo style. The legacy left by 24 nengumi artists has made a vast impression on the entire manga art form. For example, the 24 nengumi's influence resonates throughout the work of the all-female production studio known as CLAMP. CLAMP, which currently consists of Nanase Ohkawa, Mokona Apapa, Tsubaki (previously known as Mick) Nekoi, and Satsuki Igarashi, came from humble beginnings as a *doujinshi* (fan comics) group.[111] Now the "four-woman studio ranks among the most successful creators of manga, or graphic novels, in Japan and the United States."[112]

CLAMP's success in America has a lot to do with the broad appeal of their visual style. Dallas Middaugh, a manga publisher for Random House, asserts that "Clamp have been an integral part of the manga explosion that's occurred in the U.S. over the past several years. . . . Their fluid, dramatic artwork and storytelling style struck a strong chord with male and female manga readers."[113] CLAMP's manga series are visually striking, but what sets them apart from many other works of manga is their appeal to both a male and female readership. Even though CLAMP produces work for a range of different audiences, in a variety of different styles, the presence of shōjo aesthetics can still be seen in the large eyes of many of their characters, and the use of montage, as well as other innovations and conventions of shōjo manga's golden years. Full-body depictions of major characters,[114] differing shapes of thought and speech bubbles, and floating text that generally denotes thoughts and narrative asides were all innovations of the golden years of shōjo manga.[115] CLAMP are well known for their shōjo series *Cardcaptor Sakura* and *Magic Knight Rayearth*, but they have also garnered renown for their other manga such as the seinen (men's) series *Chobits*. Even though *Chobits* was not originally produced as shōjo manga, it has nonetheless been a hit with girls.[116]

Chobits tells the story of a young man named Hideki who finds an abandoned "persocom"—a personal computer in the form of a young woman. Hideki names the persocom Chi, after the only utterance the android can make at first. However, Hideki finds that Chi is able to learn, and in time, he also discovers that she is able to love. Not only is *Chobits* a sexually charged romance with many comedic moments, it is a work of science fiction as well. Perhaps some of its crossover popularity with both young men and women has something to do with *Chobits'* ability to straddle these different genres. However, visually, it is not surprising that this series is popular with teen girls because so many of the visual conventions of shōjo manga are apparent across the series. For instance, two consecutive pages from *Chobits, Volume 5*, work together as a montage image, containing a full-body portrait of Chi alongside irregularly shaped panels. Chi's full-body portrait actually interrupts the structure of the panels as her flowing hair, her dress, and her feet break into the panels' frames. The left-hand page displays Hideki and Chi in an image free of panels as the picture bleeds to the edge of the page. The pose is romantic and is rendered with soft, detailed line-work that is typically associated with shōjo manga, as opposed to the sharper drawing style that is typical of many shōnen and seinen manga. The background texture of these two pages scintillates with a pattern of stars and bubbles, giving this episode a dreamy quality. When considering CLAMP's aesthetic approach to this story along with a narrative that is (essentially) focused on a deceptively strong female character, it is no wonder that so many young women enjoy the *Chobits* series.

Moreover, the pioneering style of shōjo manga has spread outside of Japan. Prough comments:

> Manga is becoming a global style, yet one that remains inherently linked to Japan. Even though shōjo manga is a relatively small subgenre, the aesthetics of form and content cultivated within its pages have become signature features of manga, both at home in Japan and abroad.[117]

American readers appear to have had no trouble decoding the complexities of manga, including the conventions of shōjo manga that now appear frequently throughout the field. It is also notable that some of the most popular manga series have been created by women. According to Solomon, "Many of the most popular manga on both sides of the Pacific are written and drawn by women, including Rumiko Takahashi ('Ranma ½,' 'InuYasha'); Hiromu Arakawa ('Fullmetal Alchemist'); and Clamp."[118] While many of these successful titles are not shōjo manga, they have a definite female following and often feature strong female characters.

For CLAMP, success in Japan and overseas has granted them more creative power, allowing them to push the boundaries of the art form. Solomon comments, "Their many hits have given the Clamp artists the power to create pretty much whatever they choose."[119] Only a few decades ago shōjo manga was viewed as trashy in Japan and the female mangaka that created them were often artistically marginalized. Now, there are lauded female artists whose works are popular not just in Japan but in America, too, and shōjo manga's aesthetics are finally being appreciated as they have been accepted as part of what constitutes manga's visual style. In a *New York Times* interview with CLAMP, Ohkawa comments,

> While it's true that the number of female directors in the animation industry has increased over the years, it's more common for women artists to present their work in manga. . . . It's a way for them to express themselves freely. Strong female characters have become very common in manga. . . . We're in a unique position: Clamp makes a presentation to the publishers about what we want to do, receive an approval and go to work.[120]

CLAMP's popularity has liberated them and enabled the group to experiment with form, style, and genre, and, as a result of their diverse styles, they have not only become popular in Japan but have also found astounding success with American readers. In his interview with CLAMP, Solomon remarks that "[t]he women seem both pleased and surprised at their popularity in the United States."[121] CLAMP's Ohkawa explains, "For some series, we do consider the international audience. . . . But we wonder, when American girls read our manga, do the stories touch their hearts? Can they relate to the characters?"[122] Judging from American sales of manga and *anime* (Japanese cartoons), libraries' manga circulation numbers, and attendance at fan conventions, the answer is a resounding yes.

Manga in America

Manga's success in America is a fairly recent phenomenon; the art form did not gain notable popularity until the 1990s. The manga revolution arrived in the United States via an unusual medium: children's television programming. The *Sailor Moon* animated series originated as a Japanese cartoon based on the manga by Naoko Takeuchi called *Bishōjo Senshi Sērā Mūn* (which translates as *Pretty Soldier Sailor Moon*). The original cartoon, which made its debut in Japan in 1992, was dubbed into English and heavily edited (and censored) to suit a young American audience. It made its arrival in the United States in 1995 under the simplified title *Sailor Moon*.[123] American youth, already primed by the import of *Mighty Morphin Power Rangers* (adapted from the Japanese series *Kyōryū Sentai Zyuranger*) and the array of toys and products associated with the show, devoured *Sailor Moon*.[124] *Sailor Moon* was especially relevant to girls who craved an action show with female heroes. According to Benkoil, "The Japanese creators of the Sailor Moon cartoon attribute its immense popularity in Japan to the casting of strong females as central characters."[125] The American version of the show was, indeed, popular for the very same reasons: instead of the television shows common at that time that featured a majority of male heroes, the main characters in *Sailor Moon* were females in active roles. The success of the show led to a demand for translations of the manga that inspired it, and it wasn't long before other manga titles appeared in translation in America.

Some series, such as Rumiko Takahashi's shōnen-oriented *Ranma ½*, did exist in English translation before *Sailor Moon*'s American television debut. However, these manga were not well known, and at that point in time shōjo manga was virtually unheard of in the United States. Some of the first companies to successfully introduce manga to America were Viz Media, Tokyopop, and Dark Horse Comics. Viz Media, who had been publishing translated manga since 1987, found success in publishing the aforementioned *Ranma ½* in 1993.[126] But it wasn't until a new company, Tokyopop (bolstered by the success of the cartoon), translated *Bishōjo Senshi Sērā Mūn* into English that manga, especially the shōjo variety, became popular reading material for young people. Author of *The Comics Journal*'s weblog, *¡Journalista!*, Dirk Deppey, explains:

> While there had been tentative moves toward the importing of trans-lated *shoujo* manga on American shores as early as the late 1980s, the domestic revolution really got into gear with the 1990s American de-but of the animated series *Sailor Moon*, based upon Naoko Takeuchi's original manga *Bishoujo Senshi Sērā Mūn*. With its whimsical sense of fashion, thrilling adventure and complex back-story, *Sailor Moon* was like little else young girls had ever before seen on television, and miles above anything American animators were offering them. The anime led to interest in manga, which in turn became the sort of success that made the bookstore market sit up and take notice.[127]

After the success of *Sailor Moon*, the demand for English translations of manga became apparent. When fans of *Sailor Moon* ran out of the translated manga to read, new titles became available. Also, unlike American comics, there was no lack of Japanese material aimed at young girls. *Bishōjo Senshi Sērā Mūn* and other shōjo manga readily filled a void in the American comics market, and girls were able to enjoy access to a whole genre of comics meant for them. *Sailor Moon* gave girls a new type of superhero to focus on: a young teen girl with all of the awkwardness and social preoccupations of any high school student. The difference was that she just happened to have superpowers as well.

Interestingly, girls weren't the only fans of *Sailor Moon*. Because of its broad appeal, there was an even greater demand for the related manga series. Horn explains that even though *Sailor Moon* was intended for a female audience, it also "rapidly became a favorite of male readers . . . after a highly successful series of TV animated cartoons was later released."[128] The success of the *Sailor Moon* television series led to a burst of Japanese cartoons, or *anime*, being translated and introduced to an American audience. *Pokémon, Cardcaptors* (based on CLAMP's *Cardcaptor Sakura* manga series), and others, as well as the associated merchandise, were a hit with American youth. The cable channel Cartoon Network also began to air anime programming dubbed in English.

The sudden abundance of Japanese cartoons on American television had a major effect on the American comic book industry. At first, publishing companies such as Viz, Dark Horse, and Tokyopop were publishing translations of manga as single-issue comic books. But as awareness of manga increased and anime reached more households, these publishing companies began to re-release these titles in collected volumes. According to Couch, graphic novels were "distributed and sold through comic book stores, but as the number of books published expanded and as Japanese animation on television increased awareness of the properties they were able to expand their sales through bookstores."[129] The transition from comics to graphic novels and the popularity of anime led to manga branching out from fare found only in specialty shops to bound volumes found on the shelves of major retail bookstores.

Manga publishing in the U.S. reached another milestone in 2002 when Tokyopop made the decision to print new manga translations with the pages "unflipped," reading from right to left, as they are published in Japan, marketing the new format as a more authentic experience for readers. Couch recounts that "in 2002, Tokyopop began publishing unflipped manga collections, designed to be read right to left, with the sound effects untranslated. Calling this format 'real' manga, the small books provided a frisson of authenticity and were embraced—particularly by teenage girls."[130] The new books did, indeed, resemble the Japanese *tankōbon*, which are the collected volumes of manga serials that originally appeared in Japanese manga magazines.[131] Not only was this format a great marketing tool to engage fans with "authentic" material, but it also meant that Tokyopop no longer needed to dedicate time and resources to flipping the original material to read left to right in the conventional Western style. According to an announcement published on the ICv2 website, this move would "allow Tokyopop to publish its growing number of key manga titles with [a] three to six times greater frequency than the current industry standard—which [meant] that the company [would] be able to maintain a monthly schedule for some of its graphic novel series."[132] Spending less time and money on heavy re-formatting meant that Tokyopop was also able to maintain lower prices for the translations.[133]

Previous to Tokyopop's decision to leave their manga unflipped, it was generally believed that it would be difficult for Westerners to adjust to the conventions of manga, but the readers quickly caught on. In order to help direct their readers and avoid confusion, Tokyopop began printing information on how to read manga at the back of their books, so that the reader who opens a book the wrong way around would find a notice telling them that they were starting from the wrong end. They also provided an instructional guide on how to read manga.[134] Goldberg notes that "Tokyopop pushed the 'authentic' experience of their manga by creating bookstore floor displays to hold their titles (which also appealed to stores by creating more shelf space). In big red letters at the top of the display was the word *AUTHENTIC*."[135] The authentic presentation of these books pleased hardcore fans, but it was also in this way that manga secured a place in bookstores, and so became accessible to a wider readership.

Tokyopop's successful move to publish unflipped manga led the way for other publishers to do the same, and it wasn't long before bookstores were filled with manga titles. This had an enormous impact on female readership because girls who would never have stepped into a comic book specialty store had access to comics in retail stores where they were more likely to shop. These new manga translations were presented in book format and didn't bear the negative stigma attached to American comic books. Moreover, there were many titles that featured main characters who were young and female—shōjo manga was a hit.

Girls are now able to find an abundance of manga for a wide age-range featuring strong female characters. For young girls, there are characters such as Sakura from CLAMP's *Cardcaptor Sakura* and *Cardcaptor Sakura: Master of the Clow* (the latter series being one of the earliest titles to be published unflipped by Tokyopop). The two series contain a continuous fantasy story about a ten-year-old schoolgirl named Sakura Kinomoto who discovers that she has extraordinary powers, must capture the magical Clow cards, and, in the second series, has to transform them. Like *Pretty Soldier Sailor Moon*, *Cardcaptor Sakura* falls under the *mahō shōjo* (magical girl) genre, where a girl (or young woman) is revealed as having special powers, sometimes involving a transformation from a normal appearance to a magical form.[136] The *Sakura* series contain action, adventure, and a focus on relationships, as well as the main character's self-realization through her magical talents and quest.

For older girls, there is Ai Yazawa's *Nana*, a series about two young women with the same first name. Nana Osaki is a strong, independent young woman who dreams of finding success with her punk rock band BLAST. When her charismatic boyfriend and bass player, Ren, receives an offer to join another band that is about to sign a record contract in Tokyo, Nana Osaki is caught between two difficult choices. She could choose to move to Tokyo with the man whom she loves or else break up with him and stay with her band in her hometown, trying to achieve her dream of making it as a punk rock singer. Nana recalls how she simultaneously fell in love with Ren and became the singer for his band; but she is clear in stating that, although she was in love, singing in the band fulfilled her *own* needs—she never sang for Ren's sake. She says, "From that day on, I was like . . . the roar of the sea . . . swaying to Ren's gravitational pull. My heart floated . . . higher . . . higher . . . higher . . . and this voice gave voice to my inner desires. But I wasn't singing . . . for Ren. I sing every day . . . for myself."[137] Nana is torn between the love of a man, and her dreams and identity. When her guitarist, Nobu, tells her that she should move to Tokyo and that she could still be with Ren, even if they are in different bands, she tells him that it wouldn't work; she would just end up moving in with Ren and "waiting around at home, with no band of my own, making miso soup, while Ren gets famous in a band with a better girl singer."[138] No matter what Nana tells Nobu, there is still a part of her that questions whether she should follow her boyfriend. She wonders if it would be the right thing to do to move in with him in Tokyo, give up her own dreams, settle down and have children with Ren, and find a different sort of happiness, even if she would be living in Ren's shadow. Ultimately, she makes the decision to say goodbye to her boyfriend and chooses to work on her future music career. Page 154 of *Nana, Volume 1*, shows a confident Nana Osaki as she begins to gather up the remnants of her band, making plans for her future (see fig. 4.1).

The character of Nana Osaki presents a great example of a young woman making life-altering decisions that will influence her future. Even though this future is uncertain, she understands that she must take some risks in order to remain independent and true to herself in a world where it would be very easy to fall back on the man in her life. Even though it hurts, she realizes that, in order to live a fulfilling existence, she must not let anyone else dictate her future. Nana perseveres with BLAST, and almost two years after the break-up, she decides to buy herself the birthday present of a one-way ticket to Tokyo with the intention of trying to break into the music industry herself.

In contrast to Nana Osaki, Nana Komatsu is naive and clingy and has a propensity to not think about consequences. She "falls in love" too easily, and her feelings are often not returned. What's more, she attempts to change her looks, trying desperately to please the men that she is interested in. Nonetheless, like Nana Osaki, Nana Komatsu winds up moving to Tokyo, but for very different reasons than the other Nana. She wants to go to Tokyo because her friends plan to move there. After high school, she follows her best friend, Junko, to art college, where she makes friends with Kyosuke (who becomes Junko's boyfriend) and Shoji, who is interested in a relationship with Nana. However, Nana has designated Shoji as a friend and does not understand his feelings. When Junko decides to go to a university in Tokyo to further her studies in art, taking Kyosuke with her, Nana is devastated. She cries and tells Junko that she doesn't want her to leave. Nana then begs Junko's boyfriend not to go because, according to Nana's immature logic, if Kyosuke doesn't go, Junko won't go either. However, Junko sets her straight. Frustrated, she yells at Nana, saying,

Figure 4.1. *Nana, Vol. 1*., 2005, page 154.
Nana © 1999 by Yazawa Manga Seisakusho/Shueisha Inc.

"Even if Kyosuke doesn't go, I'm going anyway! I really want to study art in Tokyo!"[139] Junko has a strong sense of self and, unlike Nana Komatsu, does not allow herself to be defined by the people she chooses as friends.

Noting how upset Nana feels as her social life turns upside down, Shoji tells Nana that he, too, intends to move to Tokyo, and he asks her if she would like to join him. Nana brightens at this prospect, and she sets out to apply, rather indiscriminately, to any art university that will accept her. The panels show just how desperate Nana Komatsu is to follow her friends (see fig. 4.2). She does not want to go to a university in order to better herself with education but because she would be lost without the guiding presence of her social circle. When Kyosuke questions her reasons for her proposed move to Tokyo, Nana doesn't even have an original comeback. Directly aping what Junko had said to her previously, she yells, "Yo dude, it's my life! You're not the boss of me!"[140] Nana's anger is emphasized by the spiky form of her speech balloon, her mouth a large, angry oval, and her brow knitted together, as she lashes out at Kyosuke. Although Nana may seem passionate, the phrase that she uses in defense of her actions has been stolen from Junko. Ironically, even though Nana appears to put up a feisty argument, she doesn't *actually* want to live her own life. Instead, she prefers to mimic her friends—even down to their words.

Some adults may feel concern that characters such as Nana Komatsu are portrayed negatively and worry that manga may be reinforcing gender stereotypes. For instance, Benkoil criticizes the *Sailor Moon* cartoon (based on the manga) saying that "these so-called warriors-against-sexism characters wear miniskirts and draw their power from makeup" and that "[a]lmost all of the forces of evil in the show are older women," detracting from the show's (and the manga's) themes of female empowerment.[141] However, *Sailor Moon* should not be repudiated so easily. Looking beyond these negative details, there is no doubt that *Sailor Moon* presents girls with powerful female characters for role models as an alternative to the male action-heroes found in popular culture. As with *Go Girl!* Sailor Moon and similar manga characters send the message that girls can embrace their femininity without compromising their power. Even *Nana*'s Nana Komatsu, a relatively weak character, is balanced by the strong-willed Nana Osaki. Their friendship is a friendship of opposites: Nana Osaki is ambitious and ruled by her head, while Nana Komatsu's life

Figure 4.2. *Nana, Vol. 1.*, 2005, page 64.

Nana © 1999 by Yazawa Manga Seisakusho/Shueisha Inc.

revolves around her relationships with others—she is ruled by her heart. Together, they temper each other's personalities.

When seventeen-year-old manga devotee Qiuning Huang was asked what she thought of manga's portrayal of females, she commented rather objectively that "[some] have really strong female leads and some have really wimpy female leads that need to be rescued. It depends upon the manga."[142] Again, there are good examples and bad examples to be found in any art form, and not all manga depicts women in a stereotypical or otherwise negative manner. Just as it would be preposterous to condemn all conventional literature on the basis of a few poorly written books, manga should not be scorned because of a few negative examples.

There are plenty of manga that feature strong females as lead characters, such as Kanade Outsuka from Sakura Tsukuba's *Land of the Blindfolded, Volume 1*. Kanade is a high school student, but she is not ordinary—if she touches someone, she can glimpse that person's future. Although she is at times frightened and overwhelmed by this talent, she continues to use her power to help people. Even when warned by fellow student Arou Naitou (a boy who can see into the past) not to interfere with people and their futures, Kanade refuses to stop trying to do what she thinks is right. Arou suggests that their gifts should be used merely to observe and that it would be unfair to influence the futures of others, warning Kanade that she could get hurt herself. However, Kanade lets Arou know that she will take the risk and that she will not stand by and observe people when she could be helping them. Eventually, strong-willed yet gentle Kanade wins Arou over, and he begins to use his powers to help others. It is not long before the pair fall for each other. Not only does *Land of the Blindfolded, Volume 1*, portray a strong-willed, powerful female, but, like many shōjo titles, it shows an example of the development of a loving relationship between two individuals. The relationship between Kanade and Arou is particularly positive, because they are equally matched in power and complement one another.

Rumiko Takahashi's *InuYasha* also contains wonderful examples of strong female characters. *InuYasha* is a time-slip adventure story about a sensible high school girl, Kagome, who travels back in time to feudal Japan and has adventures with Inu-Yasha—who is half dog-demon (*inu* meaning "dog" in Japanese) and half human. The series begins when

Kagome, whose family house is also an ancient shrine, chases the family cat into the old "Bone-Eaters Well" on her fifteenth birthday. Once inside (perhaps in a subtle allusion to *Alice's Adventures in Wonderland*) she gets pulled down the well by a demon and emerges in an era where magic is possible—feudal Japan during the *Sengoku* or "Warring States" period.[143] In this time of legend, Kagome finds out that she is the reincarnation of Kikyo—priestess of the shrine and guardian of the magical Shikon Jewel. This jewel has the ability to grant power to demons and men and in the wrong hands may be used for evil purposes. During a fight for the jewel with a centipede demon, Kagome frees Inu-Yasha from an enchantment under which her previous incarnation, Kikyo, had placed him fifty years earlier. Inu-Yasha subsequently helps her to vanquish the monster, but with selfish intentions—he wants the jewel for himself.

Even though *InuYasha* is shōnen manga, the series features a strong young woman as a central character. What is even more fascinating about this series is that Kagome is introduced to her abilities (and her responsibilities as guardian of the Shikon jewel) through a powerful and wise older woman named Kaede. When Inu-Yasha attempts to take the jewel from Kagome, Kaede, who is a priestess of the shrine and the younger sister of the deceased Kikyo, throws magical prayer beads around Inu-Yasha's neck and instructs Kagome to "utter a subduing spell."[144] After some hesitation, Kagome, in a comedic moment, commands Inu-Yasha to "sit," as if he were a dog. Under this command, Inu-Yasha is flattened to the ground. Later on in this volume, the Shikon jewel is shattered when Kagome and Inu-Yasha try to recover it from another marauding demon. Their quest begins when Kagome and Inu-Yasha discover that they must work together to recover the shards. Stories like *InuYasha* empower girls, as well as provide boys with positive examples of females, both young and old. With examples of active and nonstereotypical female characters, manga is able to empower female readers and promote gender equality.

Not only does manga present an array of reading choices that feature female protagonists in active roles, but the art form has also inspired a whole new generation of comic book artists and authors. Bryan Lee

O'Malley, the creator of the popular *Scott Pilgrim* comics, explains how much of an impact manga has had on him. He says,

> I really got into *manga* in the first place because of *Sailor Moon*, which was really big on Canadian television. At first my little sister would be watching it, and I'd think "Ugh, girl's stuff!" I was 16 at the time. But she'd watch it every day, and I'd catch little bits of it. When it first premiered, it was playing every day. By the 10th or 12th episode, I was hooked![145]

Like many young people who became manga fans in the 1990s, O'Malley had his first introduction to manga through cartoon adaptations presented on North American television. This initial interest in anime would lead to engagement with manga, such as Takahashi's *Ranma ½*. O'Malley recalls:

> At the time, *manga* in English was still . . . young. *Ranma* was one of the big ones—I'd buy them in the single issue floppies when they came out. I remember first picking up Volume 3 of the *Ranma ½* graphic novel. . . . I'm not sure if I knew or not that what I was picking up was not the beginning of the story! So I probably ended up being confused, but totally and instantly obsessed with it![146]

O'Malley admits that, even though he started out drawing in the style of Naoko Takeuchi and Rumiko Takahashi (creators of *Pretty Soldier Sailor Moon* and *Ranma ½*, respectively), he later became more interested in independent comics.[147] However, manga's influence on O'Malley's style is apparent in *Scott Pilgrim*, the comics series that he is best known for. It has been shelved in both manga and Western comics sections in retail stores, and though O'Malley is generally not considered a manga artist, there are undeniable echoes of manga in the way his characters are drawn.[148] Traces of the manga technique are evident in the way in which he designs his characters; the larger-than-life eyes and miniscule noses are just some of the tell-tale signs.

Hope Larson, author-artist of critically acclaimed female-centric graphic novels such as *Chiggers*, *Grey Horses*, and *Mercury* (and, coincidentally, the wife of Bryan Lee O'Malley), was also influenced by manga in her formative years. In her introduction to Faith Erin Hicks's take on the school story in graphic novel form, *The War at Ellsmere*, Larson recounted that when she left boarding school and went to a day school she "rediscovered comics" and was introduced to manga.[149] When asked about the comics that she read as a teen, Larson comments:

> In high school, I had a bunch of guy friends who read comics, and we'd pool our money to buy volumes of *Ranma ½*—they were so expensive back then!—and pass them around at school. *Ranma ½* was, and remains, one of my favorites. I still read plenty of manga. Fumi Noshinaga (*All My Darling Daughters*), Mitsuru Adachi (*Cross Game*) and Naoki Urasawa (*20th Century Boys*) are particular favorites.[150]

Larson explains that she writes "to [her] interests, whatever they happen to be that month (gold mining, the film industry of the 1920s, *Sailor Moon*–style magical girls) in the hope that others will eventually share them."[151] Although Larson's manga influences are not overt, the subject matters that she chooses to write about, her use of montage, and other stylistic choices, such as the angled jaws of her characters, all hint toward an appreciation of manga.

Manga's Future Influence in America

Just as artists such as Larson and O'Malley were influenced by the popularization of manga in North America, so will some of today's fans inevitably become the creators of tomorrow's comic books. Manga fan and budding artist Davi Gabriel remarks that "if it weren't for manga, I don't know if I *would* be an artist. I don't know what I would be."[152] Through her introduction to manga, Gabriel found an interest in art that she continues to cultivate. She astutely comments that she has, in her recent work, tried to develop her own style, moving away from manga because "I was starting to get into a rut and . . . as an artist, I really needed to have branched out and I'm glad that I did . . . I'm a lot more proud of my work, but I won't ever deny that I had . . . manga origins."[153]

It is evident that Gabriel's artistic development is owed not only to her appreciation of manga but also from the expansion of her interest in other art forms. Strikingly, Banksy's book, *Wall and Piece*, lies casually on the sofa alongside a handful of manga volumes, as Gabriel sits for her interview. Perhaps, Gabriel's artistic style has also benefitted from the recent diversification of her comic book reading habits. Although Gabriel is primarily a manga fan, she has also begun to read Western comics, and she notes that, had she been introduced to comics initially, she might have "been into that instead of manga."[154] Gabriel explains that she has only been reading Western comics for about a year, after her father introduced her to them, and that she isn't familiar with too many titles yet.[155] However, a particular favorite of hers is Vertigo's *Fables* by Bill Willingham, which she prefers to many manga titles that she has read.[156] Nevertheless, when Gabriel further discusses the maturation of her artistic style and her future ambitions as an artist, she stresses that "if it weren't for manga or anime, I wouldn't be drawing, and I wouldn't have made the friends [that I've made]."[157]

Friends and community appear to be very much a part of manga fandom. There is even a Japanese word describing the manga fan: *otaku*, although this term can have negative implications. Ortabasi describes the meaning of the term:

> For the uninitiated, the term otaku is commonly used to designate a rabid fan/hobbyist of anime, manga, computer games, and related genres. Fans overseas have even adopted the term for themselves, thereby creating a sort of international fellowship of 'geeks' bound by their intense absorption in these popular media. Indeed, as a descriptive term, it is applied only too easily to those who seem to have a more than passing interest in such "nonintellectual" subjects. This is precisely the problem with the label, since it implies not only type and level of fandom but, from a mainstream point of view, a rejection of or challenge to society.[158]

The word literally means "your home" or "you," but it was co-opted in the 1970s by fans of science fiction animation enthusiasts.[159] Currently, in America, there are plenty of manga and anime fans that self-identify as *otaku*, using it interchangeably with "fan-boy" or "fan-girl." However, in Japan, the word has a negative connotation associated with young, socially disconnected people, consumed by their preoccupation with an unrealistic world of manga and the associated cartoons.[160] Gabriel agreed that being referred to as *otaku* is a "negative thing."[161] Gabriel compares the stereotype of the comic book fan in America to the perception of the *otaku*, stating that the general view is that they are "hard-core [and] never go out of the basement."[162] Regardless of whether an individual could be considered an *otaku* or just a loyal fan, manga enthusiasts are unified by their love of the art form. The young women who were interviewed for this book all maintain that their love of manga is a part of their social lives—whether it is shared with friends from school, at conventions, or through online communication, there is an element of community associated with this literature.

Fan unity has also contributed to major changes in the American manga publishing industry. The power of fandom made publishers such as Tokyopop highly successful. According to *Publishers Weekly*, by 2006 "manga sales . . . were about $175 million–$200 million."[163] However, these strong numbers have since plummeted, as U.S. manga sales "declined by as much [as] 50% since sales peaked in 2007."[164] As a consequence of these failing numbers, in May 2011 Tokyopop made the announcement that it would be "shutting down its Los Angeles–based U.S. publishing division. . . . A Hamburg, Germany, office which handles European publishing and global rights will remain open, and film and television projects will remain unaffected."[165] How could an industry leader such as Tokyopop decline so rapidly? When Tokyopop laid off Lillian Diaz-Przybyl and Troy Lewter, two of their longstanding editors, as well as other staff members, CEO Stuart Levy, blamed the bankruptcy of bookstore retail chain Borders for their deterioration.[166] However, at least a part of Tokyopop's (as well as the entire industry's) rapid decline in sales point toward what was once the source of their success—the fans.

Many fans of manga have, in recent years, turned to reading *scanlations*—manga translated by amateurs, digitally scanned, and shared on the Internet, generally without the consent of the creator or publisher.[167] A large number of manga's fans are young people, and for many teens a manga reading habit can become unaffordable over time. Teenage readers Davi Gabriel and Qiuning Huang both admit to reading manga online, yet neither of the girls appear to be aware that scanlations often infringe upon copyrights and are considered digital piracy. It is also unclear what exactly Gabriel and Huang mean when they say that they read "online." Nonetheless, Gabriel points out that when she was collecting manga at about ten dollars per volume, "it started becoming really expensive . . . when you have twenty-plus issues of a series."[168] For her, reading online is a "good alternative to just spending forty bucks every time you go to Borders."[169]

Huang, a connoisseur of manga, offers another reason why fans enjoy scanlations: sometimes "fan translations are better."[170] Huang speculates fans care more about the material because they love it, unlike the publishing companies whose primary concern, she implies, is to get the books published quickly and turn a profit.[171] It must be noted that many scanlation groups attempt to be conscientious about their scanning activity by only translating and uploading manga that hasn't yet been published in translation and by removing material that is scheduled to be officially translated.[172] None of this, of course, could have been accomplished without the use of the Internet, and in many ways, scanlation activity hasn't always adversely affected the publishing industry. In fact, scanlations have even been useful to publishers in that they are able to provide insight as to what titles interest fans.[173] In this way, the scanlations that appear on the Internet essentially provide publishers with a valuable source for market research, comparable to a giant focus group.

The major problems currently facing publishers are the economic downturn, the development of new technologies such as e-readers and other digital phenomena, and a sheer inability to keep up with the demand of the fan base. It is impossible to predict the future of American manga publishers. In order to survive these challenges, manga publishers will have to adapt. It was announced at the 2011 annual San Diego Comic-Con that "[t]he 39 publishers that make up the Japanese Digital Comics Association have organized Jmanga.com as an effort to address declining sales of manga."[174] The Jmanga website intends to offer some free content as well as merchandise for purchase. Jmanga.com will also include a social component, putting an emphasis on the fan community.[175] However, Reid observes that "the site is also clearly an effort to confront pirate manga scanlation sites that attract millions of fans each month by illegally aggregating thousands of manga scanlations."[176] Do waning manga sales throughout the industry (e.g., the demise of Tokyopop) portend a drop in interest in manga? Not necessarily. Reid writes:

Jmanga.com business manager Robert Newman noted that while U.S. manga sales have declined by as much 50% since sales peaked in 2007, attendance at manga conventions and fan shows continue to show strong growth. Newman said the decline was due to several factors—scanlations included—among them, too few new titles, limited manga information in English, difficulty finding relevant works and a licensing process that is long and expensive.[177]

While American manga publishers are experiencing a time of uncertainty, there is little sign that the fans, themselves, are wavering. Their dedication is apparent at conventions, as well as in their high circulation in public libraries.[178] Librarian Justin Azevedo reports: "I have observed heavy interest [in manga] from both females and males, though I definitely see a slight edge toward females. Many of the comic-related requests I get at the reference desk are for hard-to-find volumes of shōjo and josei series by female patrons."[179] Librarian Chelsea Couillard concurs that manga is so popular that "[t]here are even manga series for preteens now, so they can feel like the teens."[180] It would seem that the demand for manga is only increasing—even if this interest is no longer reflected in actual sales. Alvin Lu of Viz Media predicts:

> The audience will continue to grow and to widen, but at the same time, the Japanese titles will still pick up a new audience. We'll see the American comics market respond with a greater convergence of what we call "comics" and what we call "manga." I don't know how long using those terms [as separate categories] will be applicable to differentiate between the two.[181]

This "convergence" is already evident in the appearance of original English language manga, or OEL manga, for short. An example of this would be Chynna Clugston's series, *Blue Monday*—a series about a teenage girl named Bleu and her comedic, rock-and-roll-fueled escapades. Although written to be read from left to right, there is no doubt that Clugston utilizes the manga aesthetic for this series. Perhaps an even better example would be the previously mentioned *Scott Pilgrim* series, which continues to defy categorization and has been so popular that it has been made into a major motion picture.

Regardless of the direction of manga's future, the popularity that Japanese comics have garnered in America has helped to focus attention on Western comics, particularly the graphic novel. Manga has injected the concept of mature and often novel-length comics for mass consumption rather than just a fringe following. It is also apparent that exposure to a mainstream group of readers may mean that comics are not only changing in the eyes of popular culture but are gaining acceptance as literature and art as well.

Notes

1. Will Eisner, "Foreword," in *Faster than a Speeding Bullet: The Rise of the Graphic Novel,* by Stephen Weiner (New York: Nantier, Beall, Minoustchine, 2003), ix.

2. Mila Bongco, *Reading Comics: Language, Culture, and the Concept of the Superhero in Comic Books* (New York: Garland, 2000), 126.

3. Frederik L. Schodt, "Foreword: Japan's New Visual Culture," in *Japanese Visual Culture: Explorations in the World of Manga and Anime,* ed. Mark W. Mac-Williams (Armonk, NY: M. E. Sharpe, 2008), vii.

4. Davi Gabriel, interview by author, June 22, 2011.

5. Gabriel interview.

6. Gabriel interview.

7. Gabriel interview.

8. Gabriel interview.

9. Gabriel interview.

10. Jean-Marie Bouissou, "Manga: A Historical Overview," in *Manga: An Anthology of Global and Cultural Perspectives,* ed. Toni Johnson-Woods (New York: Continuum, 2010), 22.

11. Neil Cohn, "Japanese Visual Language: The Structure of Manga," in *Manga: An Anthology of Global and Cultural Perspectives,* ed. Toni Johnson-Woods (New York: Continuum, 2010), 200.

12. Robert S. Petersen, *Comics, Manga, and Graphic Novels: A History of Graphic Narratives* (Santa Barbara, CA: Praeger, 2011), 39.

13. Petersen, *Comics, Manga, and Graphic Novels,* 39.

14. Bouissou, "Manga," 22.

15. Petersen, *Comics, Manga, and Graphic Novels,* 40–41.

16. Petersen, *Comics, Manga, and Graphic Novels,* 41.

17. Petersen, *Comics, Manga, and Graphic Novels,* 41.

18. Petersen, *Comics, Manga, and Graphic Novels,* 37.

19. Petersen, *Comics, Manga, and Graphic Novels,* 37–39.

20. Petersen, *Comics, Manga, and Graphic Novels*, 39.

21. Petersen, *Comics, Manga, and Graphic Novels*, 42.

22. Petersen, *Comics, Manga, and Graphic Novels*, 42.

23. Petersen, *Comics, Manga, and Graphic Novels*, 42.

24. Petersen, *Comics, Manga, and Graphic Novels*, 43.

25. Petersen, *Comics, Manga, and Graphic Novels*, 43.

26. Petersen, *Comics, Manga, and Graphic Novels*, 44.

27. Petersen, *Comics, Manga, and Graphic Novels*, 44.

28. Petersen, *Comics, Manga, and Graphic Novels*, 126.

29. Petersen, *Comics, Manga, and Graphic Novels*, 126.

30. Petersen, *Comics, Manga, and Graphic Novels*, 126.

31. Frederik L. Schodt, *Manga! Manga! The World of Japanese Comics* (Tokyo: Kodansha International, 1983), 38.

32. Schodt, *Manga! Manga!* 38.

33. Petersen, *Comics, Manga, and Graphic Novels*, 126.

34. Schodt, *Manga! Manga!* 41.

35. Petersen, *Comics, Manga, and Graphic Novels*, 127.

36. Schodt, *Manga! Manga!* 40.

37. Petersen, *Comics, Manga, and Graphic Novels*, 127.

38. Schodt, *Manga! Manga!* 40.

39. Schodt, *Manga! Manga!* 40.

40. Schodt, *Manga! Manga!* 40.

41. Schodt, *Manga! Manga!* 40.

42. Schodt, *Manga! Manga!* 40.

43. Schodt, *Manga! Manga!* 41.

44. Schodt, *Manga! Manga!* 41.

45. Schodt, *Manga! Manga!* 41.

46. Schodt, *Manga! Manga!* 41.

47. Schodt, *Manga! Manga!* 41.

48. Schodt, *Manga! Manga!* 42.

49. Schodt, *Manga! Manga!* 42.

50. Petersen, *Comics, Manga, and Graphic Novels*, 128.

51. Petersen, *Comics, Manga, and Graphic Novels*, 128.

52. Schodt, *Manga! Manga!* 42.

53. Schodt, *Manga! Manga!* 42.

54. Schodt, *Manga! Manga!* 42.

55. Schodt, *Manga! Manga!* 43.

56. Schodt, *Manga! Manga!* 43.

57. Schodt, *Manga! Manga!* 43.

58. Schodt, *Manga! Manga!* 45.

59. Schodt, *Manga! Manga!*, 45, 48.

60. Schodt, *Manga! Manga!* 45.

61. Schodt, *Manga! Manga!* 48.

62. Schodt, *Manga! Manga!* 48.

63. Schodt, *Manga! Manga!* 48-49.

64. Schodt, *Manga! Manga!* 49.

65. Schodt, *Manga! Manga!* 49.

66. Schodt, *Manga! Manga!* 51.

67. Schodt, *Manga! Manga!* 51.

68. Schodt, *Manga! Manga!* 51.

69. Schodt, *Manga! Manga!* 51.

70. Schodt, *Manga! Manga!* 51.

71. Schodt, *Manga! Manga!* 51.

72. Schodt, *Manga! Manga!* 56.

73. Schodt, *Manga! Manga!* 55–56.

74. Schodt, *Manga! Manga!* 56.

75. Schodt, *Manga! Manga!* 61.

76. Akiko Hashimoto, "Blondie, Sazae, and Their Storied Successors: Japanese Families in Newspaper Comics," in *Imagined Families, Lived Families: Culture and Kinship in Contemporary Japan*, ed. Akiko Hashimoto and John W. Traphagan (Albany: SUNY Press, 2008), 21.

77. Hashimoto, "Blondie, Sazae," 22.

78. Schodt, *Manga! Manga!* 97.

79. Mark W. MacWilliams, "Introduction," in *Japanese Visual Culture: Explorations in the World of Manga and Anime*, ed. Mark W. MacWilliams (Armonk, NY: M. E. Sharpe, 2008), 3.

80. Schodt, *Manga! Manga!* 96-97.

81. Petersen, *Comics, Manga, and Graphic Novels*, 175.

82. Schodt, *Manga! Manga!* 63.

83. Petersen, *Comics, Manga, and Graphic Novels*, 175.

84. Susanne Phillipps, "Characters, Themes, and Narrative Patterns in the Manga of Osamu Tezuka," in *Japanese Visual Culture: Explorations in the World of Manga and Anime*, ed. Mark W. MacWilliams (Armonk, NY: M. E. Sharpe, 2008), 68.

85. Petersen, *Comics, Manga, and Graphic Novels*, 175.

86. Phillipps, "Characters, Themes, and Narrative," 73.

87. Phillipps, "Characters, Themes, and Narrative," 69.

88. Phillipps, "Characters, Themes, and Narrative," 69, 73.

89. Petersen, *Comics, Manga, and Graphic Novels*, 181.

90. Mizuki Takahashi, "Opening the Closed World of *Shōjo Manga*," in *Japanese Visual Culture: Explorations in the World of Manga and Anime*, ed. Mark W. MacWilliams (Armonk, NY: M. E. Sharpe, 2008), 127.

91. Takahashi, "Opening the Closed World."

92. Jennifer Prough, "Shōjo Manga in Japan and Abroad," in *Manga: An Anthology of Global and Cultural Perspectives*, ed. Toni Johnson-Woods (New York: Continuum, 2010), 94.

93. Prough, "Shōjo Manga," 94–95.

94. Prough, "Shōjo Manga," 95.

95. Prough, "Shōjo Manga," 95.

96. Prough, "Shōjo Manga," 95.

97. Prough, "Shōjo Manga," 95.

98. Takahashi, "Opening the Closed World," 130.

99. Takahashi, "Opening the Closed World," 130.

100. Prough, "Shōjo Manga," 95.

101. Takahashi, "Opening the Closed World," 130.

102. Takahashi, "Opening the Closed World," 130.

103. Takahashi, "Opening the Closed World," 130.

104. Takahashi, "Opening the Closed World," 131.

105. Schodt, *Manga! Manga!* 91.

106. Takahashi, "Opening the Closed World," 124.

107. Prough, "Shōjo Manga," 97.

108. Prough, "Shōjo Manga," 97.

109. Prough, "Shōjo Manga," 97.

110. Prough, "Shōjo Manga," 97.

111. CLAMP, *Chobits, Volume 5*. Los Angeles: Tokyopop, 2003, "CLAMP: About the Creators."

112. Charles Solomon, "Four Mothers of Manga Gain American Fans with Expertise in a Variety of Visual Styles," *New York Times*, November 28, 2006, accessed August 15, 2011, http://www.nytimes.com/2006/11/28/arts/design/28clam.html?8dpc.

113. Solomon, "Four Mothers."

114. Takahashi, "Opening the Closed World," 125.

115. Prough, "Shōjo Manga," 97.

116. J. D. Considine, "Manga Mania Comes to the West; Japanese Comics and Graphic Novels Are No Longer Just a Niche Market in North America— Manga Is Flooding into Bookstores Thanks to Girls' Buying Power," *Globe and Mail (Canada), The Globe Review*, July 17, 2003, R3.

117. Prough, "Shōjo Manga," 104.

118. Solomon, "Four Mothers."

119. Solomon, "Four Mothers."

120. Solomon, "Four Mothers."

121. Solomon, "Four Mothers."

122. Solomon, "Four Mothers."

123. Dorian Benkoil, "Move Over, Power Rangers; Here Comes Japan's Sailor Moon," *The Free Lance-Star*, February 18, 1995, Section E.

124. Benkoil, "Move Over."

125. Benkoil, "Move Over."

126. James Rampant, "The Manga Polysystem: What Fans Want, Fans Get," in *Manga: An Anthology of Global and Cultural Perspectives*, ed. Toni Johnson-Woods (New York: Continuum, 2010), 222.

127. Dirk Deppey, "She's Got Her Own Thing Now," *The Comics Journal*, no. 269 (July 2005): 10.

128. Maurice Horn, *Women in the Comics; Revised and Updated, Vol. 3* (Broomall: Chelsea House Publishers, 2001), 221.

129. N. C. Christopher Couch, "International Singularity in Sequential Art: The Graphic Novel in the United States, Europe, and Japan," in *Manga: An Anthology of Global and Cultural Perspectives*, ed. Toni Johnson-Woods (New York: Continuum, 2010), 213.

130. Couch, "International Singularity," 214.

131. Couch, "International Singularity," 213.

132. ICv2, "Tokyopop to Publish Manga in Japanese Format: Change Will Affect Publisher's Entire Line-up," January 30, 2002, accessed August 4, 2011, http://www.icv2.com/articles/news/1067.html.

133. ICv2, "Tokyopop."

134. Wendy Goldberg, "The Manga Phenomenon in America," in *Manga: An Anthology of Global and Cultural Perspectives*, ed. Toni Johnson-Woods (New York: Continuum, 2010), 287.

135. Goldberg, "Manga Phenomenon," 287.

136. Mio Bryce and Jason Davis, "An Overview of Manga Genres," in *Manga: An Anthology of Global and Cultural Perspectives*, ed. Toni Johnson-Woods (New York: Continuum, 2010), 36.

137. Ai Yazawa, *Nana, Vol. 1.* (San Francisco: Viz Media, 2005), 144–48.

138. Yazawa, *Nana*, 153.

139. Yazawa, *Nana*, 60.

140. Yazawa, *Nana*, 64.

141. Benkoil, "Move Over."

142. Qiuning Huang, interview by the author, June 25, 2011.

143. Rumiko Takahashi, *InuYasha, Vol. 1.*, 2nd ed. (San Francisco: Viz Media, 2005), 30.

144. Takahashi, *InuYasha*, 68.

145. Deb Aoki, "Interview: Bryan Lee O'Malley; Creator of Scott Pilgrim and Lost at Sea," About.com Manga, p. 1, accessed August 2, 2011, http://manga .about.com/od/mangaartistinterviews/a/Interview-Bryan-Lee-O-Amalley.htm.

146. Aoki, "Interview: Bryan Lee O'Malley," 2.

147. Aoki, "Interview: Bryan Lee O'Malley," 2.

148. Aoki, "Interview: Bryan Lee O'Malley," 2.

149. Hope Larson, "Introduction," in *The War at Ellsmere*, by Faith Erin Hicks (San Jose: SLG Publishing, 2008).

150. Hope Larson, email interview by author, July 28, 2011.

151. Larson interview.

152. Gabriel interview.

153. Gabriel interview.

154. Gabriel interview.

155. Gabriel interview.

156. Gabriel interview.

157. Gabriel interview.

158. Melek Ortabasi, "National History as Otaku Fantasy: Satoshi Kon's Millennium Actress," in *Japanese Visual Culture: Explorations in the World of Manga and Anime*, ed. Mark W. MacWilliams (Armonk, NY: M. E. Sharpe, 2008), 277–78.

159. Bouissou, "Historical Overview," 31.

160. Richard A. Gardner, "Aum Shinrikyō and a Panic about Manga and Anime," in *Japanese Visual Culture: Explorations in the World of Manga and Anime*, ed. Mark W. MacWilliams (Armonk, NY: M. E. Sharpe, 2008), 209–210.

161. Gabriel interview.

162. Gabriel interview.

163. Kai-Ming Cha, "Viz Media and Manga in the U.S.," accessed August 2, 2011, http://www.publishersweekly.com/pw/by-topic/new-titles/adult-announcements/article/3065-viz-media-and-manga-in-the-u-s-.html.

164. Calvin Reid, "Japanese Publishers Launch Jmanga.com Manga Portal at Comic-Con," *Publishers Weekly* (Digital), July 22, 2011, accessed August 2, 2011, http://www.publishersweekly.com/pw/by-topic/digital/content-and-e-books/article/48109-japanese-publishers-launch-jmanga-com-manga-portal-at-comic-con.html.

165. Heidi MacDonald, "Manga Pioneer Tokyopop Shuts Down U.S. Publishing," *Publishers Weekly* (Book News), April 15, 2011, accessed August 2, 2011,

http://www.publishersweekly.com/pw/by-topic/book-news/comics/article/46885-manga-pioneer-tokyopop-shuts-down-u-s-publishing.html.

166. Reid, "Japanese Publishers Launch Jmanga.com."
167. Petersen, *Comics, Manga, and Graphic Novels*, 185.
168. Gabriel interview.
169. Gabriel interview.
170. Huang interview.
171. Gabriel interview.
172. Petersen, *Comics, Manga, and Graphic Novels*, 185.
173. Gabriel interview.
174. Reid, "Japanese Publishers Launch Jmanga.com."
175. Reid, "Japanese Publishers Launch Jmanga.com."
176. Reid, "Japanese Publishers Launch Jmanga.com."
177. Reid, "Japanese Publishers Launch Jmanga.com."
178. Justin Azevedo, interview by author, July 23, 2011.
179. Azevedo interview.
180. Chelsea Couillard, interview by author, July 22, 2011.
181. Kai-Ming Cha, "Viz Media and Manga in the U.S."

GIRLS' COMICS TODAY
Different Formats, Expanding Readership

Comics specialty retail, in the majority a trade run by men, is no longer the only vendor of comics and graphic novels. Thanks in part to the popularity of manga, girls are now able to go into their local public libraries, as well as most bookstores, and be exposed to comics. The previous unavailability of comics outside of the comic book specialty shop may have prevented many female readers from exploring the art form in the past. Comic book specialty stores, most of which focus on mainstream superhero comics, have long catered more to the needs of male customers than female customers. When asked about how she feels about shopping in comic book stores, teenager Qiuning Huang remarked that she sometimes feels "out of place."[1] In addition, Huang mentioned that she also feels as though she has been treated differently because of her sex while shopping at comic book specialty stores and that she is more comfortable visiting the comics shop when accompanied by her male friends.[2]

However, not all comic book retailers create such a biased atmosphere, and many are highly aware of the way in which their store is arranged and managed—and how this affects female clientele. Jared Rudy of A-1 Comics in Sacramento, California, discusses his philosophy on how a comic book shop should serve its patrons. When asked about what his store does to encourage female readers and provide a comfortable, inclusive atmosphere, Rudy explains, "There is no designated section for men or women; we use the standard A-Z alphabet, and sections like trades, back issues, manga, and new comics, etc. I encourage all customers regardless of age, gender, or other factors to get interested in comics and related items. I approach them and ask if they need help, and if they are a little lost, I ask questions to help narrow things down so I can help them find what they want."[3] A-1 Comics and Rudy offer an exemplary model for how a comic book store should be managed, and there are plenty of comic book specialty shops like A-1 that strive to offer a neutral space for female customers, offering titles for all ages and genders. Nonetheless, comics specialty stores are still associated with maleness, for the time being at least. Now that manga has been introduced to bookstores and libraries, girls who do not shop at comic book stores will be exposed to these titles. Moreover, the manga boom has also strengthened interest in Western comics, particularly graphic novels.

However, the widespread consumption of manga is not the only reason why comics are enjoying a renaissance. Recently there has been a great output of film adaptations of comics and graphic novels. Not only are superhero comics enjoying a resurgence in popularity through the film industry, but independent comics are gaining exposure as well. The kids who grew up reading independent comics have become today's filmmakers, publishers, teachers, and librarians. As early as 2003, the late Will Eisner was quick to point out growth in the awareness of comics. In his introduction to Stephen Weiner's *Faster than a Speeding Bullet: The Rise of the Graphic Novel* (2003) Eisner explains,

> Superhero comics are mined by the motion picture industry for ideas, plots, and audiences. Motion picture adaptation of comics is now widespread. . . . Meanwhile, establishment bookstores are assigning shelf space for Pulitzer Prize and other award winners as well as serious graphic novels that address adults. The most significant evidence of comics' arrival, however, is their acceptance and acknowledgment by public librarians. The inclusion of graphic novels in their collections is a most welcome happening and, I might say, about time.[4]

The Validation of Comics through the Graphic Novel Format

Many bookstores and public libraries now contain graphic novels—and not just "serious" graphic novels aimed at an adult audience. All manner of graphic novels are now widely available for children and teens, as well as for adults, and in an array of subjects. Eisner was correct to assume that libraries that welcome the graphic novel are major contributors to a colossal change in how the field is perceived. When asked if he believes that comics and graphic novels can have equal weight (i.e., literary value) compared to conventional literature, teen services librarian Justin Azevedo replied:

> I absolutely feel that comics have equal literary weight to other sorts of books. This is especially true for young or reluctant readers; comics give these readers a taste of following character arcs and watching a story develop. I think that ascribing an arbitrary sense of literary worth to comics in general can be a tricky proposition. True, there is plenty of fluff to balance the notable "literary" graphic novels; but just as with conventional literature, that's a criticism of public taste rather than the medium itself.[5]

Youth services librarian Chelsea Couillard's comparison of comics to conventional literature is similar to Azevedo's. She explains:

> I think the only difference between graphic novels and traditional literature is the medium through which they tell the story. Graphic novels, by definition, use text and images to convey the story, but the story can have as much complexity and depth as any great piece of text, particularly if the artist/author is creative and truly uses the medium to its full advantage. Comics [serialized comic books] can work in the same way, though I tend to think of comics as shorter and more episodic and graphic novels as longer, stand-alone works of literature. That is how I differentiate the two. But the medium is essentially the same.[6]

More librarians, like Azevedo and Couillard, understand that comics have literary and artistic value equal to traditional books and welcome them in their libraries. Nonetheless, some misunderstandings about the art form still exist, even within librarianship. Couillard discusses this matter:

> I have never personally experienced a challenge to a children's or teen graphic novel. More often, I run into fellow professional librarians who are scared of graphic novels and so ill-informed about the medium and what is being published that they are afraid to purchase any for their collections. I think certain aspects of the professional discussion on the topic feed into this confusion because discussion of graphic novels so often includes discussion about challenges. Why does it have to be that way? As someone

who worked closely with an intellectual freedom information service during grad school, I can assure you that EVERYTHING gets challenged, including some of the most beloved and seemingly innocuous picture books of all time. I think we need to be more careful about characterizing graphic novels as more of a problem than traditional texts. They aren't, at least in my experience. We need to make sure our peers can learn more about them without feeling as if they are entering into something dangerous.[7]

While considering graphic novels, especially those aimed at teens, some adults are uncomfortable with visual representations of certain subject matters. Parents sometimes feel comfortable with their teens reading traditional novels dealing with such issues as sexuality but turn squeamish when faced with those same topics in a visual medium. Azevedo recalls only one instance in his career where a graphic novel was challenged, and it was because of a "sexually suggestive panel."[8] This particular book was an adult graphic novel that Azevedo explains had been "mistakenly placed in the teen area, making us culpable for the issue and bringing to light the problems that arise when people assume that all comics are for young readers."[9] Azevedo adds, "That being said, I found it interesting that the challenge concerned a sex scene with no actual nudity depicted, whereas nothing at all was said about the graphic violence found elsewhere in the book."[10] The implications about what this incident says about our culture aside, there seems to be a great distinction between content that can be read, silently, and the visual representation of similar content. Couillard comments on this phenomenon and offers a rational response to those who are nervous about exposing teens to explicit material in graphic form:

Textual literature for teens can be very explicit, but I know many people argue that it is different when the content is visual. I don't necessarily disagree with that, but I don't think we can deny that sexuality and violence exist in the lives of many teens, and even those who are sheltered have questions that good literature can help answer. If a graphic novel is focused on a teen and a teen's experiences, if it is well-written and thoughtful and authentic and isn't using the graphic medium for exploitation, then I can't justify keeping it out of a teen collection simply because someone might find it offensive. Not every book is for every reader, particularly in a teen collection that spans 6–12 grades, and that is as true of graphic novels as it is of traditional texts.[11]

It is important to remember that young adults have a need for literature in which they can see their problems and their particular state in life represented. Many graphic novels are well written, are of high quality, and fulfill these needs, and teens should not be denied access to this type of literature. As Couillard says, even the most benign literature can be challenged, therefore, librarians must not allow their fears of the comics medium to deter them from acquiring graphic novels for their libraries' collections and upholding intellectual freedom.

Couillard notes that graphic novels appear to be increasingly popular among the younger set. While teens seem to check out more manga, tweens and even younger children tend to be drawn to Western comics. She explains,

> I think the interest in graphic novels for preteens, elementary schoolers, and even early readers has increased exponentially in the past five years. There are many more high-quality titles out there on a variety of subjects and for very different audiences. It's not just a teen/adult thing anymore. Younger kids see teens reading graphic novels and want to pick them up themselves.[12]

Couillard also observes what appears to be an increase in literary Western comics for young adults:

> The variety of [Western graphic novel] titles has increased. While non-manga titles for teens don't circulate as much as manga titles, there have been a number of wonderful graphic novels for teens in the past five years on very diverse and complex topics such as cultural identity, the Holocaust, racial identity, sexual identity, and fencing! They aren't as mainstream, but for a certain audience, they have an important place, and they demonstrate that graphic novels can be a medium through which to tell powerful and relevant contemporary stories.[13]

The opinions of librarians like Azevedo and Couillard mark a definite shift in attitude toward comics. Moreover, librarians realize the importance of cultivating a collection and an atmosphere that attracts readers of either sex. Azevedo comments: "Having grown up in comic shops myself, I too can attest to them having a bit of a 'boys' club' feel, at least back then. I am very proud of the fact that the library is as welcoming to comic-reading girls as it is to boys."[14]

Librarians are in a special position to offer a gender-neutral space where young people are able to explore comics that they might not have had exposure to otherwise, because of a reluctance to visit specialty stores. Couillard was asked if awareness of this issue has a hand in guiding her collection development—for example, if she collects specifically female-oriented titles to attract girls. She replied,

> I do think that I am keenly aware of finding those graphic novels that would appeal to girls. But that carries into every aspect of my collection development. I'm always trying to make sure I have enough traditional fiction that will appeal to boys and enough graphic novels that will appeal to girls.[15]

Providing a venue in which girls can comfortably explore graphic novels fills a void for girls in numerous communities, and many librarians like Azevedo and Couillard are dedicated to providing a well-rounded collection to do just that.

What Is a Graphic Novel? Taking a Step Back through History

While it is the involvement of libraries that has the power to bring comics to the attention of those who would not normally encounter them, it is the graphic novel format that has made comics more accessible for librarians to acquire for their collections and for booksellers to add to their shelves. Will Eisner defines graphic novels as "book-length comic books that are meant to be read as one story."[16] Eisner was at the genesis of what we commonly refer to as the graphic novel today. Although there are many examples of early graphic novels, the gravity and success of Eisner's *A Contract with God and Other Tenement Stories* (1978) popularized the term.

Earlier in his career, Eisner helped open up the comics field to original and inspired themes fraught with the reality of an adult world. Weiner points out that comics have long been considered a children's format: "Newspaper comic strips were always recognized as something read by everyone, but from the beginnings of the new medium, comic books were perceived as a format for children."[17] Contrary to this notion, Eisner's vision was to create comics that were both mature and complex works of art. As an example of Eisner's progressive attitude toward comics, Scott McCloud writes, "Around 1940, Will Eisner . . . gave an interview to the *Baltimore Sun* in which he proposed that comics were a legitimate *literary* and *artistic* form."[18] Eisner wrote challenging stories with complicated heroes such as "The Spirit" (*The Spirit*, 1940–1952) who dealt with the realities of adult life as well as the role of a mysterious crime fighter. However, it wasn't until the late 1970s that Eisner would create *A Contract with God and Other Tenement Stories* that his artistic and literary goals as a cartoonist would be fully realized. Artistically, *A Contract with God* broke away from the typical comics form of regular panels, at times doing away with frames altogether, as well as utilizing montage, full-page images, and close-ups. With its gritty tales of 1930s Bronx tenement life in a predominantly Jewish community, in addition to its artistic originality, Eisner's first graphic novel would blaze a trail for future cartoonists.

The timing was right. Eisner's graphic novel was an indirect result of the enforcement of the Comics Code. The graphic novel emerged after a time of great upheaval in the comics industry. The horror comics panic, spearheaded by Wertham, had done much to mar the reputation of comics, yet the creation of the Comics Code instigated some changes that may be viewed in a positive light. Weiner states:

> The boom in sales in crime and horror comics in the 1950s had led to the publication of a lot of sensationalistic material that was produced hurriedly and with little care. The quality of comic book product rose once the sensationalistic stories that flooded much of the comic book market had been minimized. Comic book publishers tried their hand at different genres whose stories could entertain within the confines of the regulations imposed by the Comics Code.[19]

According to Nyberg, "the Comics Code demanded that 'all comic books that wished to carry the seal [of approval] had to be suitable for the child reader.'"[20] The Code prohibited references to crime, horror, nudity, and gratuitous slang; practically anything that preached values outside of the conservative mainstream was banned. The restrictive nature of the Comics Code forced the hand of comic book artists and writers into creating comics that had "lost their social relevance."[21] However, this did not quell the interest in and the production of comics but rather caused the field to reinvent itself. In Nyberg's article, Roger Sabin is quoted as saying "the code left the way open for juvenile and teen-oriented material to flourish."[22] Not only did children's comics explode, but in the 1960s the superhero genre also grew within the constraints of the Comics Code. Stan Lee is credited with creating the new superhero, one that is more human. Lee envisioned an imperfect superhero who has to deal with the day-to-day problems of his own humanity in addition to thwarting evildoers.[23] The revitalization of the superhero was a great success and fomented the organization of the first comic book conventions. Weiner explains,

> Comic book conventions and fanzines assured comic book readers that Dr. Wertham had been wrong; they weren't delinquents or crazy; in fact, several of them had gone on to achieve success in real life, but they still liked comic books.[24]

The fans of comics' first days had grown up, and a fandom was born.

In addition to the dawning of comic book conventions, another important factor in comic book culture developed: the specialty shop. The success of the comic book conventions made it obvious that there was a market in comic book retail ready to be tapped.[25] Prior to the advent of the specialty shop, comics were typically sold in newsstands or in spinner racks in drugstores; but, as Weiner writes, "entrepreneurs saw that by going directly to the readers, a profit could be made."[26] Along with the ideas gleaned from the fan conventions, the sale of *comix* in head shops helped encourage the creation of the comic book specialty shop.[27]

As previously discussed, the 1960s ushered in the underground comix movement. In rebellion against the Comics Code, these comics featured fresh ideas, often politically charged. Weiner states, "The undergrounds were comic books written and drawn by young adults for their peers. . . . They were totally and intentionally opposed in every way to the standards set by the Comics Code."[28] Comix sprang up in counterculture shops, coinciding with the "hippie" movement—R. Crumb's *Zap Comix* being an iconic example of this new development.

This newfound freedom of structure and expression was taken up by pioneers like Eisner and what occurred was a field enriched by new ways of using the comics art form. After *The Spirit* ended its run in 1952, Eisner focused on an enterprise creating instructional comics for businesses and for the military.[29] However, Eisner's earlier work, particularly *The Spirit*, continued to be lauded by the growing fan culture. A turning point in Eisner's career occurred in 1971 when a man named Phil Seuling, who helped cultivate the direct market approach to selling comics (which led to the creation of the comic book specialty store),[30] asked Eisner to be a guest at a New York comics convention.[31] Here, Eisner met Art Spiegelman (who would go on to found *RAW* and would also find major acclaim with his Pulitzer-winning *Maus*) and Denis Kitchen (founder of Kitchen Sink Press as well as the Comic Book Legal Defense Fund) and was exposed to the fresh and gritty new perspectives of underground comics.[32] According to Weiner,

> The environment inspired Eisner: here were young cartoonists using the comics medium in the ways that he'd always hoped it could be used, as a vehicle for personal and political statements rather than as a medium restricted to regurgitated genre stories. . . . Inspired by the innovation of the underground cartoonists, Eisner said he was intent on pushing the form "into areas that had not been done before."[33]

Eisner was so impressed by what he had seen that he divested himself of the educational comics company[34] and refocused his efforts on pioneering a new type of comics narrative—what would become *A Contract with God and Other Tenement Stories*.

The introduction of the graphic novel was groundbreaking because it allowed comics to expand the art form in new directions, and the book format also made it easier for a broader section of the population to discover. Furthermore, modern graphic novels have come directly out of the form-bending tradition of underground comics. The underground had clearly risen up to the mainstream of literature, carrying with it a potential to explore narrative in a different form from the typical novel.

Marketing Comics as Literature

Traditionally, comics in America have been used as the scapegoat for societal maladies like youth crime. As seen in chapter 1, the modern distaste for comics owes much to these moral panics and to a bias against working-class fiction as a whole. However, the comic book is an ever-changing art form that continually pushes boundaries and explores new modes of expression, and in recent decades the popular opinion of the graphic novel has begun to change. The graphic novel has garnered much critical acclaim, due in part to the cachet of its book format, the generally higher standard of quality of the output, and its greater accessibility. As Michaels points out,

> Single-issue comic books, usually about twenty or fifty pages long, were for years the primary format for American comics. Released monthly on cheap, flimsy paper with poor image and colour quality, they are still mostly sold in comic and hobby shops, meaning that people outside the comic book subculture don't tend to run across them.[35]

Michaels goes on to talk about how the graphic novel has changed all of this. With graphic novels, the quality of production is better, they are more widely distributed, and "[t]hey also afford much greater durability. . . . In addition, graphic novels are often released by mainstream publishers, and have ISBNs, making it easier for 'regular' bookstores and libraries to order them."[36] Therefore, a wider section of the population is gaining access to these works. Robbins comments that it is indeed graphic novels that are drawing girls into the field of comics:

> Comics, although no longer cheap, are still flimsy, and the majority of them are superhero comics, read mostly by boys. Enter graphic novels— comics with a difference—printed on heavy stock and sturdy enough to stand on a shelf alongside YA and children's books. Some of these are tailor made for girls, with young female protagonists. Many are created by women and published by independent presses.[37]

The graphic novel is a format that serves as a bridge extended from the specialty market and the underground toward those who would have not encountered them before, including girls. Libraries and bookstores are beginning to offer this exposure, because there is now no denying that comics have made a major contribution not only to literacy but to those vessels of human experience, the arts and humanities. Wilkins writes:

> Despite my lengthy defense of the graphic novel in terms of its value for librarians, graphic novels do not require a defensive attitude. . . . There is now a wealth of material of genuine quality which fully justifies a place on our shelves in its own right, without consideration to where they may lead in terms of personal reading development.[38]

The literary and cultural complexity of graphic novels and the value of the stories that they tell are apparent in Spiegelman's Maus series, Joe Sacco's *Palestine* (1993), and Marjane Satrapi's *Persepolis* (2003) and *Persepolis 2* (2004). What Will Eisner started with *A Contract with God and Other Tenement Stories* is having an effect on the way comics are viewed in American culture, and this may have a powerful impact on female readers as they are finally being reached by the medium in the form of the graphic novel and its placement in bookstores and public libraries. Recent graphic novel adaptations of popular young adult books, such as Neil Gaiman's *Coraline* (illustrated by P. Craig Russell) or Stephenie Meyer's *Twilight* (illustrated by Young Kim), and the addition of the graphic novel *Black Is for Beginnings* to Laurie Faria Stolarz's text series *Blue Is for Nightmares* is only more proof that graphic novels are expanding their female readership.

New Heroes: The Maturation of the Female Role in Comics

It is obvious that the roles of females in comics are changing. Betty and Veronica have given way to the more realistic takes on the lives of teenage girls represented in Clowes's *Ghost World* and Tomine's *Optic Nerve*. These teens are fleshed out so well that the reader has the sensation of staring through the keyhole at adolescence at its most awkward moments. Comics are also moving beyond the body-objectifying portrayals of the female superheroes of the past. Naifeh's *Courtney Crumrin* balances the lessons of growing up with displaying the power one little girl can hold, turning the tables on a patriarchal society that expects female children to be complacent and meek yet rewards male children who display boldness and tenacity. All of these different comics bear literary value and significance for the female reader as they are both insightful and empowering portrayals of females.

Persepolis: The Story of a Childhood is an autobiographical account of Satrapi's own girlhood during the political and religious upheaval of the Islamic Revolution in Iran. The graphic novel begins its chronicle of Satrapi's youth in 1980, when she is ten years old, through her early teens when she is sent away from the chaos of the revolution to Austria. Satrapi visually examines what it is to be a child living in a time that is changing, a time of increasing oppression for liberal Iranians and especially for females. When she is ten years old, her school insists on the wearing of the veil. Satrapi makes it very clear that these are average children dealing with a situation that they do not understand as political unrest boils in their country.[39] This panel shown in figure 5.1 depicts the children joining in various games that they have invented with the veil; some skipping rope with it, some "playing horse" with the garment used as reins, while the text states, "We didn't really like to wear the veil, especially since we didn't understand why we had to."[40] Here, Satrapi combines text and image to form a complementary narrative exploring the children's reaction to wearing the garment.

The young Marjane grew up in a modern, liberal family whose peace was shattered by the Islamic Revolution. Satrapi does an excellent job of conveying the mixed reactions to the politics of this time. Figure 5.2

Figure 5.1. *Persepolis: The Story of a Childhood*, 2003, page 3. **The children, unaccustomed to wearing the veil, devise inventive games with the garment instead of wearing it, while in the background two girls enact a political scene, showing that children are aware of what is happening in the world around them, even if they don't fully understand what is going on.**
From *Persepolis: The Story of a Childhood* by Marjane Satrapi, translated by Mattias Ripa and Blake Ferris, translation copyright © 2003 by L'Association, Paris, France. Used by permission of Pantheon Books, a division of Random House, Inc.

Figure 5.2. *Persepolis: The Story of a Childhood*, 2003, page 6. Marjane is caught between tradition and modernity.

From *Persepolis: The Story of a Childhood* by Marjane Satrapi, translated by Mattias Ripa and Blake Ferris, translation copyright © 2003 by L'Association, Paris, France. Used by permission of Pantheon Books, a division of Random House, Inc.

shows Marjane's reaction: "I really didn't know what to think about the veil. Deep down I was very religious but as a family we were very modern and avant-garde."[41] This statement is underscored by the image of the young, unsmiling Marjane, literally bisected by the two influences of her cultural background—the modern, represented by the gears and tools of an age influenced by industry, on which side her dress is liberal and her head bare, and the other side defined by the icon of latticework associated with tradition. This half of Marjane is clad in the conservative veil. Inside, little Marji (as she is nicknamed) wants to be a prophet. She has conversations with God that are handled with both sensitivity and humor. Yet Satrapi goes on to explore how a child's beliefs can be shaken in a world that does not always make sense. She eventually embraces Marxism (which she learns all about from a comic book called "Dialectic Materialism") as a substitute for religion. Marji feels a great pull toward demonstrating against the Islamic extremist regime, and God symbolically walks out of the door at this point in Marji's life (fig. 5.3), suggesting that she has embraced a political ideology (her modern side) over religion (the side of Marji that has always felt a spiritual connection associated with tradition). This also may be read as Marji's innocence falling away in the wake of the political upheaval; the simplicity of her trust in God is replaced by the desire for meaning that she finds in Marxism.

Through the juxtaposition of a relatively straightforward textual narrative with images of political uprising and its effects, Satrapi is able to balance the voice of a child with the visual representations' grisly realities (fig. 5.4). However, over the course of this graphic novel, not only is the reader witness to an account of history that does not censor violence and death, but also the reader is treated to the celebration of the life of a young girl, who through all this strife still manages to grow up and enjoy what she can of childhood. *Persepolis* is an important graphic novel for young females, because it is based on the true story of a successful female growing up against a backdrop of crisis in the history of Iran. Most importantly, this work values a young girl for being her own hero, providing a fresh cultural perspective on the lives of marginalized young women in the Middle East.

In her introduction to the graphic novel, Satrapi states of her mother country:

> This old and great civilization has been discussed mostly in connection with fundamentalism, fanaticism, and terrorism. As an Iranian who has lived more than half of my life in Iran, I know that this image is far from the truth. This is why writing *Persepolis* was so important to me. I believe that an entire nation should not be judged by the wrongdoings of a few extremists.[42]

The historical context and brutal realism of *Persepolis* can be closely compared to Spiegelman's *Maus*, but *Persepolis* is an important graphic novel not only because of the history it relates but because it represents the voice of a young girl from a culture that may often be misunderstood in America

Figure 5.3. *Persepolis: The Story of a Childhood*, 2003, page 16.
From *Persepolis: The Story of a Childhood* by Marjane Satrapi, translated by Mattias Ripa and Blake Ferris, translation copyright © 2003 by L'Association, Paris, France. Used by permission of Pantheon Books, a division of Random House, Inc.

Figure 5.4. *Persepolis: The Story of a Childhood*, **2003, page 18.**
From *Persepolis: The Story of a Childhood* by Marjane Satrapi, translated by Mattias Ripa and Blake Ferris, translation copyright © 2003 by L'Association, Paris, France. Used by permission of Pantheon Books, a division of Random House, Inc.

today. The fact that it is an *autobiographical* work written by a female and told through the eyes of her child-self imbues this graphic novel with an undeniable reality that the young reader can relate to. What Marji does not witness firsthand, she cannot help imagining, which Satrapi depicts through the visual narrative (see fig. 5.5 for an example). Panel 2 shows Marji listening in on her parents' conversation about the Shah's men burning down a cinema full of people. Panels 3 through 8 contain a caption functioning as a "voice-over" relating the event. This may be the adult Marjane's narrative or her parents', but it is obvious that the illustrations represent Marjane's imagining of the tragedy.

As she grows into a young teenager, Marjane's nearly constant exposure to injustice and violence only fuels her defiant attitude toward the fundamentalist regime. However, one incident in particular emboldens her. One Saturday afternoon when she is out shopping with a friend, Marjane hears an explosion. Soon, a store radio announces that a missile has just exploded in her neighborhood. Marjane quickly runs home, fearing what she might discover there. Once she arrives near her house, a bystander informs her that one of the buildings at the end of the street was hit. Only two buildings were at the end of the street: Marjane's home and that of her neighbors the Baba-Levys, who have a daughter close to Marjane's age whom she enjoyed visiting from time to time.[43] Marjane pushes through the crowd to get to her house and, much to her relief, finds her mother running toward her. Her family is safe. However, the Baba-Levys were not so lucky. Their home had been razed to the ground. When Marjane comments, "At least they weren't home!"[44] her mother appears troubled. She explains that it was Shabbat, the Jewish Sabbath, and the Baba-Levys, being Jewish, might have been at home.[45] However, Marjane's mother quickly suggests that the Baba-Levys weren't particularly observant and that they were most likely away that day, and she hastily changes the subject.[46]

As Marjane's mother takes her by the hand and guides her back home, Marjane notices something sticking out of the rubble of the house next door. The next few panels lack any spoken dialog, but Marjane's narration explains, "I saw a turquoise bracelet. It was Neda's. Her aunt had given it to her for her fourteenth birthday . . ."[47] The next panel shows Marjane with her hand covering her mouth in shock. She narrates: "The bracelet was attached to . . . I don't know what . . ."[48] The following panel displays Marjane with her hands covering her eyes, and her mouth a wavering line. There are no words. The subsequent panel is completely black, save for the caption that reads: "No scream in the world could have relieved my suffering and my anger."[49] From that moment forward, Marjane becomes actively seditious toward figures of authority that support the current regime. She explains, "After the death of Neda Baba-Levy, my life took a new turn. In 1984, I was fourteen and a rebel. Nothing scared me anymore."[50]

Persepolis 2: The Story of a Return picks up where *Persepolis* leaves off. After continued bombing incidents and Marji's continued run-ins with authority figures, her parents, fearing that her spirited behavior could get her killed, decide to send her to live in Vienna. The night before she is to

Figure 5.5a. *Persepolis: The Story of a Childhood*, 2003, page 14. **Marji overhears her parents talking about the atrocity. The images represent her imaginings of these frightening events.**
From *Persepolis: The Story of a Childhood* by Marjane Satrapi, translated by Mattias Ripa and Blake Ferris, translation copyright © 2003 by L'Association, Paris, France. Used by permission of Pantheon Books, a division of Random House, Inc.

depart for Austria, Marji's grandmother spends the night and gives her advice that will serve as an important guide in the coming years, a theme that features heavily in the second volume. She advises, "Always keep your dignity and be true to yourself."[51] As she prepares to leave, Marji's family assure her that they will come to see her, but the second volume reveals that she wouldn't see her mother again for nineteen months.[52]

Figure 5.5b. *Persepolis*, 2003, page 15.

Persepolis 2 follows Marjane through a painful period of adjustment as she struggles to maintain her sense of identity in a country where her peers have never known violence and persecution and where she herself feels the bitterness of prejudice. After the Mother Superior at the boarding house where Marjane is living insults her ("It's true what they say about Iranians. They have no education"), the feisty teenager lashes out verbally and is kicked out of her lodgings.[53] From that point on there is little stability in Marjane's life. At first, Marjane tries to fit in and assimilate into Viennese society, but in doing so she betrays herself. Marjane explains, "The harder

I tried to assimilate, the more I had the feeling that I was distancing myself from my culture, betraying my parents and my origins, that I was playing a game by somebody else's rules."[54]

Marjane cuts her hair and spikes it, adopting the punk style of her newly found friends, and even pretends to smoke joints to gain their approval. Outwardly, Marjane appears to have a blossoming social life, but on the inside, she feels isolated and ashamed of herself. She begins to feel guilty when she talks to her parents on the telephone and avoids any mention of the strife in Iran on the news.[55] She explains, "I felt so guilty that whenever there was news about Iran, I changed the channel. It was too unbearable."[56] When an acquaintance asks her if she is worried about what is going on in her homeland, Marjane replies, "No, it's okay! I talked to my parents. They're fine."[57] In the same panel, the captioned narrative reads: "I was lying. I knew nothing and I didn't want to know more."[58] In the subsequent panel, Marjane continues, "I wanted to forget everything, to make my past disappear, but my unconscious caught up with me."[59] This panel displays Marjane asleep in her bed as images from Iran—happy memories, sad ones, as well as those that are frightening—float above her, haunting her dreams. Though she tries to avoid her connection to Iran, her unconscious mind will not let her forget who she is. Nevertheless, in her waking hours, Marjane attempts to distance herself further from her past. While at a party thrown at her school, Marjane tries to pass herself off as French to a boy named Marc who appears interested in her. In her shame, Marjane comments, "I even managed to deny my nationality . . . and when I got back that night, I remembered that line my grandmother told me: 'Always keep your dignity and be true to yourself!'"[60]

One of the greatest turning points in the story occurs a few days after this incident. While at a café, Marjane overhears Marc's sister, Anna, and her clique talking about her in the next booth over. The group calls her a liar for saying that she is French, and they also insult her looks. One of the girls says, "I don't know if you've noticed, but she never talks about either her country or her parents," to which Anna replies, "Well, of course! She lies when she says that she's known war. It's all to make herself seem interesting."[61] The next panel shows a close-up of Marjane; her shoulders are hunched up around her ears, her brows set at sharp angle, and steam is shown spewing from her nostrils as she fumes in an exaggeration of the fury that is welling up inside of her. A speech balloon emanates from the right hand side of the panel, as an unseen commenter states, "Anyway, her parents clearly don't care about her, or they wouldn't have sent her alone."[62]

The irony of this statement and its hurtfulness overwhelms Marjane. In the caption at the bottom of this panel, she narrates, "That was too much, I saw red."[63] In the panel that follows, an incensed Marjane reveals herself to the gossips and says, "You are going to shut up or I am going to make you! I am Iranian and proud of it!"[64] She then flees the café and bursts into tears. Once she has left the café and has calmed down, she makes an important realization: she had just stood up for herself and her culture, regaining the dignity her grandmother had tried to instill in her. She comments, "I had nothing to cry about. / I had just redeemed myself. / For the first time in a year, I felt proud. I finally understood what my grandmother meant. If I wasn't comfortable with myself, I would never be comfortable."[65] A smile plays across Marjane's face in this last panel, as she begins to comprehend this personal triumph.

The rest of the graphic novel details Marjane's teenage years, her eventual return to Iran, and her transition into womanhood. However, the vignette at the café is one of *Persepolis 2*'s most salient moments, especially for a teenage readership. At this point in the graphic novel, Marjane learns to value herself. Most teenagers go through a period in which they are developing a sense of self, and this is often a turbulent experience. Marjane's tribulations and triumph in accepting herself should resonate with adolescents as well as adults.

Satrapi could have written a traditional autobiography. However, the graphic format lends something to the story that words alone could not capture. In fact, Satrapi's artistic style is so essential to the telling of this story that the animated film adaptation (which encompasses both volumes of *Persepolis*) retains the bold black and white cartooning technique found in the books. Satrapi agreed to the film adaptation of her autobiographical comics, but she "demanded full creative control" over the project.[66] Consequently, the adaptation process has not weakened the storytelling. Chute describes the importance of preserving the artist's original style:

> Satrapi's insistence that the film version resemble the book so closely points up just how crucial the question of style in the book really is. Both the film and the book do the work of witnessing by visually approaching trauma through the abstraction provided by minimalist black-and-white, hand-drawn lines.[67]

This film would not have had the same visual impact if it had been rendered in full-color animation or if it had been portrayed by live actors—changes such as these would have only diminished the story. Chute comments on the fidelity to Satrapi's original work:

> She insisted on an artisanal mode of production, so her team of roughly one hundred, working in Paris, hand-traced images on paper—an art that has long been obsolete in animation, replaced by computer technology. . . . She also insisted—as for the graphic narrative—on black and white, a rarity for contemporary animated films.[68]

The result is a striking film that tells the author's story from her point of view, without distorting it beyond recognition. The filmmaker's attention to detail confirms that Satrapi's story of atrocity, difference, and courage during a (sometimes shaky) coming of age could not be properly expressed without the acuity of her dramatically poignant visual style.

Similarly, Brian Talbot's *The Tale of One Bad Rat* (1994, 1995) deals with the subject of childhood sexual abuse and incest from a child's viewpoint. This may seem like a controversial subject for a graphic novel that may reach young readers, but there are plenty of books *without* images that tackle the subject within the broader field of children's literature, such as *I Was a Teenage Fairy* (1998) by Francesca Lia Block (which received ALA recognition) and Anne Provoost's award-winning book *My Aunt Is a Pilot Whale* (1994). The comic format, however, is able to deal with the matter visually, allowing the silenced victim a voice of her own through the visual narrative. Allwood asserts that "the main problem with incest . . . is silence: On the one hand the silence resulting from the hypocrisy surrounding all violence in the family, and on the other hand the silence of the survivors. Not only does the survivor's silence contribute to the invisibility of incest, but it is often also interpreted as a form of consent."[69]

The Tale of One Bad Rat addresses the silence of the victim through the use of images, which allows the survivor's story to be told without the need for verbal confession. Although the images are disturbing, Talbot always represents the situation tastefully and with respect for victims of abuse. He employs text as well as the manipulation of perspective (such as the "head shot" when portraying moments of abuse), keeping more explicit details "off screen." Talbot illustrates the abuser, Helen's father, and references to the abuse using red hues. The "flashback scenes" that refer to the abuse display this color, as do scenes that indirectly recall the abuse—for example, when Helen, the survivor, posts a letter to her father and mother near the end of the graphic novel in the chapter titled "Country." Only her hand is shown depositing the envelope into a bright red postbox. The utilization of red suggests a highly emotional state associated with anger, violence, and sexuality. Figure 5.6 (panels 1–6) features Helen's father washed in shades of red, turning into a darker and deeper hue as the panels cinematically "zoom" in on his face which seems to take on an increasingly villainous glare as the reader is confronted with Helen's father. The red used in these

Figure 5.6. *The Tale of One Bad Rat*, 1995, panels 1–6. Helen's father is featured in red hues, evoking the memory of the abuse.
The Tale of One Bad Rat™ © 2012 Bryan Talbot.

panels is also suggestive of devilishness as he throws Helen in the midst of a psychological battle causing her to confuse sexual favor with paternal love. This is Helen's perspective, and the reader is allowed to look directly into his face as it looms "closely," becoming more menacing. There is the glow of inferno in the abuser's eye, offsetting the darkness in his pupil, making him seem evil and almost supernaturally powerful.

The story is not a sensationalistic account of sexual abuse. It is a complicated story about a girl who is much more than a victim; she is a person, a blossoming young woman and artist. The protagonist, Helen Potter, has an affinity with the children's author and artist of a similar name, Helen Beatrix Potter. Helen clings to the innocence of her younger days with her Potter books, taking them with her when she runs away from home. The dream of following in the footsteps of that other Potter that is integral to Helen's self-liberation, as she follows her instincts to the home of Beatrix Potter in England's Lake District. Beatrix Potter escaped from a claustrophobic home life in London to great freedom and autonomy in the Lake District, which Helen comments on in figure 5.7. It is obvious from these panels that it is Helen's fondest wish to escape her bonds, as did her hero, and eventually she succeeds.

Talbot uses the image of the rat as a metaphor for the stigma that sexual abuse imprints on its survivors. Rats are often feared for their role in the black death and their uncanny ability to adapt to human communities. But rats are also intelligent and resourceful, and, most importantly, they are *survivors*. Victims of sexual abuse often feel, or are made to feel by their abusers, as if they are bad and that it is their fault that the abuse occurred. Talbot draws parallels to the misunderstood rat and how victims of sexual abuse are misunderstood in society. The rat also functions as an alternative narrative. Helen uses her relationship with her pet rat as a way of communicating her inner feelings and as a way of escaping into herself. Moreover, her discussions with her rat, even after its death, act as an interior dialog, as seen in figure 5.7 when she discusses Beatrix Potter, revealing her desire for the liberation and success that her hero had achieved. There are many narrative threads and strategies at work representing the voice of Helen in *The Tale of One Bad Rat*. This is an example of Bakhtin's notion of polyphony as explained by McCallum:

> By making the "speaking person" a condition of the novel, Bakhtin defines the novel as an inherently dialogic, or "polyphonic" form, which is

Figure 5.7. *The Tale of One Bad Rat*, 1995, panels 1–4. Talking to her dead rat, Helen discusses Beatrix Potter's escape from oppression. This functions as an interior dialog that has been exteriorized.

The Tale of One Bad Rat™ © 2012 Bryan Talbot.

characterized by: (1) the variety and range of narrative strategies used to represent the discourse (speech, thoughts and "language world views") of others; (2) its capacity to appropriate and represent a multiplicity of social and ideological discourses and viewpoints; and (3) its capacity to represent characters and narrators as speakers and as subjects.[70]

The Tale of One Bad Rat fits Bakhtin's description of the novel, only it does so partly in visual form. It is this multilayering of dialog through the different visual and textual narratives that defines Talbot's work as a complex graphic novel. At the end of *One Bad Rat*, Helen has worked through much of her anger and self-hatred surrounding the abuse. Like Beatrix Potter, she has escaped a caged life, which is summarized by the fantasy of finding the manuscript for "The Tale of One Bad Rat" (fig. 5.8). This also functions as an intertextual play on Beatrix Potter's *The Tale of Two Bad Mice* (1904), in which two rodents invade and ransack a dolls' house. In this story, the "bad" mice disrupt the silence and paralysis of the dolls that live inside, filling the house with life where there was a deathly stillness before. This parallels Helen's own escape from the silence of guilt through her personal journey in finding her voice, literally and artistically, as the manuscript encapsulates the story of Helen's abuse and her triumph over adversity (see fig. 5.9), setting her free to purge her demons through her artistic talent.

Talbot's *The Tale of One Bad Rat* exemplifies a tough subject matter handled artfully through the graphic novel medium. Even though it tackles a controversial topic, it's an issue that many girls have to face and

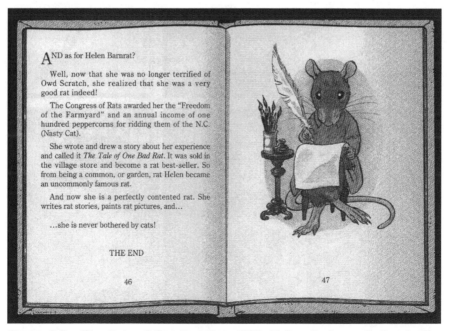

Figure 5.8. *The Tale of One Bad Rat,* **1995. Helen finds resolution in the imagining of "A Tale of One Bad Rat" (an intertextual reference to Potter's** *The Tale of Two Bad Mice***).**
The Tale of One Bad Rat™ © 2012 Bryan Talbot.

Figure 5.9. *The Tale of One Bad Rat*, 1995.
The Tale of One Bad Rat™ © 2012 Bryan Talbot.

suggests that there is hope in speaking out. For readers who have not experienced abuse, it makes young readers aware of the problems that incest survivors face. Regardless of whether or not the reader has experienced abuse, through the polyphony of the graphic novel format and the ability of images to speak without words, this graphic novel aids in breaking the cycle of silence.

Often, the *length* of the graphic novel affords a depth comparable to the prose novel, such as Satrapi's and Talbot's works. However, there are also plenty of serialized comic books (as well as some comic strips) that have great narrative depth. Sometimes, these are collated and reprinted as *trade paperbacks*, a term borrowed from the publishing world to distinguish these large-format paperbacks from the smaller mass-market editions. But the term also refers simply to comic books or strips that are collected and bound into paperback form. ("Trade paperback" is sometimes used, erroneously, as a term that is interchangeable with "graphic novel.") The collection of serialized comics into a book format makes these comics available to a wider market—one that includes more girls.

Beyond Graphic Novels: The Digital Age of Comics Has Arrived

In addition to the widening availability of graphic novels and trade paperbacks in bookstores and in libraries, digital media have also expanded; comics are now reaching readers through such innovations as webcomics and e-readers. Media and technology have pushed the boundaries of comics as an art form exponentially within a relatively small amount of time. One of the earliest explorations of digital media was found in *The Complete Maus* (1994)—a CD-ROM containing Spiegelman's original comics along with in-depth historical information as well as biographical information that contributed to the creation of the graphic novels.[71] Unfortunately, this early form of digital comics was imperfect; the digital format of the "page" was unwieldy, and viewing the content of the CD-ROM was limited by the speed of the machine it was being viewed upon.[72] Interestingly, it appears that some of the concepts explored through *The Complete Maus* CD-ROM have been updated to be included in the supplemental DVD for the new book *Meta Maus* (2011), a sort of "making-of" companion to the graphic novels.

In 2000, Scott McCloud not only discussed the shortcomings of the CD-ROM format[73] but predicted a future of "digital delivery" (or online distribution)—which he defines as "comics that travel as *pure information* from *producer* to *reader*"—in his book *Reinventing Comics*. McCloud accurately described what has now occurred: "as the *quantity* of bandwidth *increases*—vast *qualitative* changes may render the Web a very *different place* in a very *short time*."[74] When McCloud wrote this, the concept of webcomics was still in its infancy. McCloud explains, "a *small* but *growing* number of artists are creating comics *exclusively* for viewing on *the Web*," and he describes the digital medium as a new "frontier."[75] At the time that he wrote this, McCloud posited that "digital delivery is the *real thing*—a genuine full-scale *revolution*—but . . . the first *wave* of that change has yet to *reach shore* as I write this. When the time comes, comics will *ride that wave* alongside any form that can be transmitted as *pure information*."[76] Currently, McCloud's vision of the future is now a reality. Cell phone manga was introduced in 2004 when Japanese cell phone companies partnered with manga publishers, making access to manga as easy as pulling your phone out of your pocket, and this digitized medium has become increasingly popular.[77] Now that comics are being offered in a format that makes them easily accessible and even portable, the comic-reading audience has a new chance to broaden. Petersen tellingly observes that "[a]lthough women represent only a minority of print manga readers, they constitute more than 70 percent of the readers of cell phone manga"; that older women, in particular, enjoy the privacy that reading manga on a phone affords them.[78] In the United States, the iPad and later the Kindle Fire allowed access to comics on portable e-readers in full color.

The digitization of comics means that comics are more accessible than ever, thanks to cell phones, tablet computers, and e-book readers. The success of such devices has allowed the comic book industry to expand their digital offerings. *Publishers Weekly* recently published a report of major announcements made at the 2011 San Diego Comic-Con International, stating that

> Marvel plans to begin simultaneous release [of] print and digital editions of a limited number of series, joining Archie and now DC Comics, which will begin "day and date" print and digital release in September

with the relaunch of its entire line of comics. And among the biggest manga events, Viz Media has launched VizManga.com, a new manga portal site, offering for-pay digital access to 40 initial series, and the 39 member Japanese Digital Comics Association announced plans to launch JManga, an industry-sponsored manga portal, and in this case, a mostly free, promotional website meant to be the opening salvo in a collective effort to lure fans away from illegal scanlation sites.[79]

Both DC and Marvel utilize ComiXology—a company whose proprietary "Guided View" technology "automatically takes the reader panel by panel through the comic," greatly improving usability and the digital comic book–reading experience, making what McCloud had envisioned over a decade ago a reality.[80]

Independent comics creators have been digitizing for quite some time. Webcomics—comics that are specifically created to be read via web-pages—began to flourish in the 1990s.[81] Early webcomics were limited by bandwidth, but this hurdle has slowly been surmounted, as high-speed (broadband) Internet has largely replaced the use of dial-up access.

Webcomics have opened up new possibilities for fledgling artists to create comics and distribute them inexpensively. Before the arrival of webcomics, self-publishing in color was an expensive investment for comic book creators. But webcomics have made it easy for almost anyone to publish comics and get them distributed to a broad readership. Cutting out large monetary costs as well as middlemen (distributors, specialty shops, etc.) has opened up the medium for the experimentations of a diverse range of creators. Not only does this mean that more female creators may now have an opportunity to bypass the "boys club" of the mainstream comics industry through self-publishing, but it also means that comics may be reaching more female readers. There is even a webcomics magazine called *Girlamatic*, dedicated to publishing comics that appeal primarily to young women. *Girlamatic* was established in 2002 by Joey Manley as part of the Modern Tales family of webcomics subscription sites.[82] Currently, *Girlamatic* is edited by Diana McQueen and is a member of the *ComicSpace* family, which hosts webcomics and supports a social network of comics creators and fans.[83] According to the *Girlamatic* website,[84]

Girlamatic's mission, along with ComicSpace, is twofold: to empower comic creators and readers while also proving, again and again, that women and girls enjoy comics, read comics, and make comics. . . . Girlamatic is committed to scouting and publishing professional, high-quality, creator-owned, gender-spanning comic series and related content online and, very soon, in print. As the only professional webcomics publication aimed at both women and men with the default mode: girl, we take pride in the fact that we, and our readers, don't fit in the usual "target demographics."[85]

With websites like *Girlamatic* that create communities based on webcomics and comics fans, girls are taking notice of webcomics. Artists such as the award-winning Hope Larson and up-and-coming author-artist Leigh Dragoon have both launched their careers from their humble beginnings in webcomics.

Writer and artist Leigh Dragoon began her comics career with the creation of her webcomic *By the Wayside* (2002–2011), a supernatural and often comedic adventure story that won her the Kim Yale Award for Best New Female Talent in 2006. *By the Wayside* tells the story of nineteen-year-old Adele Davies, a class-four mage and exorcist, and her friend, Maddie, a seventeen-year-old runaway and witch. Together they investigate and dispel hauntings. When Adele takes on an exorcism job that is beyond her skill level, and the house that she has been hired to clear gets consumed by a spirit, she gets in trouble with Triune—the agency she works with that also keeps tabs on magical people. A Triune agent is swiftly sent out to "contain" Adele, and there is the distinct possibility that she will be stripped of her powers. Meanwhile, Maddie has her own problems. She lives under the cloud of a troubled past that is not yet explained—the reader is left wondering what happened in her life that made Maddie run away. These questions are, as yet, unanswered. The production of *By the Wayside* is currently on hiatus, as Dragoon has been working on other projects.

Since she began *By the Wayside*, Dragoon has written scripts for the two *Faerie Path: Lamia's Revenge* graphic novels (a Tokyopop/HarperCollins venture developed from Frewin Jones's young adult novels and illustrated by Alison Acton), a story for The Jim Henson Company and Archaia's *Fraggle Rock* comics series (2010), as well as an adaptation of Richelle Mead's *Vampire Academy, Vampire Academy: A Graphic Novel* (2011), illustrated by Emma Vieceli. The second installment of the series, *Frostbite*, also adapted by Dragoon, is due to come out in 2012. Currently, Dragoon is working on the third volume of the *Vampire Academy* graphic novel series, as well as a project with Sam Kieth. She also has a story in the upcoming anthology *Greek Myths Retold*.[86] Dragoon has found success in the comics industry, but it all started when she began to self-publish her comics on the Internet. Dragoon explains:

> I started out doing *By the Wayside* on my own website. However, when it came time to do the second volume, I decided I wanted to do something to increase the viewership. By sheer coincidence, I found out about Girlamatic around that time. I emailed to ask if they were going to be open for submissions and turned out I had 2 months![87]

After working furiously to get her comics pitch in order, Dragoon submitted her work. She recounts, "A few days after I submitted [the proposal], Girlamatic's editor Lisa Jonte called me to tell me I was in!"[88] Due in part to the attention that her webcomics garnered, Dragoon began to embark on a career in print comics. When asked if she feels that there is more flexibility or freedom in webcomics Dragoon replied,

> I do think there's a certain amount of freedom in web comics. Self-publishing and print on demand services for authors are gaining more traction and respectability right now, but comics has a long history of self-publishing, and more people seem to take for granted that really amazing comics are self-published all the time. I think the web is a wonderful format for new comics artists, because it gives you a chance to post your work and gain an audience without a huge financial investment. Back in the day you had to publish physical copies of comics, and the cost was significant: something like 1K for a single issue print run. If you could scrape up the money, you then had to go through a distribution company called Diamond, and if they decided your book wasn't getting enough orders, they would refuse to carry it, which would pretty much kill your book.[89]

Unlike independent comic book creators and self-publishers of the past, today's artists are not constrained by the financial limitations that Dragoon describes. There are now cheap and effective alternatives to be found in publishing comics on the Internet, and this is opening up the field to artists who may not have previously been able to afford to publish independently. Dragoon also notes that even though she is now involved with the publishing industry, she would still consider publishing webcomics. She remarks, "I do have a project I want to pitch, but if no company picks it up, I'm sure I'll go ahead and publish it as a web comic. It helps that I do web development for my day job, so I can handle all the web maintenance and design issues on my own."[90] Regarding her transition from webcomics to print, Dragoon is extremely modest. She comments, "I was very lucky, and happened to meet people, some through conventions, some through the Internet, who liked my work and thought I would be a good fit for their projects. I've had the chance to work with some really amazing people and I'm just grateful for my good fortune."[91]

Hope Larson, author of *Grey Horses* (2006), *Chiggers* (2008), and *Mercury* (2010), also got her start with webcomics. Her first full-length graphic novel, *Salamander Dream* (2005), was originally published online and soon after made its way to print. Larson explains, "I put *Salamander Dream* online and made it known that I was looking for a publisher. Ad-House Books picked it up, and I haven't gone back to the web since."[92]

Although Larson is more involved with the world of printed comics now, she praises webcomics' ability not only to reach a wide audience but also to attract valuable feedback that can help a budding artist develop her skills. The Internet affords comics creators an incredible experimental space, where fresh new ideas and styles can be explored and where an artist may hone their talents with little monetary investment. It is a space where new talent and new ideas can thrive—where artists are able to break new ground through webcomics, just as Larson has. Larson explains her unique approach to her art: "I was a comics fan, but I didn't intend to become a cartoonist until Scott McCloud encouraged me to give it a shot. I don't have a passion for comics so much as a passion for visual storytelling."[93] This enthusiasm was further encouraged by Larson's foray into webcomics. She elucidates:

> I read webcomics as a teen, made them in my early 20s, and stopped in my mid-20s when I made the transition to print. The web is a great place for a developing artist because you can make work, get it in front of an audience, and get feedback within a few hours. Lather, rinse, repeat, and gradually you learn what works and doesn't work, and what it is that readers are responding to.[94]

Through the webcomics medium, the poignant graphic novel *Salamander Dream* was realized. *Salamander Dream* is an emotional tale about a girl named Hailey who grows up and realizes that she must leave her child-hood behind. The story begins "Once upon a time, there was a little girl very much like you" and proceeds to follow Hailey from being a young girl having adventures with her friend, Salamander, to the beginning of adulthood.[95] Salamander is never explained; he is rendered as an anthropomorphic, shadowy form with a face that appears to be a representational mask. His depiction suggests an imaginary friend, and the mask seems to infer that this form is merely a guise representing ideas such as innocence and childhood or perhaps even a friendly spirit of nature. Salamander is all of these things to Hailey, and she seeks him out each summer on her walks in the woods near her house, "where it was easier to believe in magic."[96] Together, they explore the flora and fauna that surrounds them and Salamander entertains her with wondrous stories about his adventures in the forest.

As time progresses, Hailey and Salamander see each other with less frequency. Both move on and spend more time with other friends, and as the case is with many childhood relationships, they grow apart. One day, while playing hide-and-go-seek, Hailey stumbles upon Salamander in the woods. Salamander helps her find a good hiding spot up in a tree and they attempt to catch up with each other.[97] Hailey asks Salamander why she hasn't seen him in so long, and he replies, "I've been around . . . I just thought you were busy. You have so many friends!" to which Hailey replies, "But not any good ones, obviously."[98] Salamander appears to be saddened by this exchange; he is shown slumped over with a rueful expression upon his face.[99] His speech balloon contains only an ellipsis, which conventionally represents a loss for words in comics.[100] However, Hailey relents, informing Salamander that he will be forgiven if he tells her another story, and Salamander tells her about his birthday flight with Hawk. Nevertheless, the story ends on a note of sadness as both Hailey and Salamander realize that they did not celebrate Salamander's birthday together.[101] When Hailey hears her friends calling, "Ollie Ollie oxenfree," she tells Salamander that she has to go.[102] Salamander replies, "I know," and hugs her tight before saying goodbye.[103] There is a sense of finality to this parting, yet the two friends meet one more time, in the late years of Hailey's adolescence. It is summer, once more, when Hailey comes to the woods, and the time looms near when she will go away to college. She seeks out Salamander and informs him that she is leaving for school on a scholarship.[104] At this last meeting, Hailey decides to tell Salamander a story. In an almost entirely wordless sequence, Hailey takes Salamander on a journey through the palm of her hand, through her pores, through her red blood cells into the nucleus of one of her cells to her DNA, and finally, to the very center of her atoms, reaching the atomic nucleus. In a double-page spread (see fig. 5.10), Hailey and Salamander are shown floating in among a magical substance filled with leaves, stars, and all of the creatures of the wood from Salamander's stories.[105]

There is no textual narrative that provides exposition for what has been explained visually, but this sequence seems to imply that, even though Hailey has grown up and will soon leave Salamander and the woods behind, Salamander and the magic of nature and the childhood joy that he represents will always be a part of her—down to her subatomic particles. When she says goodbye to Salamander at the end of the graphic novel, it is a bittersweet departure. Poetically, the story ends similarly to how it began, with "Once upon a time, there was a girl very much like you . . . and one day she

Figure 5.10. *Salamander Dream*, 2005, pages 84–85.
Copyright 2005, Hope Larson.

began to grow up."[106] The text continues to explain how change, inevitably, occurred; the suburbs encroached upon the woods and, eventually, the little girl moved away, perhaps forgetting about Salamander.[107] Yet the story ends on a hopeful note, suggesting, "but maybe she found another place in the world with a wood, and a field with a creek running through it, where it was easier to believe in magic."[108]

With her spare, fluid lines, minimalist use of color, and economy of words, Larson creates a subtle, yet deeply touching story that is particularly timely for readers who are just on the verge of womanhood. Cutting through the sadness of this transition, there is a greater reassurance that the magic and wonder of the universe it not something that ever truly leaves.

Webcomics such as Dragoon's *By the Wayside* and Larson's *Salamander Dream* focus on young, strong female characters and thus have the potential to attract girls to comics. Of her inclination to write comics that appeal to this demographic, Dragoon says,

> I think it's probably unintentional, but [it] probably has a lot to do with [the] frustration I feel about poorly written or stereotyped female characters. It also probably has a lot to do with the fact that some of the most complicated relationships I've had in my life have been friendships with other women, so I think I end up exploring a lot of that in my work.[109]

Hope Larson echoes these sentiments, asserting that she does not set out to write for any specific age group. She describes her surprise upon discovering that she could be considered an author of young adult graphic novels: "I always write the books I want to read. It didn't occur to me that I was writing YA until after I completed the script for *Chiggers*, when my agent told me I'd written a YA book. I was so clueless!"[110]

Many female comics creators are now filling in the gaps in the comics industry, writing comics that appeal to them, and incidentally to girls. However, there are even some women working in the industry, such as Leigh Dragoon, who have been relatively sheltered from gender biases in the field. Dragoon comments,

> I was actually unaware of the gender bias in comics for a long time. I was protected from the knowledge that comics was mainly a "boy's club." The first series I really got into was Elfquest, which was created

by a woman named Wendy Pini. I absolutely love Pini's artwork (I'd say she's easily one of my biggest artistic influences). Her artwork is consistently amazing. I love how expressive her characters' faces are, and the attention she pays to body language. Once I got to college, I read a lot of underground comics by Roberta Gregory and Donna Barr. I actually didn't figure out until much, much later, well after I'd started doing my own comics, that women were not equally represented in the comics industry. This is something I really feel is changing, though. There are lots of amazing female creators working in the biz now.[111]

Whether or not female creators of comics are putting out material with the intention of combating gender inequalities in the field or if they are simply producing these comics to fulfill a personal need, these authors and artists are changing the future of comics and how they are perceived.

Many male authors and artists are also part of this revolution, creating comics that feature main characters who are girls. Barry Deutsch's *Hereville: How Mirka Got Her Sword* (2010) is a webcomic that has been re-published in print form. Deutsch's graphic novel about Mirka Hirschberg, an eleven-year-old Orthodox Jewish girl who battles trolls and bucks traditions, originated as a webcomic for *Girlamatic* in 2004 but later got picked up by Amulet Books in 2010.[112] Reading *Hereville*, it is not hard to see why the webcomics were picked up by a major publisher. This quirky tale introduces the reader to an unconventional girl living in a traditional community, yet Mirka is a character that *any* girl who has ever daydreamed can relate to. She has an intelligently questioning personality and enjoys testing her elders' boundaries.

One of the most charming aspects of *Hereville* is the unique way in which Deutsch manages to upend the comics hero trope as well as fairy tale conventions. Mirka doesn't care to learn how to knit and she doesn't dream of her future husband, like her sisters do. Instead, Mirka fantasizes about being a hero—specifically, a slayer of dragons. She also keeps a non-Jewish book, "The Big Book of Monsters," hidden underneath her mattress, even though children in Hereville are forbidden to do so.[113] Mirka isn't what one might typically expect a hero to be; she is an eleven-year-old girl from a pious Jewish community that has little contact with gentiles. She lives with her siblings under her father and stepmother's roof. Her stepmother Fruma (a name meaning "pious"), is not evil but loving and caring. Although she can sometimes come across as harsh, with her penchant for debates, her strict sense of order, and her severe look, she is the anchor of the Hirschberg household. Mirka appears to have a good relationship with her father, but it is Fruma who spends time with Mirka, helping her develop her intellect, coaxing her to be a critical thinker, and guiding her to become a person with integrity, not just a future homemaker.

Through the values that Fruma instills in her, Mirka is able to negotiate with a witch who eventually tells her how she might acquire the sword that will allow her to become a dragon-slaying hero. The witch informs her that, in order to attain her sword, she must fight a troll. Cryptically, the witch states, "Whatever you need to know to beat this troll, you can learn from your stepmother."[114] In the story's climax, Mirka defeats the hungry troll (who would like to eat her with rye toast)[115] using a weapon that her stepmother has taught her to hone, a weapon sharper than any sword point—her mind.

Russian-born American comics creator Vera Brosgol also experimented with webcomics before making her debut in print. Brosgol, who is also an illustrator as well as a storyboard artist for Laika Inc. (where she worked on the film adaptation of Neil Gaiman's *Coraline*), began creating webcomics in high school with her series *Return to Sender*.[116] She was also involved in the Girlamatic webcomics site. However, Brosgol has since discontinued work on *Return to Sender*, moving on from webcomics to work on a larger project: her first full-length graphic novel, *Anya's Ghost* (2011), which has received starred reviews from both *Booklist* and *Kirkus*.

In *Anya's Ghost*, teenaged Anya Borzakovskaya, like many girls her age, is hyperaware of her appearance and social status and wishes to "fit in" with the crowd. Anya is body conscious—she sees herself as chubby, although she is quite average in physique. Anya came to this country from Russia when she was about five years old, and she is painfully insecure about being an immigrant. She loathes having to associate with Dima, a boy from her private high school who gets picked on for being "nerdy" and for having a Russian accent.[117] Although her mother encourages her to be friends with Dima, Anya is afraid that if she were to be seen with him it would give her classmates a reason to pick on her. She explains, "I got bullied for years for talking funny, I did my time in ESL, I don't have an accent! It's hard enough to fit in at that school without him as a handicap!"[118] She only has one true friend at school, another social outsider—a tomboy named Siobhan.

Anya's Ghost is rendered entirely in bold black, stark white, and various shades of bleak, dusky purple befitting a ghost story. The almost monochromatic, bruised coloring helps set the tone for what turns out to be a terrible day for the graphic novel's protagonist. Anya's story begins when she leaves for school one morning and sees a cute boy at the bus stop who appears to wave at her. As she waves back, Anya finds that she was mistaken—he hadn't been waving at her but at his girlfriend. Anya feels mortified. Directly after this misunderstanding, Dima walks up to the bus stop and waves at her, which only serves to irritate Anya. On top of these indignities, she has a tiff with her friend Siobhan. When the bus comes to take them all to school, Anya doesn't get on. Feeling overwhelmed by the morning's events, Anya decides to skip school and head toward the park. Here is where her day takes an even worse turn. Occupied by her gloomy thoughts, Anya does not pay attention to where she is walking and she falls down an old, abandoned well. Once she gathers her senses and looks around, Anya realizes that she is trapped in the well with no way out. When she lights a match from her rucksack in order to see her surroundings a little better, Anya receives a second shock—a human skeleton lies nearby on the floor of the well (see fig. 5.11). Anya's fear intensifies when she discovers that she is not alone with the human remains. The ghost of the deceased appears to her. At first, Anya thinks that she is hallucinating, but it soon becomes clear that she is stuck in the well with the spirit of a teenage girl.

During the two days that Anya is stuck down the well, the ghost relays the gruesome story of her excruciatingly protracted death after falling down there some ninety years earlier. When Anya asks if the ghost could help her by flying up out of the hole and getting the attention of a passerby, the apparition explains that she can't stray far from her bones. However, on the last day of Anya's time in the well, a young man walks through the park and discards a soda can that inadvertently falls down the hole. The sound rouses the ghost girl, and she makes a decision to help Anya. She wakes Anya and urges her to yell for help. While Anya is being hoisted out of the well, she is overjoyed as she looks forward to going home again, but when she turns her head to see the ghost of the girl who had helped her to escape; a look of sadness and guilt shows on

Figure 5.11. *Anya's Ghost*, 2011, page 16.
Pages 16 and 113 from *Anya's Ghost* by Vera Brosgol, copyright © 2011 by Vera Brosgol and reprinted by arrangement with Henry Holt and Company, LLC.

her face as she gazes upon the dejected figure who will remain behind after she is gone.[119]

When Anya returns to school, everything seems like it is back to normal—until Anya discovers that the ghost has managed to follow her. The ghost emerges while Anya is in the girls' bathroom and Anya, surprised and angry, confronts her, saying, "I thought that you couldn't leave your hole!!!"[120] The ghost explains that while that is true, one of her bones—part of what used to be her little finger—had left the well with Anya.[121] Anya guesses that the bone managed to find its way into her rucksack when she had hastily packed up her belongings during the rescue. Perturbed by the apparition's reappearance, Anya informs the ghost that she will deposit the bone back down the well after school. After all, Anya can't have a ghost following her around school—she feels awkward enough as it is. However, the ghost eventually wins her over when she helps Anya cheat on her science test.[122] It isn't long before the ghost is helping her with every aspect of her school life, and the two girls—one living and one dead—become fast friends. The ghost reveals that when she was alive her name was Emily Reilly, and that her life was a sad story. She tells Anya that she was once in love, but her fiancé died in World War I.[123] Emily also relates the horrific circumstances behind her own death. She had woken up one night to find that her parents' lodger had killed them. The murderer, noticing Emily, pursued her into the woods, knife in hand until she tumbled down the well and was left there to die.[124] Her story brings Anya closer to Emily and propels Anya's desire to help solve her ghostly friend's murder.

Emily works hard to make herself indispensable to Anya and tries to help her with her social life. She observes that Anya has developed a crush on Sean, the boy from the bus stop, even though Sean already has a girlfriend—the sunny-natured Elizabeth Standard. Anya is resentful of Elizabeth because she appears to have everything that Anya would like for herself: "Nice grades, nice legs, nice nice nice."[125] From all outward appearances, Elizabeth seems perfect to Anya—almost too perfect. She comments to Siobhan, "I just wish that she'd get a zit or something to prove that she's full of pus like the rest of us."[126] Anya feels inferior to Elizabeth and she also feels that she is out of Sean's league—Sean is popular and a star player on the school's basketball team. However, Emily helps build up Anya's confidence, flattering her and telling her, "that

Sean boy could really like you! You're much more interesting than that Elizabeth girl"; she makes it her mission to help Anya get Sean's attention.[127] Emily even orchestrates a situation in which Anya joins Sean and Elizabeth at another student's party, in order to get Anya closer to Sean.

At first, Emily seems to be the greatest friend that Anya could have hoped for. Her grades go up and Emily's attempts to get Sean to notice Anya seem to be working. Anya is so happy with this new friendship that she affixes Emily's bone to a cord that she can wear as a necklace, so that she can easily take Emily wherever she goes.[128] However, Anya learns that success is rarely won without effort, as her triumphs quickly turn out to be quite hollow. As Emily pushes Anya to win Sean away from Elizabeth, Anya breaks more school rules, lies to her family, and alienates her one living friend. When Siobhan attempts to warn Anya that Sean may be "kind of a dirtbag," Anya gets angry with her and accuses Siobhan of being unsupportive.[129] Frustrated, Siobhan replies, ""I'm just trying to keep you from getting hurt!" but Anya does not want to hear her friend's advice.[130] Anya storms off, telling Siobhan, "You know what?! I don't need this. I've got other friends I can talk to."[131] Of course, the only other friend that Anya really seems to have is a ghost. Without realizing it, Anya has allowed her desire to be with Sean and to "fit in" to drive a wedge between her and her best friend.

Eventually Anya's acceptance of Emily's "help" proves to be destructive, and the wispy ghost girl turns out to be more sinister than Anya could have imagined. Anya's friendship with Emily begins to deteriorate the night of the party. While Emily is picking out an outfit for Anya to wear, Anya is plagued by doubts about Sean. She asks Emily if she thinks that Siobhan could be right about him, but Emily replies, "No. She's crazy. Your love is pure and real." Then she adds, "Trust me, I know what love is."[132] Emily's response seems misplaced—Anya has never professed her love for Sean, only a crush, and it seems strange that Emily should equate such feelings with love. While this may foreshadow the notion that there is something wrong with how Emily perceives the situation, Anya does not appear to notice. However, when Anya expresses uncertainty about the outfit, Emily becomes forceful. She is depicted with her ghostly arms folded, with a slightly unpleasant expression on her ethereal face and she asserts, "This is exactly the kind of thing men like nowadays. Now go! Try it! I won't look."[133] Anya's face appears full of worry, but she obeys.[134] The next page displays Anya in the foreground struggling to squeeze herself into her party attire, while in the background Emily is shown facing her own reflection in the mirror.[135] As Anya tells Emily how nice it is to have someone to get dressed up with, and how it is exactly the type of thing that Siobhan would loathe, the images provide a contrapuntal narrative. While Anya is preoccupied with dressing, a transformation takes place: Emily is shown gazing unhappily into the mirror in one panel, and in the next panel her expression changes to an intense look of anger or concentration, and in the subsequent panel, her reflection is drastically altered (see fig. 5.12). The ghostly girl in the mirror has longer hair, her jaw-line is more slender, and she appears slightly taller. The reader may observe that this new visage eerily resembles Elizabeth Standard. However, Anya prattles on and does not notice this shape shifting—as soon as Anya turns around to look at her, Emily reverts back to her original form.

Anya continues to express her discomfort with the outfit that Emily has picked out for her, saying, "This feels kind of slutty," as she tugs her clothes down, her arm crossed over her body in an act of modesty.[136] It is obvious from her facial expression as well as the depiction of her body language that she is still unhappy with her appearance and the exposure of her flesh, no matter how much encouragement Emily gives her. The ghost snaps at Anya, saying, "Do you want Sean to notice you or not?"[137] Cowed by Emily's stern reproach, Anya answers "Yeah . . ." unconvincingly, to which Emily curtly replies, "So wear it!"[138] In the next panel Emily cushions her bullying demands with an appeal to Anya's sympathies as she explains, "I wish I could wear stuff like that. I wish could wear anything other than this."[139] The guilt trip works, and Anya placates her by allowing Emily to instruct her on how she should wear her makeup.[140]

Anya's discomfort increases when she arrives at the party, and it is clear from the visual narrative that she feels as though she does not belong there. The house is crowded with people, and many of them appear to be drinking. In a wordless panel, Anya is depicted as a tiny, unhappy figure surrounded by a sea of cheerful partygoers. When she finally takes her jacket off, she holds the jacket in front of her defensively, but that does not stop one of the boys at the party from leering at her and commenting, "Anya, I have to tell you something very important. Your boobs . . . look spectacular in that shirt."[141] This objectifying comment makes Anya feel even more self-conscious. When she eventually gets up the nerve to look for

Figure 5.12. *Anya's Ghost*, 2011, page 113.

Pages 16 and 113 from *Anya's Ghost* by Vera Brosgol, copyright © 2011 by Vera Brosgol and reprinted by arrangement with Henry Holt and Company, LLC.

Sean, Anya finds disappointment. Sean is inside the upstairs bathroom and Elizabeth Standard is waiting for him outside of the door. Every illusion that Anya had of Sean is crushed when she realizes that he is in the bathroom with another girl and Elizabeth has, unbelievably, been left to guard the door. Right in front of his girlfriend, Sean even goes so far as to sleazily invite Anya into the bathroom to "hang out" with them.[142] Amazed, Anya asks Elizabeth why she puts up with Sean's behavior, to which Elizabeth pathetically explains, "Sure, he gets . . . bad at parties. But I'm the one he's seen with. I'm the one people look at and know—'That's his girlfriend!' Don't you understand? I love him!"[143] Disgusted, Anya leaves the party straight away. It is at this point that Anya learns that external appearances aren't always what they seem to be, and, unlike Elizabeth Standard (a last name that implies mediocrity), Anya is unwilling to give up her dignity in order to maintain a popular image or "keep a man."

Although this revelation marks a milestone in Anya's life, Anya's troubles are only beginning. Emily is incensed when Anya rejects Sean, complaining that Anya has ruined all of her "hard work."[144] It is then that Anya realizes that Emily may have had her own agenda all along. She confronts Emily, asking her, "What exactly did you want out of this?"[145] Emily replies, "I want you to be happy! You're in love! You should be with him!"[146] However, far from being the concerned friend, Emily's face is contorted in an ugly rage. Anya finally understands that a good friend should want to protect her and not push her into a potentially harmful situation, and it begins to dawn on Anya that Emily is projecting her desires onto her. After this argument, they make their way back home in silence.

The next day, Emily is still obsessed with getting Anya to pursue Sean. Anya is also disturbed to find that Emily has fully manifested herself in the likeness of Elizabeth Standard (though Anya never verbally compares the two, this mimicry is made overt by the visual narrative). At this point, it becomes obvious that Emily has Anya's future completely planned out—crazily, she expresses her intentions to follow Anya to college and to "help" Anya get married to Sean. However, Anya has no intention of seeing Sean again, never mind marrying him. Once she realizes that Elizabeth is deeply flawed, Anya snaps out of her own self-loathing and begins to stand up for herself. Through her experiences at the party, Anya has learned the importance of self-respect. She cannot accept the sort of treatment that Elizabeth has chosen to endure, and she is unwilling to allow Emily to control her future and live vicariously through her. Anya realizes that not only is Elizabeth and Sean's relationship diseased but that Emily's desire for Anya to pursue Sean is pathological as well. Furthermore, Emily's expectation that Anya should marry Sean may come from her ninety-year-old values. Before the women's liberation movement of the 1960s, many women saw marriage (and motherhood) as the only way to fulfill themselves as females. Fortunately today Emily's way of thinking is obsolete.

It is clear that Anya will never be rid of Emily unless she takes action. She decides that the only way to rid herself of the ghost is to solve Emily and her family's murders. She begins by leaving the bone necklace at home so that Emily can't follow her when she goes to the library to find information on the Reilly murders. Once there, Anya runs into Dima, who helps her search the microfilm archives for information on Emily Reilly and her family. During the long searching process, Dima admits to Anya that he finds school life difficult in America and asks her how she manages to fit in so well. Although Dima is a brilliant student, he finds that he does not fit in with the other students and is constantly getting picked on by his classmates. Anya replies, "Dude, I have like one sucky friend. My life is total crap."[147] However, Dima insists, "But you are a regular American kid! No one bothers you."[148] In an offhand and callous remark, Anya says, "Ha! I'm sorry, but the cards are kind of stacked. You're a nerd, and you're a little foreign kid. You can't really blame them."[149] As soon as she says this, Anya begins to regret it. Sympathetically, Anya explains how she was bullied when she first came to America, too. She admits to Dima, "I was fat, my clothes were from Goodwill, and I had an accent. People might think that five-year-olds can't be cruel, but I have some strong evidence to the contrary."[150] Dima registers surprise, saying, "Really? But . . . you seem so cool now!"[151] Anya retorts, "Oh, please. I'm such a loser. The only thing that's different about me now versus then is that I got some better clothes and got rid of my accent."[152] Helpfully, she adds, "You'll probably lose yours, too. But even if you don't, this is just high school. Impressing a bunch of snooty teenagers is a pretty lame life goal to have."[153] When Anya gives Dima this thoughtful advice, she shows that she has finally realized that she does not have to be ashamed of her cultural background.

After poring over the microfilms for a time, Dima and Anya stumble across some information about Emily Reilly. Anya is shocked to find that Emily had lied—Emily's family wasn't murdered. In fact, Emily wasn't a victim at all. The microfilm displays a newspaper headline that reads: "Local Girl Missing after Double Murder."[154] A wordless sequence follows showing how Emily, in a jealous rage, had locked a young couple inside their house, barring the door from the outside. She then set the house ablaze with the lovers trapped inside. Silently, through images alone, Brosgol depicts the horrific burning of the house in the moonlight and the subsequent search by the townspeople. The final panel in this sequence is a small, dark, and highly stylized depiction of the woods where Emily's life ended, but not her story.

Once Anya realizes the truth behind Emily's death, she rushes home to rid herself of this dangerous ghost. However, when she gets back, Anya discovers that the bone-necklace is missing and that Emily appears to have acquired the power to move solid objects. When Anya tries to find the bone in order to get rid of the ghost, Emily fights back, making several attempts on the lives of Anya's family members. In the end, Anya is able to find the bone and throw it back into the well, but not before Emily makes her last effort to stay with Anya. Anya firmly rejects the ghost, telling her that Emily always needed her more than she needed Emily. Anya is about to cast the bone down the well, when Emily asks Anya if she could pass her on to Siobhan.

When Anya refuses, Emily begins to point out all of the negative behavior that she has observed during her stay with Anya, saying, "Oh, right, suddenly you care so much about other people. You're the most selfish person I've ever *met*! If Siobhan's so important to you, why haven't you called her in two weeks? And you love your precious family so much that you lie about your last name. You're no saint, Anya. You're just like me."[155] However, due in part to her recent experiences, Anya has developed a strong sense of self-respect and refuses to accept Emily's abuse. She lets Emily know that she will not allow her to prey on anybody else. Emily, enraged, attempts to push Anya down into the well, but her spirit-form passes through Anya without enough substance or strength to make Anya fall. Nonetheless, Emily's skeleton returns from out of the hole and gropes Anya's ankle in one last attempt to pull Anya down into her grave.

Anya is able to fight her off and begins to run away when she appears to realize how pathetic Emily is. Though she has summoned all of her power to crawl back out of the well with her bones, she is weak—Emily can barely speak Anya's name and she is shedding small bones. Proving that Anya was right to tell Emily that she was the one who needed Anya, it is apparent that Emily has used the last of her strength in her attempt to keep Anya with her forever. When Anya sees what Emily has been reduced to, she feels sympathy for her and tells her, "I know—I know I said before I wasn't like you . . . it's not true. I'm enough like you to know how you feel. Wanting how others look, what they have, who they have! Everyone's life seems so much easier. . . . But that's all you know! What *you* want! You don't know what's going on inside anyone else's head." Anya ends her speech to Emily saying, "Why don't you go? What you want . . . What you want doesn't even exist."[156] With this explained, Emily's spirit finally departs, and both Emily and Anya are free.

Ironically, it is Anya's experience with Emily that leads to her to understand that the people who had once seemed to her to be so perfect— who had appeared to have everything that she desired for herself—were flawed or deeply unhappy. Through Emily's unhealthy desire to live another's life, Anya learns to value her own identity. *Anya's Ghost* contains a metaphor; many of us have been haunted by our desire to be more popular, more beautiful, to have what others seem to gain so easily, but the truth is that the people whom we envy have their own set of problems. When Anya realizes this truth, she is able to dispel not only the ghost but also the feelings that have been haunting her, leading to a new sense of self-appreciation and wholeness.

Through their initial experimentation with webcomics, comics creators like Vera Brosgol have been able to carve a niche for themselves outside of the bounds of mainstream comics publishing. As Scott McCloud had predicted, webcomics have become the new frontier where pioneers are able to experiment with fresh ideas without restriction. Not unlike the underground comix movement that occurred in the wake of Comics Code censorship, artists have found a new creative venue. The Internet is an almost boundless medium in which to experiment with sequential art, and out of this creative space, an interesting phenomenon is occurring. Webcomics that explore girlhood narratives are making their appearance, and many of these webcomics have earned so much attention that they have jumpstarted careers in printed publishing. Like Larson's *Salamander Dream*, and Deutsch's *Hereville: How Mirka Got Her Sword*, some lengthy webcomics featuring stories about girls are starting to be acquired by publishers and are being printed as graphic novels. Publishers who previously may not have wanted to take the risk of printing comics aimed at girls under the erroneous assumption that girls don't want to read comics, now have free and telling market research available to them through the Internet. As Trina Robbins says, "Girls, indeed, do not read comics if there are no comics published for them"; so it is possible to envision a future where more girls are reading more comics.[157] This is not to suggest that girls do not read outside of girl-specific comics—there are plenty of girls who enjoy superheroes, mainstream comics, and other titles. However, they have, for a long time now, made up a minority of readers consuming comics. Webcomics are making a difference. They have changed how the art form is disseminated to readers. Furthermore, the graphic novel format is helping to change the perception of comics. It has taken a long time, but it appears that educators, critics, parents, and society as a whole are finally beginning to recognize the importance and value of comics and graphic novels, whether printed or electronic, with or without an ISBN. Now, thanks to these changes, girls are being offered more comics in which they can see girls like themselves being represented.

Conclusion

Comics have been on a journey toward wider recognition in recent years, though it has taken a while to get to this point. Proving their growing popularity is the recent increase of film adaptations of comics. Films like *Frank Miller's Sin City* (2005), *Scott Pilgrim vs. the World* (2010), and *Kick-Ass* (2010) explore a living visualization of comic book narratives. Even the old, iconic superheroes have received a digital, cinematic makeover with *Spiderman* (both one and two; 2002, 2004), *Superman Returns* (2006), and the new Batman films (*Batman Begins*, 2005, *The Dark Knight*, 2008, and *The Dark Knight Rises*, 2012). Powerful females can be found making their appearance in films such as *Elektra* (2005), *Watchmen* (2009), *The Avengers* (2012), and the *X-Men* films. Interestingly, young females are also appearing in film in non-superhero roles such as the screen adaptation of *Ghost World* (2001) and the film adaptation of *Persepolis* (2007). This may indicate that a female audience is beginning to be targeted in comics' recent foray onto the big screen.

Comic book and graphic novel creators such as the ones mentioned throughout this book are presenting female readers with new heroes that need no capes, heroes that are definitely complicated and female. These female heroes have ascended a long road from the underground, mirroring women's own endeavors toward equality with the second wave of feminism. The women's movement began in the form of underground protests and has since moved to the political forefront and cultural mainstream. This is not unlike the history of modern-day comics and graphic novels. The oppression of the Comics Code era did not quell the tenacity and grit of comics creators; it only forced them underground, creating new modes of expression within the field. From the underground has emerged the female voice in an art form that has long been perceived as catering almost exclusively to a male readership. Many of these new comics feature strong role models that may be significant for young females to discover, as much of art, literature, and popular culture impinges on female self-perception and the formation of social roles.

Perhaps more importantly, comics' ability to give voice to the voiceless with its boundary-breaking style makes the medium an ideal messenger to bear the stories of females and the struggle for equality. Comics, webcomics, and graphic novels are exceptionally capable of representing the female experience because of the nature of the medium. Their hybrid form opens up dialogic possibilities for textual and visual storytelling and the interaction of the two, making comics unique in their transmission of different narrative streams. This polyphonic expression allows the female point of view to be examined from different angles. The stories of those females who are marginalized and silenced are articulated through interior dialog and the nonverbal communication of images, lending itself, particularly, to representations of girlhood and adolescence.

Art and literature have always been on the edge of sociopolitical change. This new surge of female narratives in comics, especially those of girlhood and adolescence, suggests that there may be something afoot in the way comics are viewed—and in turn the way girls are viewed. It is a provocative notion that the two may be related. Although the female readership of comics may be, at the moment, a minority, hopefully the new innovations and interest generated in the field, as well as the understanding of its importance by teachers and librarians, will expose more girls and young women to this one of a kind art and literary form.

Notes

1. Qiuning Huang, interview by the author, June 25, 2011.
2. Huang interview.
3. Jared Rudy, interview by the author, July 21, 2011.
4. Will Eisner, "Foreword," in *Faster than a Speeding Bullet: The Rise of the Graphic Novel*, by Stephen Weiner (New York: Nantier, Beall, Minoustchine, 2003), ix.
5. Justin Azevedo, interview by the author, July 23, 2011.
6. Chelsea Couillard, interview by the author, July 22, 2011.
7. Couillard interview.
8. Azevedo interview.
9. Azevedo interview.
10. Azevedo interview.
11. Couillard interview.
12. Couillard interview.
13. Couillard interview.
14. Azevedo interview.
15. Couillard interview.
16. Eisner, "Foreword," xi.
17. Stephen Weiner, *Faster than a Speeding Bullet: The Rise of the Graphic Novel* (New York: Nantier, Beall, Minoustchine, 2003), 3.
18. Scott McCloud, *Reinventing Comics* (New York: Paradox Press, 2000), 26.
19. Weiner, *Faster than a Speeding Bullet*, 8.
20. Amy Kiste Nyberg, "Poisoning Children's Culture: Comics and Their Critics," *Contributions to the Study of Popular Culture* 75 (2002): 170.
21. Weiner, *Faster than a Speeding Bullet*, 8.
22. Nyberg, "Poisoning Children's Culture," 181.
23. Weiner, *Faster than a Speeding Bullet*, 10.
24. Weiner, *Faster than a Speeding Bullet*, 11.
25. Weiner, *Faster than a Speeding Bullet*, 14.
26. Weiner, *Faster than a Speeding Bullet*, 14.
27. Weiner, *Faster than a Speeding Bullet*, 14.
28. Weiner, *Faster than a Speeding Bullet*, 12.
29. Weiner, *Faster than a Speeding Bullet*, 17–18.
30. Robert S. Petersen, *Comics, Manga, and Graphic Novels: A History of Graphic Narratives* (Santa Barbara, CA: Praeger, 2011), 166–67.
31. Weiner, *Faster than a Speeding Bullet*, 18–19.
32. Weiner, *Faster than a Speeding Bullet*, 18–19.
33. Weiner, *Faster than a Speeding Bullet*, 19.

34. Weiner, *Faster than a Speeding Bullet*, 19.

35. Julia Michaels, "Pulp Fiction," *The Horn Book Magazine* (May/June, 2004): 299–300.

36. Michaels, "Pulp Fiction," 300.

37. Trina Robbins, "Contemporary Graphic Novels for Girls: A Core List," *Booklist* (February 1, 2004): 985.

38. John Wilkins, "'Who Are We Protecting Them From?' The Selection of Graphic Novels in the London Borough of Camden," in *Graphic Account: The Selection and Promotion of Graphic Novels in Libraries for Young People*, ed. Keith Barker (Newcastle-Under-Lyme: The Library Association Youth Libraries Group, 1993), 23.

39. Marjane Satrapi, *Persepolis: The Story of a Childhood*, trans. L'Association, Paris, France (New York: Pantheon Books, 2003), 3.

40. Satrapi, *Persepolis*, 3.

41. Satrapi, *Persepolis*, 6.

42. Satrapi, *Persepolis*, "Introduction."

43. Satrapi, *Persepolis*, 137.

44. Satrapi, *Persepolis*, 141.

45. Satrapi, *Persepolis*, 141.

46. Satrapi, *Persepolis*, 141.

47. Satrapi, *Persepolis*, 142.

48. Satrapi, *Persepolis*, 142.

49. Satrapi, *Persepolis*, 142.

50. Satrapi, *Persepolis*, 143.

51. Satrapi, *Persepolis*, 150.

52. Marjane Satrapi, *Persepolis 2: The Story of a Return*, trans. Anjali Singh (New York: Pantheon Books, 2004), 46.

53. Satrapi, *Persepolis 2*, 23–24.

54. Satrapi, *Persepolis 2*, 39.

55. Satrapi, *Persepolis 2*, 39.

56. Satrapi, *Persepolis 2*, 40.

57. Satrapi, *Persepolis 2*, 40.

58. Satrapi, *Persepolis 2*, 40.

59. Satrapi, *Persepolis 2*, 40.

60. Satrapi, *Persepolis 2*, 41.

61. Satrapi, *Persepolis 2*, 42.

62. Satrapi, *Persepolis 2*, 42.

63. Satrapi, *Persepolis 2*, 42.

64. Satrapi, *Persepolis 2*, 43.

65. Satrapi, *Persepolis 2*, 43.

66. Hillary L. Chute, *Graphic Women: Life Narrative and Contemporary Comics* (New York: Columbia University Press, 2010), 169.

67. Chute, *Graphic Women*, 170.

68. Chute, *Graphic Women*, 169.

69. Gill Allwood, *French Feminisms: Gender and Violence in Contemporary Theory* (London: UCL Press, 1998), 112.

70. Robyn McCallum, *Ideologies of Identity in Adolescent Fiction: The Dialogic Construction of Subjectivity* (New York: Garland., 1999), 28.

71. Petersen, *Comics, Manga, and Graphic Novels*, 228.

72. Petersen, *Comics, Manga, and Graphic Novels*, 229.

73. McCloud, *Reinventing Comics*, 209.

74. McCloud, *Reinventing Comics*, 163.

75. McCloud, *Reinventing Comics*, 165.

76. McCloud, *Reinventing Comics*, 174.

77. Petersen, *Comics, Manga, and Graphic Novels*, 229.

78. Petersen, *Comics, Manga, and Graphic Novels*, 230.

79. Heidi MacDonald and Calvin Reid, "Comics, Digital Delivery and a Few Movies Rule Comic-Con 2011," *Publishers Weekly,* July 29, 2011, accessed October 5, 2011, http://www.publishersweekly.com/pw/by-topic/industry-news/trade-shows-events/article/48173-comics-digital-delivery-and-a-few-movies-rule-comic-con-2011.html.

80. Brigid Alverson, "Comixology Launches Retailer Digital Storefronts, Upgrades App.," *Publishers Weekly,* August 29, 2011, accessed October 7, 2011, http://www.publishersweekly.com/pw/by-topic/book-news/comics/article/48496-comixology-launches-retailer-digital-storefronts-upgrades-app.html.

81. Petersen, *Comics, Manga, and Graphic Novels*, 234.

82. Girlamatic, "About," accessed October 21, 2011, http://girlamatic.com/about/.

83. Girlamatic, accessed October 21, 2011.

84. ComicSpace (website), accessed October 21, 2011, http://comicspace.com.

85. Girlamatic, accessed October 21, 2011.

86. Leigh Dragoon, interview by the author, August 12, 2011.

87. Dragoon interview.

88. Dragoon interview.

89. Dragoon interview.

90. Dragoon interview.

91. Dragoon interview.

92. Hope Larson, interview by the author, July 28, 2011.

93. Larson interview.

94. Larson interview.

95. Hope Larson, *Salamander Dream* (Richmond: AdHouse Books, 2005), 1.

96. Larson, *Salamander Dream*, 1.

97. Larson, *Salamander Dream*, 45.

98. Larson, *Salamander Dream*, 45.

99. Larson, *Salamander Dream*, 45.

100. Larson, *Salamander Dream*, 45.

101. Larson, *Salamander Dream*, 45–57.

102. Larson, *Salamander Dream*, 60.

103. Larson, *Salamander Dream*, 60–61.

104. Larson, *Salamander Dream*, 70.

105. Larson, *Salamander Dream*, 84–85.

106. Larson, *Salamander Dream*, 95.

107. Larson, *Salamander Dream*, 95.

108. Larson, *Salamander Dream*, 96–97.

109. Dragoon interview.

110. Larson interview.

111. Dragoon interview.

112. Barry Deutsch, "Steven Bergson's 'Jews-And-Comics Book Montage,'" Hereville.com, accessed April 24, 2012, http://www.hereville.com/steven-berg sons-jews-and-comics-book-montage/.

113. Barry Deutsch, *Hereville: How Mirka Got Her Sword* (New York: Amulet Books, 2010), 29.

114. Deutsch, *Hereville*, 74.

115. Deutsch, *Hereville*, 122.

116. Vera Brosgol, "Updates," *Return to Sender* (webcomic), accessed November 13, 2011, http://rts.lunistice.com/.

117. Vera Brosgol, *Anya's Ghost* (New York: First Second, 2011), 97.

118. Brosgol, *Anya's Ghost*, 97.

119. Brosgol, *Anya's Ghost*, 38.

120. Brosgol, *Anya's Ghost*, 49.

121. Brosgol, *Anya's Ghost*, 49, 50.

122. Brosgol, *Anya's Ghost*, 55.

123. Brosgol, *Anya's Ghost*, 89.

124. Brosgol, *Anya's Ghost*, 91.

125. Brosgol, *Anya's Ghost*, 105.

126. Brosgol, *Anya's Ghost*, 105.

127. Brosgol, *Anya's Ghost*, 99.

128. Brosgol, *Anya's Ghost*, 103.

129. Brosgol, *Anya's Ghost*, 105–106.
130. Brosgol, *Anya's Ghost*, 106.
131. Brosgol, *Anya's Ghost*, 106.
132. Brosgol, *Anya's Ghost*, 112.
133. Brosgol, *Anya's Ghost*, 112.
134. Brosgol, *Anya's Ghost*, 112.
135. Brosgol, *Anya's Ghost*, 113.
136. Brosgol, *Anya's Ghost*, 114.
137. Brosgol, *Anya's Ghost*, 114.
138. Brosgol, *Anya's Ghost*, 114.
139. Brosgol, *Anya's Ghost*, 114.
140. Brosgol, *Anya's Ghost*, 114–115.
141. Brosgol, *Anya's Ghost*, 118.
142. Brosgol, *Anya's Ghost*, 123.
143. Brosgol, *Anya's Ghost*, 124.
144. Brosgol, *Anya's Ghost*, 127.
145. Brosgol, *Anya's Ghost*, 127.
146. Brosgol, *Anya's Ghost*, 127.
147. Brosgol, *Anya's Ghost*, 149.
148. Brosgol, *Anya's Ghost*, 149.
149. Brosgol, *Anya's Ghost*, 149.
150. Brosgol, *Anya's Ghost*, 150.
151. Brosgol, *Anya's Ghost*, 151.
152. Brosgol, *Anya's Ghost*, 151.
153. Brosgol, *Anya's Ghost*, 151.
154. Brosgol, *Anya's Ghost*, 153.
155. Brosgol, *Anya's Ghost*, 179.
156. Brosgol, *Anya's Ghost*, 211.
157. Trina Robbins, *The Great Women Cartoonists* (New York: Watson-Guptill, 2001), 117.

BIBLIOGRAPHY

Allwood, Gill. *French Feminisms: Gender and Violence in Contemporary Theory.* London: UCL Press, 1998.

Alverson, Brigid. "Comixology Launches Retailer Digital Storefronts, Upgrades App." *Publishers Weekly* (August 29, 2011). Accessed October 7, 2011. http://www.publishersweekly.com/pw/by-topic/book-news/comics/article/48496-comixology-launches-retailer-digital-storefronts-upgrades-app.html.

Aoki, Deb. "Interview: Bryan Lee O'Malley; Creator of Scott Pilgrim and Lost at Sea." About.com, 1–5. Accessed August 2, 2011. http://manga.about.com/od/mangaartistinterviews/a/Interview-Bryan-Lee-O-Amalley.htm.

Appleyard, J. A. *Becoming a Reader: The Experience of Fiction from Childhood to Adulthood.* Cambridge: Cambridge University Press, 1994.

Archie Comics Digest Magazine, no. 38, October, 1979. New York: Archie Comic Publications, 1979.

Avgerinou, Maria. "What Is 'Visual Literacy?'" *International Visual Literacy Association (IVLA).* Accessed June 27, 2011. http://www.ivla.org/org_what_vis_lit.htm.

Azevedo, Justin. Interview by the author, July 23, 2011.

Baldick, Chris. *The Concise Oxford Dictionary of Literary Terms,* s.v. "chapbook." Oxford: Oxford University Press, 1990.

Barker, Martin. *Comics: Ideology, Power and the Critics.* Manchester: Manchester University Press, 1989.

Benkoil, Dorian. "Move Over, Power Rangers; Here Comes Japan's Sailor Moon." *The Free Lance-Star,* February 18, 1995, Section E.

Black, Holly, and Ted Naifeh. *The Good Neighbors, Book One: Kin.* New York: Graphix, 2008.

Black, Holly, and Ted Naifeh. *The Good Neighbors, Book Two: Kith*. New York: Graphix, 2009.

Blake, Quentin. *Clown*. New York: Holt, 1995.

Bongco, Mila. *Reading Comics: Language, Culture, and the Concept of the Superhero in Comic Books*. New York: Garland, 2000.

Bosman, Julie. "Picture Books No Longer a Staple for Children." *New York Times*, October, 7, 2010. http://www.nytimes.com/2010/10/08/us/08picture.html?pagewanted=1.

Briggs, Raymond. *The Snowman*. New York: Dragonfly Books, 1978.

Brosgol, Vera. *Anya's Ghost*. New York: First Second, 2011.

Brosgol, Vera. "Updates." *Return to Sender* (webcomic). Accessed November 13, 2011. http://rts.lunistice.com/.

Burningham, John. *Aldo*. New York: Crown, 1991.

Burningham, John. *Granpa*. New York: Crown, 1985.

Calling All Girls magazine, issues September, 1942; October, 1957; April, 1959; May, 1959; October, 1960.

Castellucci, Cecil, and Jim Rugg. *Janes in Love*. New York: Minx, 2008.

Castellucci, Cecil, and Jim Rugg. *The Plain Janes*. New York: Minx, 2007.

Cech, John. *Angels and Wild Things: The Archetypal Poetics of Maurice Sendak*. University Park: The Pennsylvania State University Press, 1995.

Cha, Kai-Ming. "Viz Media and Manga in the U.S." Accessed August 2, 2011. http://www.publishersweekly.com/pw/by-topic/new-titles/adult-announcements/article/3065-viz-media-and-manga-in-the-u-s-.html.

Chute, Hillary L. *Graphic Women: Life Narrative and Contemporary Comics*. New York: Columbia University Press, 2010.

CLAMP. *Chobits, Volume 5*. Los Angeles: Tokyopop, 2003.

Clowes, Daniel. *Ghost World*. 6th softcover ed. Seattle: Fantagraphics Books, August 2001.

Collins, Max Allan. *Patriotic Pin-Ups*. Portland: Collector's Press, 2002.

ComicSpace (website). Accessed October 21, 2011. http://comicspace.com.

Considine, J. D. "Manga Mania Comes to the West; Japanese Comics and Graphic Novels Are No Longer Just a Niche Market in North America—Manga Is Flooding into Bookstores Thanks to Girls' Buying Power," *Globe and Mail (Canada), The Globe Review*, July 17, 2003, R3.

Cooper, Linda Z. "Supporting Visual Literacy in the School Library Media Center: Developmental, Socio-cultural, and Experiential Considerations and Scenarios." *Knowledge Quest* 36, no. 3 (January/February 2008): 14–19.

Curti, Merle. *Probing Our Past*. New York: Harper, 1955.

Daniels, Les. *Wonder Woman: The Life and Times of the Amazon Princess; The Complete History*. San Francisco: Chronicle Books, 2000.

Denning, Michael. *Mechanic Accents: Dime Novels and Working-Class Culture in America*. London: Verso, 1998.

Deppey, Dirk. "She's Got Her Own Thing Now." *The Comics Journal*, no. 269 (July 2005): 10–20.

De Souza, Steven E. "Annotations by Stephen E. de Souza." In *The Best of the Golden Age Sheena, Queen of the Jungle, Vol. 1*. Ed. Stephen Christy. Chicago: Devil's Due Publishing, 2008.

Deutsch, Barry. *Hereville: How Mirka Got Her Sword*. New York: Amulet Books, 2010.

Deutsch, Barry. "Steven Bergson's 'Jews-And-Comics Book Montage.'" Accessed April 24, 2012. http://www.hereville.com/steven-bergsons-jews-and -comics-book-montage/.

Doonan, Jane. *Looking at Pictures in Picture Books*. Stroud: The Thimble Press, 1993.

Eisner, Will. *Comics and Sequential Art: Principles and Practices from the Legendary Cartoonist*. New York: Norton, 2008.

"Elizabeth H. Marston, Inspiration for Wonder Woman, 100" (obituary). *New York Times*, April 3, 1993, Saturday, Late Edition, Section 1, 11.

Girlamatic. "About." Accessed October 21, 2011. http://girlamatic.com/about/.

Graham, Judith. "Texts That Teach: Wordless Picture Books." *Language Matters*, no. 1 (1987): 22–24.

Haenigsen, Harry. "A Week with Penny" (cartoon). *Calling All Girls* magazine, October 1957.

Haining, Peter, ed. *The Penny Dreadful Or, Strange, Horrid and Sensational Tales!* London: Victor Gollancz, 1976.

Hajdu, David. *The Ten-Cent Plague: The Great Comic-Book Scare and How It Changed America*. New York: Farrar, Straus and Giroux, 2008.

Hale, Shannon, Dean Hale, and Nathan Hale. *Rapunzel's Revenge*. New York: Bloomsbury, 2008.

Harris, Benjamin. "Blurring Borders, Visualizing Connections: Aligning Information and Visual Literacy Learning Outcomes." *Reference Services Review* 38, no. 4 (2010): 523–35. doi:10.1108/00907321011090700.

Hashimoto, Akiko. "Blondie, Sazae, and Their Storied Successors: Japanese Families in Newspaper Comics." In *Imagined Families, Lived Families: Culture and Kinship in Contemporary Japan*. Ed. Akiko Hashimoto and John W. Traphagan. Albany: SUNY Press, 2008.

Hemming, Judith, and Jane Legget. *Comics and Magazines*. Exeter: The English Centre, 1984.

Hicks, Faith Erin. *The War at Ellsmere*. San Jose, CA: SLG Publishing, 2008.

Horn, Maurice. *Women in the Comics; Revised and Updated, Vol. 3*. Broomall: Chelsea House Publishers, 2001.

Humphries, Stephen. *Hooligans or Rebels? An Oral History of Working-Class Childhood and Youth, 1889–1939*. Oxford: Blackwell, 1995.

Hutchins, Pat. *Rosie's Walk*. New York: Macmillan, 1968.

ICv2. "Tokyopop to Publish Manga in Japanese Format: Change Will Affect Publisher's Entire Line-up." January 30, 2002. Accessed August 4, 2011. http://www.icv2.com/articles/news/1067.html.

Iser, Wolfgang. *The Implied Reader: Patterns of Communication in Prose Fiction from Bunyan to Beckett*. Baltimore: The Johns Hopkins University Press, 1990.

Johnson-Woods, Toni, ed. *Manga: An Anthology of Global and Cultural Perspectives*. New York: Continuum, 2010.

Johnston, Allyn, and Marla Frazee. "Why We're Still in Love with Picture Books (Even Though They're Supposed to Be Dead)." *The Horn Book Magazine*, May/June 2011, 10–16.

Kieth, Sam, Alex Pardee, and Chris Wisnia. *Ojo*. Portland: Oni Press, 2005.

Krashen, Stephen D. *The Power of Reading: Insights from the Research*. 2nd ed. Westport, CT: Libraries Unlimited, 2004.

Larson, Hope. *Salamander Dream*. Richmond: AdHouse Books, 2005.

Lewis, David. "The Jolly Postman's Long Ride, or, Sketching a Picture-Book History." *Signal*, no. 78 (September 1995): 178–92.

MacDonald, Heidi. "Manga Pioneer Tokyopop Shuts Down U.S. Publishing." *Publishers Weekly* (Book News), April 15, 2011. Accessed August 2, 2011. http://www.publishersweekly.com/pw/by-topic/book-news/comics/article/46885-manga-pioneer-tokyopop-shuts-down-u-s-publishing.html.

MacDonald, Heidi, and Calvin Reid. "Comics, Digital Delivery and a Few Movies Rule Comic-Con 2011." *Publishers Weekly*, July 29, 2011. Accessed October 5, 2011. http://www.publishersweekly.com/pw/by-topic/industry -news/trade-shows-events/article/48173-comics-digital-delivery-and-a -few-movies-rule-comic-con-2011.html.

MacWilliams, Mark W., ed. *Japanese Visual Culture: Explorations in the World of Manga and Anime*. Armonk, NY: M. E. Sharpe, 2008.

McCallum, Robyn. *Ideologies of Identity in Adolescent Fiction: The Dialogic Construction of Subjectivity*. New York: Garland, 1999.

McCloud, Scott. *Reinventing Comics*. New York: Paradox Press, 2000.

McCloud, Scott. *Understanding Comics: The Invisible Art*. New York: Paradox Press, 1993, 2000.

Meek, Margaret. *How Texts Teach What Readers Learn*. Stroud: The Thimble Press, 1988.

Michaels, Julia. "Pulp Fiction." *The Horn Book Magazine*, May/June, 2004, 299–306.

Miss America magazine, vol. 1, no. 92, September 1958, Miss America Publishing Corp.

Miss America magazine, vol. 7, no. 2, September 1947, Miss America Publishing Corp.

Moi, Toril. *The Kristeva Reader*. Oxford: Blackwell, 1986.

Naifeh, Ted. *Courtney Crumrin and the Coven of Mystics*. 1st ed. trade paperback. Portland: Oni Press, 2003.

Naifeh, Ted. *Courtney Crumrin and the Night Things*. 1st ed. trade paperback. Portland: Oni Press, 2002.

Nikolajeva, Maria, and Carole Scott. "The Dynamics of Picturebook Communication." *Children's Literature in Education* 31, no. 4 (2000): 225–39.

Nyberg, Amy Kiste. "Poisoning Children's Culture: Comics and Their Critics." *Contributions to the Study of Popular Culture* 75 (2002): 167–86.

Nyberg, Amy Kiste. *Seal of Approval: The History of the Comics Code*. Jackson: University Press of Mississippi, 1998.

Petersen, Robert S. *Comics, Manga, and Graphic Novels: A History of Graphic Narratives*. Santa Barbara, CA: Praeger, 2011.

Pulaski, Mary Ann Spenser. *Understanding Piaget: An Introduction to Children's Cognitive Development*. New York: Harper & Row, 1971.

Radicalesbians. "The Woman Identified Woman." In *The Second Wave: A Reader in Feminist Theory*. Ed. Linda Nicholson. New York: Routledge, 1997.

Rathmann, Peggy. *Good Night, Gorilla*. New York: G. P. Putnam's, 1994.

Reid, Calvin. "Japanese Publishers Launch Jmanga.com Manga Portal at Comic-Con." *Publishers Weekly* (Digital), July 22, 2011. Accessed August 2, 2011. http://www.publishersweekly.com/pw/by-topic/digital/content-and -e-books/article/48109-japanese-publishers-launch-jmanga-com-manga -portal-at-comic-con.html.

Reynolds, Kimberley. *Girls Only? Gender and Popular Children's Fiction in Britain, 1880–1910*. New York: Harvester Wheatsheaf, 1990.

Robbins, Trina. "Contemporary Graphic Novels for Girls: A Core List." *Booklist*, February 1, 2004, 985–86.

Robbins, Trina. *From Girls to Grrrlz: A History of Female Comics from Teens to Zines*. San Francisco: Chronicle Books, 1999.

Robbins, Trina. *The Great Women Cartoonists*. New York: Watson-Guptill, 2001.

Robbins, Trina, and Anne Timmons. *Go Girl!* 1st ed. trade paperback. Milwaukie, OR: Dark Horse Comics, 2002.

Rosenblatt, Louise M. *Literature as Exploration*. New York: D. Appleton-Century-Crofts, 1938.

Saraceni, Mario. *The Language of Comics*. London: Routledge, 2003.

Satrapi, Marjane. *Persepolis: The Story of a Childhood*. Trans. L'Association, Paris. New York: Pantheon Books, 2003.

Satrapi, Marjane. *Persepolis 2: The Story of a Return*. Trans. Anjali Singh. New York: Pantheon Books, 2004.

Schodt, Frederik L. *Manga! Manga! The World of Japanese Comics*. Tokyo: Kodansha International, 1983.

Scieszka, Jon, and Lane Smith. *The Stinky Cheese Man and Other Fairly Stupid Tales*. New York: Viking, 1992.

Sendak, Maurice. *Caldecott & Co.: Noted on Books and Pictures*. New York: Farrar, Straus and Giroux, 1988.

Sendak, Maurice. *In the Night Kitchen*. New York: Harper & Row, 1970.

Sendak, Maurice. *We Are All in the Dumps with Jack and Guy: Two Nursery Rhymes with Pictures*. New York: HarperCollins, 1993.

Shulevitz, Uri. "What Is a Picture Book?" In *Only Connect: Readings on Children's Literature*. 3rd ed. Ed. Sheila Egoff, Gordon Stubbs, Ralph Ashley, and Wendy Sutton. Toronto: Oxford University Press, 1996.

Solomon, Charles. "Four Mothers of Manga Gain American Fans with Expertise in a Variety of Visual Styles." *New York Times*, November 28, 2006. Accessed August 15, 2011. http://www.nytimes.com/2006/11/28/arts/design/28clam. html?8dpc.

Soryo, Fuyumi. *Mars Vol. 8*. Los Angeles: Tokyopop, [1996] 2002.

Spiegelman, Art. *Maus: A Survivor's Tale. I: My Father Bleeds History*. New York: Pantheon Books, 1986.

Spiegelman, Art. *Maus: A Survivor's Tale, II: And Here My Troubles Began*. New York: Pantheon Books, 1991.

Springen, Karen. "Don't Write the Obit for Picture Books Yet." *Publishers Weekly* 257, no. 49 (2010): 15.

Springhall, John. *Youth, Popular Culture and Moral Panics: Penny Gaffs to Gangsta-Rap, 1830–1996*. London: Macmillan, 1998.

Stanley, John, and Irving Tripp. *Little Lulu: Lulu Goes Shopping*. Milwaukie, OR: Dark Horse Books, 2004.

Stimson, James. *Thirteen O'Clock*. San Francisco: Chronicle Books, 2005.

Takahashi, Rumiko. *Inu Yasha, Vol. 1*. 2nd ed. San Francisco: Viz Media, 2005.

Talbot, Bryan. *The Tale of One Bad Rat*. Milwaukie, OR: Dark Horse Books, 1995.

Tamaki, Mariko, and Steve Rolston. *Emiko Superstar*. New York: Minx, 2008.

Tamaki, Mariko, and Jillian Tamaki. *Skim*. Toronto: Goundwood Books, 2008.

Tan, Shaun. *The Arrival*. New York: Arthur A. Levine Books, 2007.

"Tizzie's Private Practice Session" (story). *Calling All Girls* magazine, April, 1959.

Tomine, Adrian. *Optic Nerve*, no. 3, August 1996. Montreal: Drawn and Quarterly Publications, 1996.

Weiner, Stephen. *Faster than a Speeding Bullet: The Rise of the Graphic Novel.* New York: Nantier, Beall, Minoustchine, 2003.

Wertham, Frederic. *Seduction of the Innocent.* New York: Rinehart, 1954.

Whelehan, Imelda. "Feminism and Trash: Destabilising 'The Reader.'" In *Gendering the Reader.* Ed. Sara Mills. New York: Harvester Wheatsheaf, 1994.

Wilkins, John. "'Who Are We Protecting Them From?' The Selection of Graphic Novels in the London Borough of Camden." In *Graphic Account: The Selection and Promotion of Graphic Novels in Libraries for Young People.* Ed. Keith Barker. Newcastle-Under-Lyme: The Library Association Youth Libraries Group, 1993.

Yazawa, Ai. *Nana, Vol. 1.* San Francisco: Viz Media, LLC, 2005.

INDEX

20th Century Boys, 158
24 nengumi, 141–43
Ace Comics, 5
Action Comics, 5
Acton, Alison, 201
Adachi, Mitsuru, 158
AdHouse Books, 203
Aldo, 46, 48, 49
Alice; or, The Adventures of an English Girl in Persia, 10
Alice's Adventures in Wonderland, 156
All My Darling Daughters, 158
Allwood, Gill, 123, 192
Ally Sloper, 4
alternative press, 31, 32
Arnheim, Rudolph, 103
anime, 146, 147, 148, 157, 159
Anya's Ghost, 208–10, 211–13, 214, 215–17, 218
Apapa, Mokona, 144
Appleyard, J. A., 103, 104
Arakawa, Hiromu, 145
Archaia, 201
Archie, 13, 14, 15, *15, 16*
Archie, 13–15, *16*, 92, 199

The Arrival, 66, 67, 68, 69
Asahi, 135
Asahi Graph, 135
The Avengers, 219
Azevedo, Justin, 162, 173–76

Bakhtin, Mikhail, 77, 194, 195
Baltimore Sun, 177
Barker, Martin, 11, 18
Barr, Donna, 207
Batman, 5, 219; *Batman Begins*, 219; *The Dark Knight*, 219; *The Dark Knight Rises*, 219
Bayeux Tapestry, 3
Beadle and Adams, 9
Becoming a Reader: The Experience of Fiction from Childhood to Adulthood, 103, 104
Benkoil, Dorian, 147, 153
Betty, 13, 14, *15*, 92, 181
Betty and Veronica, 14
Bigot, George, 133, 134
Bishōjo Senshi Sērā Mūn. See Sailor Moon
Black Is for Beginnings, 181

Black, Holly, 45, *47*
Blake, Quentin, 38, 60–63
Block, Francesca Lia, 192
bloods. *See* penny dreadfuls
Blue is for Nightmares, 181
Blue Monday, 162
Bolter, Jay David, 76
Bongco, Mila, 13, 129
Booklist, 208
booksellers, 32, 78, 123, 147, 148, 149, 160, 171, 172, 176, 180, 181, 198
bookstores. *See* booksellers
Borders Group, Inc., 160, 161
Bosman, Julie, 78, 79
Bouissou, Jean-Marie, 131
Box of Curios, 135
Briggs, Raymond, 63–66
Bringing Up Father, 135
Brosgol, Vera, 208, *210*, *214*, 217–18
Buell, Marjorie Henderson, 19
Burningham, John, 46, 49, 59, 60
By the Wayside, 201–2, 206
Byfield, Mary, 11

Caldecott & Co.: Notes on Books and Pictures, 66
Calling All Girls, 22–23, 25, *26*, 27, *28–29*, 29–30
Cardcaptor Sakura, 144, 148, 150
Cardcaptor Sakura: Master of the Clow, 150
Cardcaptors (cartoon), 148
caricature, 5–6, 64, 131–32, 134
Cartoon Network, 148
Castellucci, Cecil, 1, 54–57
Caxton, William, 4
CCA. *See* Comics Code Authority
CD-ROM, 198
Cech, John, 65–66

cell phones. *See* digital delivery
censorship, 10, 17–18, 106, 136–38, 173–75, 218
challenged books. *See* censorship
chapbooks, 6
cheap library, 9
Chiggers, 157, 203, 206
Chobits, 144–45
Chute, Hillary L., 191–92
CLAMP, 144–46, 148, 150
Clowes, Daniel, 2, 101, *102*, 181
Clown, 60, 61–63
Clugston, Chynna, 162
Coffman, William, 74
cognitive development, 75, 76
collector's market, 32, 136
Collins, Max Allan, 27
Columbine High School massacre, 10
comic book conventions, 146, 161–62, 178–79, 203
Comic Book Legal Defense Fund, 179
comic book specialty shops, 31–32, 123, 129, 148–49, 171–72, 175–76, 178–80, 200
Comic-Con. *See* San Diego Comic-Con International
Comic Cuts, 4
comic strips, 4–6, 9, 30–31, 64, 66, 134–39, 176, 198
comics: composite text in, 52, 220; controversial topics in, 101, 103, 173–75, 192 193–95, 196, 197; crime, 5–6, 13, 16–17, 19, 177; digital delivery of, 199 (*see also* e-readers; webcomics); digital media in, 161, 198, 199, 200; fantasy in, 46, 104, 107, 121, 140, 150; film adaptations of, 162, 191, 219; frameless panels in, 86, *88*;

horror, 5–6, 13–14, 16–17, 19, 177; literary value of, 32, 69, 82, 92, 163, 177, 179, 181; mechanics of, 69; "pause panel" in, 86; perception of time in, 86–89; realism in, 1, 101, 103–4, 184, 186; romance, 18–19, 129; slice of life in (*see* realism in captions in, 64–65, 69, 82–83, *84*, 85, 186); speech balloons in, 83, 85, 132, 153, 190; thought bubbles in, 69, 82–83; unreliable narrator in, 52, 105; violence in, 6, 12, 16–17, 174, 184

Comics and Magazines, 30

Comics and Sequential Art: Principles and Practices from the Legendary Cartoonist, 3, *91*

Comics Code, 17, 18, 130, 177, 178, 218, 220

Comics Code Authority (CCA), 17

The Comics Journal, 147

Comics: Ideology, Power and the Critics, 11

ComicSpace, 200

comix. *See* underground comics

ComiXology, 200

complementary narrative, 41–42, *43*, 44, 69, *81*, 82, 115, 182

The Complete Maus, 198. *See also Maus*

Comstock, Anthony, 9, 16

A Contract with God and Other Tenement Stories, 90, *91*, 176–77, 179, 181

contradictory narrative, 40–41, 46, 49, *50–51*, 52, 69

contrapuntal narrative, 41, 44–46, *47*, 48, 82, 106, 213

convention culture. *See* comic book conventions

Cooper, Linda Z., 74–76

Coraline, 181; film adaptation of, 208

Couch, N. C. Christopher, 148

Couillard, Chelsea, 162, 173–76

counterpoint. *See* contrapuntal narrative

Courtney Crumrin, 1, 83, *84*, 86, *89–90*, 107, *108*, *110–11*, 112, *113*, 115, *116*, 117, 181

crime. *See* juvenile delinquency

Cross Game, 158

Crumb, R., 178

Curti, Merle, 9, 11

Dalziel, Margaret, 7

Dango Kushisuke Man'yu-ki, 136

Dark Horse Comics, 147, 148

DC Comics, 12, 14, 18, 199–200

Debes, John, 73–74

Deppey, Dirk, 147

Detective Comics, 5

Deutsch, Barry, 1, 207, 218

dialogism, 77, 82–83, 92, 104, 194, 195, 220. *See also* interior narrative; polyphony

Diamond (distribution), 202

Diaz-Przybyl, Lillian, 160

dime novel, 8–9, 11, 16

Disney, 65, 139

distributers, 200, 202

Doonan, Jane, 52–53, 59, 77, 103

doujinshi, 144

Dragoon, Leigh, 201–3, 206–7

"Dylan and Donovan," 104–6

e-books. *See* e-readers

e-readers, 32, 161, 198, 199

EC. *See* Entertaining Comics

Eightball, 101

Eisner, Will, 2, *3*, 3–4, 7, 12, 59, 90–91, *91*, 129, 172, 176–79, 181

INDEX

Elektra (film), 219
Elfquest, 31, 206–7
Elliot, Freeman, *26*, 27, *28*
emaki, 132
Emiko Superstar, 42–43, 93
enhancing interaction, 41, 42, 43
Entertaining Comics, 16, 17
etoki hoshi, 132

Fables, 159
Faerie Path: Lamia's Revenge, 201
fan culture. *See* fandom
fandom, 178–79, 201. *See also* otaku
fantasy genre, 104, 107. *See also*
    comics, fantasy in
Fantomah, 12
*Faster Than a Speeding Bullet: The Rise
    of the Graphic Novel*, 129, 172
female stereotypes, 14–15, *15*, 19, 22–
    23, *24*, 25, *28–29*, 29–30, 92–93,
    123, 153, 155–56, 206
feminism, 2, 12–13, 22–23, 31, 49,
    107, 114, 117, 120–121, *122*,
    123, 220. *See also* second wave of
    feminism; theory of difference;
    women's rights movement
"Feminism and Trash: Destabilising
    the Reader," 106
fierce plates, 7
Fleischer, Max, 139
formalism, 40
Fraggle Rock, 201
Frank Miller's Sin City, 219
Frazee, Marla, 78
*From Girls to Grrrlz: A History of
    Female Comics from Teens to Zines*,
    5, 14
Frostbite, 201
Fullmetal Alchemist, 145

Gabriel, Davi, 130–31, 158–60
Gaiman, Neil, 181, 208
Gaines, William, 16, 17
gender discrimination, 171, 206–207.
    See also sexism
Gentleman Jim, 66
gestalt, 90, 91
Ghost World, 2, 101–4, *102*, 181
Ghost World (film), 219
Girl's Own Paper, 10
Girlamatic, 200–2, 207
*Girls Only? Gender and Popular
    Children's Fiction in Britain, 1880–
    1910*, 10–11
girls' magazines, 22–23, 25–27, 30
Go Girl! 117–23, *118*, *120*, *122*, 154
Goldberg, Wendy, 149
Golden Age (comics/of comics), 5
The Good Neighbors, Book Two: Kith,
    46, *47*
Goodnight Gorilla, 44–45
Graham, Judith, 64
Granpa, 59, 60
graphic novels, 32, 104, 123, 129,
    137, 148, 163, 171–77, 179–81,
    196–98, 218–20; adaptations of
    books as, 181, 201–2
graphic treatment of text, 90,
    90–91
The Great Women Cartoonists, 18
Greek Myths Retold, 202
Gregory, Roberta, 207
Grey Horses, 157, 203
guided view technology, 200

Haenigsen, Harry, 29
Hagio, Motō. *See* 24 nengumi
Haining, Peter, 7
Hajdu, David, 15, 18–19

Hale, Dean, 49, *50–51*
Hale, Nathan, 49, *50–51*
Hale, Shannon, 49, *50–51*
A Harlot's Progress, 5
HarperCollins, 201
Harris, Benjamin, 76
Hasegawa, Machiko, 138–39
Hashimoto, Akiko, 138–39
Hemming, Judith, 30
Hereville: How Mirka Got Her Sword, 1, 207–8, 218
Hicks, Faith Erin, 158
hieroglyphs, 3
Hōchi, 135
Hogarth, William, 5
Hokusai Manga, 132
Hokusai, Katsushika, 131–32
Hooligans or Rebels? An Oral History of Working-Class Childhood and Youth, 1889–1939, 7
Horn, Maurice, 31, 148
The Horn Book Magazine, 78
How Texts Teach What Readers Learn, 77
Huang, Qiuning, 155, 160–61, 171
Humphries, Stephen, 7
Hutchins, Pat, 44

I Was a Teenage Fairy, 192
icon, 59, 77, 90
ICv2, 149
Igarashi, Satsuki, 144
Iger, S. M., 12
Ikeda, Riyoko. *See* 24 nengumi
Illustrated London News, 133
The Implied Reader: Patterns of Communication in Prose Fiction from Bunyan to Beckett, 39–40
In the Night Kitchen, 64–66

independent comics, 2, 31, 92, 157, 172, 180; self publishing of, 31–32, 202, 220
index, 90–91
Ingarden, Roman, 39–40
integrated text, 42, 53–59, 96–98, 132; *See also* graphic treatment of text
interior narrative, 82–83, 92–93, 104, 194, *195*, 220; *See also* dialogism
International Visual Literacy Association, 73–74
Internet, 32, 160–61, 199–203, 218–19
intertextuality, 196, *196*
Inuyasha, 145, 155, 156
Iser, Wolfgang, 39, 40
It Ain't Me, Babe, 31
IVLA. *See* International Visual Literacy Association

Janes in Love, 54, 57–58, *58*
The Japan Punch, 133–34
Japanese cartoons. *See* anime
Japanese Digital Comics Association, 161, 200
Japanese Visual Culture, 130
Jenny Diver, the Female Highwayman, 10
Jijishimpo, 135
The Jim Henson Company, 201
JManga, 161, 200
Johnston, Allyn, 78
Jones, Frewin, 201
josei, 130, 162
¡*Journalista!* 147
Jughead, 13–15, *16*
juvenile delinquency, 7–8, 15–17, 19, 79, 178–79

Katy Keene, 14, 123
Katy Keene, 14
kibyoshi, 132–33
Kick-Ass, 219
Kieth, Sam, 80, *81*, 202
Kihara, Toshie. *See* 24 nengumi
Kim, Young, 181
Kindle Fire, 199
Kirkus, 208
Kitchen Sink Press, 179
Kitchen, Denis, 179
Kitazawa, Rakuten, 135
Krashen, Stephen, 80
Krazy Kat, 5
Kristeva, Julia, 114, 115
The Kristeva Reader, 114
Kyōryū Sentai Zyuranger. See Mighty Morphin Power Rangers

Lana Lang, 121
Land of the Blindfolded, 155
The Language of Comics, 3
Larson, Hope, 157–58, 201, 203, *205*, 206, 218
Lee, Stan, 178
Legget, Jane, 30
Levy, Stuart, 160
Lewis, David, 64, 69, 82
Lewter, Troy, 160
librarians, 123, 162, 172–73, 175–76, 220
libraries, 79, 136, 162, 171–76, 180–81; intellectual freedom and, 175
literacy, 1, 37, 77–80, 82, 180
Literature as Exploration, 40, 52
Little Lulu, 19–22
Little Lulu Moppet, 19–22
Little Nemo in Slumberland, 66
Lois Lane, 121

Looking at Pictures in Picture Books, 52
Lu, Alvin, 162

Magic Knight Rayearth, 144
magical girl genre, 150, 155, 158
mahō shōjo. *See* magical girl genre
Malaeska: The Indian Wife of the White Hunter, 9
Manga, 137–38
manga, 32, 123, 129–34, 136–50, *152*, 153, *154*, 155–63, 171–72, 175, 200; aesthetics of, 142, 146, 157; American influence in, 134–136; British influence in, 134; cartoon adaptations of, 157, 146–48, 153; cell phone, 199; conventions of, 149; depiction of eyes in, 142–44, 157; influence in America of, 157–58; propaganda in, 137–38; romance in, 140–142; scanlations of, 160–62, 200; Sengoku period, 156; translation of, 147–48, 160–62; "unflipped" translations of, 148–49. *See also* Original English Language Manga
Manga Tarō, 136
mangaka, 135, 137, 139, 141–42, 145; female, 139 141–42 145
Manley, Joey, 200
"Marge." *See* Buell
Marge's Little Lulu, 19
Mars, 143
Marston: Elizabeth Holloway, 12, 13; William Moulton, 12, 13. *See also* Wonder Woman
Marumaru Chimbun, 134
Marvel Comics, 18, 22, 199–200
Maus, 92, 179, 181, 184. *See also* Spiegelman, Art

McCallum, Robyn, 194
McCay, Winsor, 66
McCloud, Scott, 2–5, 10, 86, *87–88*, 177, 199–200, 203, 218
McManus, George, 135
McQueen, Diana, 200
Mead, Richelle, 201
Meek, Margaret, 77–79
Mercury, 157, 203
Meta Maus, 198. *See also Maus*
metafictive device, 53, 105
Meyer, Stephenie, 181
Michael Rosen's Sad Book, 38
Michaels, Julia, 180
Middaugh, Dallas, 144
Mighty Morphin Power Rangers, 146, 147
Miller, Frank, 219
Millie the Model, 14–15, 18
Miss America, 22–25
Miss America, 22
Miyao, Shigeo, 136
Modern Tales, 200
Moi, Toril, 114–15
montage, 142–45, 158, 177
moral panic, 7, 8, 9, 177, 180
Ms. Magazine, 13
My Aunt Is a Pilot Whale, 192

Naifeh, Ted, 1, 46, *47*, 83, *84*, *89–90*, 107, *108*, 109, *110–11*, 112–113, *113*, 115, *116*, 117, 181
Nakahara, Jun'ichi, 140
Nankivell, Frank, 135
Nana, 151–54
Nekoi, Tsubaki, 144
New Criticism, 40
New Fun Comics, 5
New York Times, 13, 78, 146

New York World, 4, 134, 135
Nikolajeva, Maria, 40–42, 44, 46, 49, 52
Nonki na Tōsan, 135
North, Sterling, 9–10
Noshinaga, Fumi, 158
Nyberg, Amy Kiste, 9, 17, 177–78

OEL. *See* Original English Language Manga
O'Malley, Bryan Lee, 156–58. *See also Scott Pilgrim vs. the World*
Ohkawa, Nanase, 144, 146
Ojo, 80, *81*, 82
Okamoto, Ippei, 135–36
omniscient narrator, 83, *94*
Only Connect: Readings on Children's Literature, 38
Optic Nerve, 104–7, 181
Original English Language Manga, 162. *See also* manga
Ortabasi, Melek, 159
Ōshima, Yumiko. *See* 24 nengumi
Otaku, 159–60. *See also* fandom; manga
Outside Over There, 59

Palestine, 181
Pardee, Alex, 80, *81*
Patriotic Pin-ups, 27
Patsy Walker, 15, 18
Patsy Walker, 23, *24*, 25, 30
"Peace Preservation Law," 137
Penny, 29–30
The Penny Dreadful Or, Strange, Horrid & Sensational Tales! 11
penny dreadfuls, 6–11
Pep, 13
Persepolis (film), 191–92, 219

Persepolis 2: The Story of a Return, 181, 187–191

Persepolis: The Story of a Childhood, 181–82, *182*, 183, *183*, 184–85, *185*, 186, *186*, 187, *188–89*, 191

Petersen, Robert S., 12–13, 131–34, 139–40, 199

The Phantom, 5

Phillipps, Susanne, 139

Piaget, Jean, 75

pictograph, 3

pictorial storytelling, 3

picture book, 32, 37–42, 44–46, 48–49, 52–54, 58–59, 60, 63–66, 69, 77–79, 82

pin-up, 12, 14, 27

Pini, Wendy, 31, 207

The Plain Janes, 1, 54–55, *55*, 56–57

Pokémon, 148

political cartoon, 134–35

polyphony, 82, 106, 194, 198, 220. *See also* dialogism

Ponchi-e. *See* Punch Pictures

popular entertainment, 2, 6–11, 22, 30, 65, 77, 107, 220. *See also* working-class literature

post-war comics, 23

post-war Japan, 138–39, 141

Potter, Beatrix, 41, 194–96

Pretty Soldier Sailor Moon. See Sailor Moon

printing press, 4

Prough, Jennifer, 141–43, 145

Provoost, Anne, 192

Publishers Weekly, 160, 199

Pulitzer, Joseph, 134, 135

Pulitzer Prize, 172, 179

Pulp, 12, 33, 106–7

Pumphrey, George, 6

Punch, 134

Punch Pictures, 134

Radicalesbians, 114

Randhawa, Bikkar, 74

A Rake's Progress, 5

Ranma ½, 145, 147, 157–58

Rapunzel's Revenge, 49, *50–51*, 52

Rathman, Peggy, 44

Raw, 179

reader-response, 52, 59–60, 64

reader-response theory, 38–40. *See also* transactional theory

Reading Comics: Language, Culture, and the Concept of the Superhero in Comic Books, 13, 129

The Red Tree, 38

Reid, Calvin, 161

Reinventing Comics, 199

Return to Sender, 208

Reynolds, Kimberley, 10

Ribon no kishi, 139–40

Robbins, Trina, 5–6, 14, 18, 31, 117, *118*, 119–20, *120*, 121, *122*, 123, 180, 219

Rolston, Steve, 42, *43*

Rosen, Michael, 38

Rosenblatt, Louise, 40, 52, 60

Rosie's Walk, 44–45

Rudy, Jared, 171–72

Rugg, Jim, 1, 54–55, *55*, 56, 57, *58*

Russell, P. Craig, 181

Sabin, Roger, 178

Sacco, Joe, 181

Sailor Moon, 146–48, 151, 154, 157–58

Salamander Dream, 203–4, 205, *205*, 206, 218

San Diego Comic-Con International, 161, 199. *See also* comic book conventions
Saraceni, Mario, 3–6, 85, 90, 91
Satrapi, Marjane, 181–82, *182*, 183, *183*, 184, *185*, 186, *186*, *188*, 191–92, 198
Saturday Evening Post, 19
satzdenken, 39
Sazae-San, 138–39
Schodt, Frederik L., 130–31, 134–38
school story, 107, 108, 142, 158
Scieszka, Jon, 53
Scott Pilgrim, 157, 162
Scott Pilgrim vs. the World, 219
Scott, Carole, 40–42, 44, 46, 49, 52
The Second Wave: A Reader in Feminist Theory, 114
second wave of feminism, 22, 123, 220
Seduction of the Innocent, 15–16, 79
seinen manga, 130, 145
semiotics, 60, 90
Senate Subcommittee on Juvenile Delinquency, 16, 17
Sendak, Maurice, 59, 64–66
sequential art, 2–4, 7, 69, 218
Seuling, Phil, 179
sexism, 25, *26*, 27, *28*, 29–30, 119–20, 153; subversion of, 22, 115, 121–22. *See also* female stereotypes
sexuality, 93, 96, 97, 98, 99, 100, 101, 102, 106, 141
sexual orientation, 96–97, *98*, 99
sexual abuse 105, 106, 192–93, *193*, 194, 196, 198
Sheena, Queen of the Jungle, 12
shilling shockers. *See* penny dreadfuls

Shin Nippon Mangaka Kyōkai (The New Cartoonists Association of Japan), 137
Shintakarazima (New Treasure Island), 139
sho-jo. *See* shōjo manga
Shōjo Club, 137
shōjo manga, 130, 137, 139–47, 150, 155, 162; aesthetics of, 142–46. *See also* manga; montage
shōnen manga, 130, 137, 140, 143, 145, 147, 156. *See also* manga
Shōnen Club, 137
shoujo. *See* shōjo manga
Shulevitz, Uri, 38
Sin City. See Frank Miller's Sin City
Skim, 2, 93–94, *94*, 95, *95*, 96–97, *98*, 99–101
Smith, Lane, 53
The Snowman, 63–66, 69
Solomon, Charles, 145–46
Soryo, Fuyumi, 143
Spiderman, 219
Spiegelman, Art, 92, 178, 181, 184, 198
The Spirit, 177, 179
Springen, Karen, 78, 79
Springhall, John, 7–8
Stanley, John, 19
Steinem, Gloria, 13
Stimson, James, 53
The Stinky Cheese Man and Other Fairly Stupid Tales, 53–54, 58
Stolarz, Laurie Faria, 181
story paper, 9
storybook, 38
superhero, 1, 5, 12–14, 22, 117, *118*, 119–21, 123, 129, 130–31, 148, 171–72, 178, 180–81, 219

Superman, 5, 121
Superman, 5
Superman Returns, 219
symbol, 3, 32, 52, 59, 73–75, 77, 90–91
symmetrical interaction, 41, 44

*Tagosaku to Mokubē no Tōkyō
    Kembutsu*, 135
Takahashi, Makoto, 140
Takahashi, Mizuki, 140–42
Takahashi, Rumiko, 145, 147, 155, 157
Takarazuka Revue, 139
Takemiya, Keiko. *See* 24 nengumi
Takeuchi, Naoko, 146, 147, 157
Talbot, Bryan, 192, *193*, 194–95, *195*,
    196, *196–97*, 198
The Tale of One Bad Rat, 192, *193*,
    194–95, *195*, 196, *196–97*
The Tale of Peter Rabbit, 41
The Tale of Two Bad Mice, 196, *196*
Tamaki, Jillian, 2, 93, *94–95*, 96, *98*
Tamaki, Mariko, 2, 42, *43*, 93, *94–95*,
    96, *98*
Tan, Shaun, 38, 66–67, *68*
tankōbon, 149
*The Ten Cent Plague: The Great
    Comic-Book Scare and How It
    Changed America*, 18
The Terrific Register, 11
Tezuka, Osamu, 139–40, 142
theory of difference, 123. *See also*
    feminism
Thirteen O'Clock, 53
Timely Comics, 22
Timmons, Anne, 117, *118*, 119–20,
    120, *122*, 123
Tizzie, 27, 29, *29*
toba-e, 132
Tōbaé, 134

Tokyopop, 147–50, 160–61, 201
Tomine, Adrian, 104–6, 181
Töpffer, Rodolphe, 5
trade paperbacks, 32, 171, 198. *See
    also* graphic novels
transactional theory. *See* Rosenblatt
Traps for the Young, 9
Tripp, Irving, 19
Tsukuba, Sakura, 155
Twilight, 181

ukiyo-e, 131–32
underground comics, 31, 92, 130,
    178–80, 207, 218, 220
*Understanding Comics: The Invisible
    Art*, 2, *87–88*
Urasawa, Naoki, 158

Vampire Academy 201
Vampire Academy: A Graphic Novel,
    201, 202
Veronica, 14, *15*, 92, 181
Vertigo Comics, 159
vice societies, 9. *See also* censorship
Vieceli, Emma, 201
visual literacy, 32, 69, 73–77, 79
Viz Media, 147–48, 162, 200
Vizmanga.com, 200

Watchmen (film), 219
*We Are All in the Dumps with Jack and
    Guy*, 66
webcomics, 32, 198–204, 206–8, 218–
    20. *See also* comics, digital delivery
    of; Internet
Weiner, Stephen, 129, 172, 176–79
Wertham, Dr. Frederic, 6, 15–19,
    79–80, 177–78
Whelehan, Imelda, 106–7

Where the Wild Things Are, 65–66
When the Wind Blows, 66
Wilbur, 14
Wilkins, John, 180–81
Willingham, Bill, 159
Wirgman, Charles, 133–34
Wisnia, Chris, 80, *81*
The War at Ellsmere, 158
The Woman in Red, 12
Women in the Comics (Vol. 3), 31
women's rights movement, 31, 119, 216, 220. *See also* feminism
Wonder Woman, 12–13
Wonder Woman, 12–13
wordless narrative, 42, 59–64, 66–67, *68*, 205, 217

working-class literature, 2, 6–11, 107, 180
World War II, 22–23, 137–38

X-Men (films), 219

Yamagishi, Ryōko. *See* 24 nengumi
Yazawa, Ai, 150, *152*, *154*
The Yellow Kid, 5
The Yellow Kid, 4
Yōnen Club, 137
Youth, Popular Culture, and Moral Panics: Penny Gaffs to Gangsta-Rap, 1830–1996, 7

Zap Comix, 178

ABOUT THE AUTHOR

Jacqueline Danziger-Russell has an MA in children's literature from Roehampton University, London, and she is currently pursuing an MLIS at San José State University, California. Her interest in the world of comics began when she was twelve years old and picked up a copy of Art Spiegelman's *Maus: A Survivor's Tale*.